CONTENTS

LIST OF MAPS

CONTRIBUTORS

Sanjay Chaturvedi, a Liverhume Fellow of the University of Cambridge, England, is the Co-ordinator of the Centre for the Study of Geopolitics, Panjab University, Chandigarh. His research interest is geopolitics with special reference to the polar regions and the Indian Ocean. He has a considerable number of publications to his credit, the more recent one being *The Polar Regions: A Political Geography*, (John Wiley and Sons, 1996). He is currently associated with the Department of Political Science at the Punjab University in Chandigarh.

Paula Banerjee is a specialist in diplomatic history, and has worked on American foreign policy on South Asia at the University of Cincinnati, Ohio. She has been working on themes related to peace studies and has published several papers on women in conflict situations. Currently involved in writing a full-length history of borders in South Asia, she teaches in the Department of South and South Asian Studies, University of Calcutta.

Suchandana Chatterjee, presently a project fellow in Central Asian Studies at the Maulana Abul Kalam Azad Institute of Asian Studies, Kolkata, works on Tajikistan in the aftermath of the Tajik Civil War (1992). Her articles on Tajikistan have appeared in *Contemporary Central Asia, Asia Annual 2000* and *2001*. Since 1993, she has been writing on various aspects of Central Asian history and history-writing, culture, religion, popular beliefs and regionalism. She is also collaborating with CNRS (Paris) and is a regular contributor to the Teheran-based review journal *Abstracta Iranica.* She has contributed articles to the forthcoming *Turkiye Dergisi* (Ankara), *Encyclopaedia of Islam* and *Muslim World* (Macmillan Reference).

Indrani Chatterjee, presently Assistant Professor in the Department of History, Rutgers University, New Jersey, has worked on slavery at the School of Oriental and African Studies, London and at the Maulana Abul Kalam Azad Institute of Asian Studies, Kolkata. She is the author of *Gender, Slavery and Law in Colonial India* (Oxford University Press, 1999) and has contributed articles to several volumes and journals.

Anita Sengupta is associated as a researcher on Central Asia with the Maulana Abul Kalam Azad Institute of Asian Studies, Kolkata. She has been working on State formation in Uzbekistan, and has published papers on the minority question in Central Asia. She has written various articles on boundaries and State formation in Central Asia after the revolution of 1917.

Rita Manchanda is Programme Executive in the South Asia Forum for Human Rights, Kathmandu and co-ordinator of its Women and Peace and Media and Conflict programmes. Academically trained in International Relations at the Graduate School for International Studies, University of Geneva, she is a well known journalist and writer on South Asian security and human rights issues. Among her many publications are an edited volume titled *Women, War and Peace in South Asia: From Victimhood to Agency* (2001) and *States, Citizens and Refugees* of which she is the co-editor. Currently she is the Director of the Research Track of the November 2001 Colloquium of Women Waging Peace, a project of the Kennedy School of Government, Harvard University.

Ranabir Samaddar is currently Director, Peace Studies Programme at the South Asia Forum for Human Rights, Kathmandu. His two recent books are *Memory, Identity, Power: Politics in the Jungle Mahals 1890–1950* (Orient Longman, 1997) and *The Marginal Nation: Transborder Migration from Bangladesh to West Bengal* (Sage, 1999).

LIST OF ABBREVIATIONS

ASEAN	Association of South East Asian Nations
ASSR	Autonomous Soviet Socialist Republic
BJP	Bharatiya Janata Party
CBM	Confidence Building Measures
CENTO	Central Treaty Organisation
CII	Confederation of Indian Industry
CIS	Commonwealth of Independent States
CoAS	Chief of Army Staff
DGMO	Director-General of Military Operations
GoI	Government of India
IGNCA	Indira Gandhi National Centre for the Arts
INION	Institute of Scientific Information in the Social Sciences of the Russian Academy of Sciences
IOR-ARC	Indian Ocean Rim-Association for Regional Cooperation
ISI	Inter-Services Intelligence Agency
LoC	Line of Control
MFN	Most Favoured Nation
MoU	Memorandum of Understanding
NAI	National Archives of India
NAM	Non-Aligned Movement
NGO	Non-Governmental Organisation
NLC	National Library, Calcutta
NMD	National Missile Defense System
NRI	Non-Resident Indian
NRP	Non-Resident Pakistani
NWS	Nuclear Weapon States
OSCE	Organisation of Security and Cooperation in Europe
PHDCCI	Punjab, Haryana, Delhi Chambers of Commerce and Industry
PILER	Pakistan Institute of Labour Education and Research
PIPFPD	Pakistan–India Peoples' Forum for Peace and Democracy
PML	Pakistan Muslim League
PoW	Prisoners of War

RAW	Research and Analysis Wing
RGICS	Rajiv Gandhi Institute for Contemporary Studies
RGS	Royal Geographic Society, London
RSDRP	Russian Social Democratic Workers Party
RSFSR	Russian Socialist Federated Soviet Republic
SAARC	South Asian Association for Regional Cooperation
SAFHR	South Asia Forum for Human Rights
SAPTA	South Asian Preferential Trade Agreement
SEATO	South East Asian Treaty Organisation
SSR	Soviet Socialist Republic
USIS	United States Information Service

PREFACE

Today with deaths in Afghanistan ending existing geopolitical sanguinities, we have a new Great Game opening before us in Central and South Asia. The puppet governments stationed in Afghanistan and those of the future in some other Central Asian countries may aim at blocking Chinese access to the energy fields in the Middle East. The aim will also be to encircle Iran and Iraq after the US success in squeezing Syria and Lebanon between the two pro-US regional powers of Israel and Turkey. Furthermore, through its influence in Afghanistan the US may acquire the ability to enhance its influence over Kazakhstan and Turkmenistan where a considerable amount of gold and petroleum resources were recently uncovered, and also influence the internal dynamics in Iran and Iraq. Explorations into the geopolitical ramifications of the deaths on 11 September 2001, and of the subsequent war in Afghanistan can go far. These ramifications suggest a new form of war, just as the deaths of 11 September by themselves were of a new form, and as the deaths of 6 and 9 August 1945 were of a new form. In forging an alliance for this new war launched by US President George Bush against unknown enemies (but partly defined by "our" anti-terrorist bloc against "their" terrorist bloc), all kinds of required concessions to would-be allies may well result in the sacrifice of past certainties such as the National Missile Defense (NMD) system, the enlargement of NATO, and an Atlantic-based power system. Thus, India may be upgraded to the status of a strategic ally, a process that has already begun. Pakistan, downgraded to a peon or orderly that may help in strategic intrusions in the region. But here the uncertainties accelerate. For, securing a government in Kabul will require the cooperation, or at least positive neutrality, of Russia and all Afghanistan's neighbours; in return, concessions would have to be given elsewhere. This would be a new scenario that would finally draw the curtain on the Euro-centric cold war. To finally become an Asian power, the West will have to non-westernise itself, ending it's Calvinistic campaign for democracy in Muslim-majority countries, allowing countries like Iran, Uzbekistan, Kazakhstan and Russia to engage in 'constructive non-alignment' in response to the US presence in the region, resuming trade with Iran and strategically confronting China from a direction completely unanticipated by the Chinese. In this new war, China, too, has to remain neutral, as indeed it has been while unequivocally condemning the 11 September terrorist act, and probably expecting in vain that the West would cooperate in its stand against Uyghur, Tibetan and Taiwanese separatism.

The new Great Game is on. Games in Central Asia and elsewhere have always been portrayed in the literature of international politics as responses to attacks on 'civilised ways of life', reinforcing old polarities, old struggles between 'democracy' and 'totalitarianism', 'modernism' versus 'backwardness', 'pluralism' versus the 'imposition of one opinion', and rationality' versus 'fundamentalism'. In other words, the Game is a 'war of modernity and rationality against fundamentalism'. It has been always so, everywhere, wherever 'modernity' had to be carried forward in its strategic mission. It is here, it would be well to remember, the local and the global are truly linked in a 'world history', or to be more precise, linked in a world of what Sankaran Krishna terms "mimetic histories".* In this sense, the new war and the new Great Game do not signify banal geopolitics. They only bring back to our consciousness the importance that territory still holds in world politics—the 'inflammable material' of the politics of our time—and how the politics of the territory, thought to have vanished in this era of globalisation, can be found to be continuing in different ways.

In recent years, and particularly after 1989, the interest of historians and political scientists has come back to world history and issues that affect the destiny of all States and all nations. The historical element in contemporary studies has thus been reintroduced, but in a substantially different form from the grand sweeps of history as chronicled by the Spenglers and the Toynbees. World history was then conceptualised and authored by the few who had the required reach, and thus the prerogative, to think all-embracingly of the world. The access to this prerogative has become broader today with nations, hitherto considered to be burdened with a myopic 'vision of the local', now exerting their right to think globally. The uniform nature of the representation of world history is over; we now have world histories with different interpretations. In this sense, these essays on international politics can be said to be *views from the South.* In addressing some of the fundamental issues that have influenced contemporary international relations, as well as the destinies of some countries in the last one hundred years, these essays take a look at world history from an alternative viewpoint.

This volume takes up three such issues that had escaped the attention of recent international studies, proscribed as it was by a cold war framework. These are problems of space in international politics, of borders and statelessness. Even though these three issues are distinct in themselves,

---

* Krishna Sankaran, *Post–Colonial Insecurities* (New Delhi: Oxford University Press, 1999).

together they indicate how their pursuit in international studies can be more fruitful. Collectively, they highlight the grounding of the State as a political organisation, which has become fundamental to the international system today. These are not new problems, but they have become crucial in the era of post–colonial nationalism, globalisation and the restoration of the pre-cold war scenario after 1989. Thus, they call for a perusal of the historical perspective as well as of the particularity of the times.

In recent years geopolitics has come to be viewed as an antiquated field, overtaken by technology, technological superiority and systemic insights that have overcome the constraints of territoriality. The idea that international relations is fundamentally governed by the fact that a State is acutely conscious of the space it occupies as well as the space that modern empires occupy is now thought to be of the pre-Second World War, pre-cold war era. Nuclear technology, superpower status, block politics, ethnicity and other trans-border developments are assumed to have done away with the problem of space that faced an established power. But this volume examines the problematic of geopolitics to show that there are other ways – sometimes alternative ways – of looking at issues of space, territory and natural resources. In short, it first addresses the issue of geography in politics.

The volume then moves on to the question of frontiers and borders – the problem of "spaces of sharing" and "spaces of conflict". While political scientists, historians and scholars of international relations have been aware of the problematic of borders, it was seen to have been lacking a history of its own. That borders could acquire a life of their own, and as an idea, could become an extremely powerful reality influencing the behaviour of States and the imagination of any collectivity aspiring to rise into the full panoply of a political unit, was often ignored. Historians forgot that if States created borders, borders also made the emergence of the modern State an imperative. For a critical perspective in international relations, the issue then is: if we are to live with borders, can they be made spaces of sharing, inasmuch as they are spaces of conflict? This volume poses the question, but does not leave it at that; it also suggests the need for an alternative line of inquiry, and thus passes on to some concrete case studies on Central and South Asia.

The issue of territoriality, frontiers and boundaries in Central Asia in the late nineteenth century was a contentious one, particularly in the geopolitical sense, as the word 'conquest' became commonly used in describing Russian policy in the steppes and the Turkestan region. Yet a closer look may suggest this to be rather conjectural; Russian policy in the nineteenth century hardly followed a linear path of conquest. The terrain differed, the environment varied, populations and cultures mixed with one another. It could not have been pragmatic for Russia to wage war for an entire century in such terrain. Even as Great Game theories and descriptions flourished in the literature of that era, as an account in this volume shows, Russia's external dynamic policy attempted to actually settle the issue of frontiers with respect to its client and buffer states, protectorates and neutral zones; while Britain was equally dynamic in trying to ensure that Russian influence did not seep farther south. A century later, however, the question remains: what effect did these policies have on the local population? Indeed, how did the struggle for their territorial integrity impact on the territorial integrity of the region? The essay on the Central Asia of that period mirrors the problematic of territoriality involved in the issue of frontiers and boundaries that face the region today, particularly since today's Central Asia is again a subject of intense interest among the major powers.

The effect of the imperial rivalries over territory is explored in an essay on slavery in the region. This essay demonstrates that ideologies of territoriality were manipulated to suit political or moral exigencies. The slave raiding and trading occurring in the northern regions beyond their direct political authority had alarmed the British officials governing India. This concern was fuelled partly by an abolitionist ideology and partly by reports of Russian advances into Bukhara that had led to the emancipation of many Persian slaves. However, issues of territoriality, which, according to the British, conferred identity, cropped up when the financial burden of the manumission of slaves of 'Indian' origin held in Xinjiang after 1892 was being considered. The Chinese officials, on the other hand, were intent on a more holistic manumission – one that suited the needs of Sinicisation of the newly reconquered province. The essay also touches on the issues of identity, marked by imperial policies, and the "mutability of all identities in the politics and economics of survival". By choosing between their 'new' homes and their 'original' homelands, the slaves demonstrated that territory had transformed beyond mere geography to also represent social and cultural spaces.

The issue of borders was also critical in the formation of new States in Central Asia after the Russian Revolution. The idea of space has always been central to that of sovereign bounded communities called States. All political units have been characterised by physical limits, and the location of these limits had significance in the lives of the people separated by these lines. However, what was remarkable in the Central Asian situation, and possibly elsewhere, was how the exercise of delimitation always appeared as having a 'rational' basis. As the essay on the delimitation of boundaries in post–revolution Central Asia argues, without an understanding of the dynamics of rationality and the imperatives of the delimited space, the reconstitution of boundaries in modern Central Asia would have no meaning. The illogicality of ignoring trans-border realities in responding to the imperatives of delimitation calls for a dialectical examination of (a) the basis on which the borders were finally drawn in the decade after the revolution; (b) the historical basis, if any, for these borders; and (c) the problems left unsolved by this attempt at a rational delimitation along ethno-linguistic lines.

But if borders produce States, they also produce dialogues. Borders predicate these dialogues, though one can justifiably claim that dialogues in turn predicate the State. Thus dialogues across one of the most contentious borders in the world, that between India and Pakistan, are examined here in two essays to probe this dialectic. It is ironic, but perhaps understandable (given the extreme theoretical poverty in the literature of international relations today) that dialogues have been little analysed in this genre (except in the literature on bargaining) and least of all in the context of borders. This brings us to the question of understanding the workings of the State in international relations today.

People study conflicts, systems, alliances, ententes, wars and peace, and the present history of a State is assumed in these discourses. But it is worth scrutinising why this should be so: the 'state of the State' today shows that this history is not settled, that the inherence of a State lies in debris in many parts of the world, and that the globalisation of crisis in many ways is also a globalisation of the breakdown of the State. In the triumphalist literature of current history, this is represented as merely a problem of management; of adequately managing the State. The concluding essay suggests that the malaise is simply too deep to be cured by the managers of the international system, and thus this volume ends by going back to the essence of the State in the world politics of today. It shows that the very ontology of the modern State is now severely disturbed by the problems posed by borders, statelessness, massive migrations and other trans-border realities, so much so that it has become an 'elusive State' today.

A few years ago, the critical philosopher Jurgen Habermas appealed for a call back to history. But he was in despair when he found that, in the euphoric aftermath of 1989 and the German reunification, the Westward-looking vision of an Adenauerian world prevailed over every aspect of life on the Rhine. A dramatic change in the course of history had lured the German people into accepting what he called the big lies as everlasting realities; that, for instance, the events in the post–Second World War were 'normal', and fascism, the atomic holocaust in Japan, or the division of Europe after the war (or even the nineteenth century colonial wars and subsequent neo-colonial exploitation) were 'abnormal'. These essays are, in a sense, a response to that appeal. Read as a volume, the essays on geopolitics, borders and the State tie together the historical and the current in international politics. By stressing the historical element they point out the fault lines in the literature of international relations; they simultaneously suggest an alternative approach to the analysis of modern international politics. In advocating the need for a world-historical element in the understanding of international relations, I hope that the volume will also address the need for a 'view from the South' of a world that has been predominantly viewed 'from the North'.

Let us for a moment go back to the question of territory. In this volume we are dealing with the manifold implications of this problematic: territory indicates the fundamental notion of space; territory has associations with the notion of identity; territory leads to issues of nationalism, State and, ironically, to globalisation. International literature addresses the issue by conveying the idea that, while territory and space are important, they are nevertheless issues now subject to the new paradigms in international politics. Apart from the fact that globalisation has reoriented geopolitics, territory has become politically one of the most explosive themes in international studies today, as the politics of identity start competing with globalisation to acquire paramountcy in studies on international relations. In fact, the symbiotic relationship between the two issues has led some theorists to speak of the twin trends of globalisation and fragmentation. In planning this volume, the authors intended to question the received image of superpower-driven international politics, wherein nothing mattered other than global capital flows, nuclear weapons, an international media and a liberal ideology. If it was an 'end of history', it was also an 'end of international relations' that supposedly revolved round great power conflicts. By bringing back a historical perspective in international relations, the authors question not merely the received wisdom of the discipline, but also raise the question of space – one of the most abiding themes in world politics that scholars such as Kenneth Waltz, Samuel Huntington and Francis Fukuyama seem to have forgotten. By doing this, the issue of identity has been freed from the sedate chambers of cultural studies to take its place on the agenda of international relations. In this volume, however, the route this assumes is not through ethnicity; by choosing and examining some very traditional themes, such as space, border and State, by standing them on their heads, so to speak, the essays suggest new and critical ways in which the question of identity can be approached. Yet it is intriguing that, when the issue of identity was being examined by other disciplines in the humanities, international relations remained unaware of the need to study the problem. When new conflicts broke out in the aftermath of the restoration of 1989, the youngest discipline proved itself to be the first to pass into a state of atrophy.

Space, in the theory of States, plays an important role: space is territory when invested with power. Older State theories related State to territory through issues such as colonial exploitation; kinship and territorial coincidence; the scramble for capital export and earmarking of zones; integration of markets in the areas over which it held sway and finally, the horizontal structuring of society. Political power found its greatest articulation in the territorial form via the operation of 'capital logic'. This meant that capital unified the space that the State occupied internally, but it also led to an external dividing and, paradoxically, an externally unifying trend as well. Conflicts signified spatial discontinuities, while consolidation and stability meant situating people as subjects of a State firmly in a place – an empire, nation, region or municipality. Yet the diaspora, confederal union and ethnicity harboured 'extra-territorial' spaces. In the twentieth century, however, the associational ethic began to change, along with the surge of democracy in various forms. The crucial problematic in international politics today is to discover the forms of this meeting of space and democracy. Fortunately, as these essays show, we do not have far to seek, since we can find the hazy forms of such a union in the events of the last two centuries. We have only to step aside from the tired path of the study of nationalism or (conversely) great power politics to see how the relational dynamic of State and space has proceeded. Thus, if space invested with power produces territory, the changes in the configuration of power, or a different notion of power, produces other possibilities of that relationship. It is thus not without reason that today's received discipline of international relations is being investigated by historical inquiries into forms of power – a task that realist gurus like Waltz and Hans J. Morgenthau did not consider important. Their examination of the possibilities of power was cursory at best; in a world of institutionalised nation-states, pundits whose theories of international relations centred around the power of the States were going to derive little comfort from the flux that nation-states produced. Theorists like Michael Mann invested too much in the State, and disregarded the contests that would invariably face the nation-state in its position as a unit of macro-sociological theory. To rewrite the history of power on an international scale is an enormous task, but the present essays hope to indicate one of the many ways in which that task can be approached.

In preparing this volume my thanks are first to the contributors who were more than willing to contribute their essays. They took the trouble of going into the set of writings, and suggested editorial revisions, for which I remain similarly grateful to the anonymous reader at Orient Longman. I would particularly like to thank Anita Sengupta for the preparation of the bibliography. Three of the eight essays were presented at a seminar organised by the Maulana Abul Kalam Azad Institute of Asian Studies, on a related theme in New Delhi in 1998 on the occasion of the fiftieth year of the Asian Relations Conference; the rest were especially commissioned for this volume. I would like to express my heartfelt gratitude to the Institute and its staff. Finally, it remains for me to thank Orient Longman and Afried Raman who persevered with the volume amid trying times.

It is my pleasure to dedicate this volume to Professor Barun De. With his healthy scepticism towards what often passes for new thinking in the social sciences, I am apprehensive that on receiving these essays in printed form Barun De will demand more critical analyses of the themes that have been negotiated here.

Ranabir Samaddar

ONE

Can There be an Asian Geopolitics?

SANJAY CHATURVEDI

Introduction

Geopolitics, in its *academic* sense, can be defined as "an interdisciplinary field of study straddling political science and geography. At the same time it also draws heavily on history, economics and demography, paying particular attention to migrations of populations."[1] However, geopolitics in its *practical* sense, both 'old' and 'new', is an ongoing process of spatialising world politics; the 'mapping of a world order' by certain practitioners of statecraft – a rather privileged community of State bureaucrats, national leaders, foreign policy experts and advisors who comment upon, influence and conduct the activities of nations. As Gearóid Ó Tuathail and John Agnew put it, "[t]he study of geopolitics in discursive terms, therefore, is the study of the socio-cultural resources and rules by which geographies of international politics get written."[2] The 1990s were a time of crisis in geopolitics – an old geopolitical order characterised by stability based upon a rigid adherence to an antagonistic-alliance system was crumbling; a new order is yet to emerge.[3]

Asia and its sub-regions too are affected by this situation, which needs to be approached and understood from a new perspective. Geopolitics can no longer be seen in terms of the impact of *fixed* geographical conditions and configurations (heartlands/rimlands, lifelines, choke-points, critical strategic zones, etc.) upon the activities of the Great Powers engaged in the pursuit of primacy. Asian polities, societies and economies today are deeply – though unevenly – affected by the 'geopolitical disorder' in the Western world from which no single, dominant geopolitical template has yet emerged by which to re-define divisions in the world. With a highly dynamic economy replacing classical State-centric geopolitics as the fundamental context for world politics and 'foreign' policy, post–cold war Asia is confronted with the need for both continuity and change.[4] At the same time, a growing awareness of the power of 'regionalism' and 'globalism' in international relations is increasingly – yet again unevenly – integrating Asia into this world economy.

This essay has three major parts. It begins with an account of how 'Asia' has come to be imagined, constructed and represented in what John Agnew calls the three ages of geopolitics: three specific epochs or eras – civilisational, naturalised and ideological – that developed over the period from the early nineteenth century to the 1980s.[5] The essay then evaluates the possibility of a critical geopolitics in contesting the new geopolitical constructions of Asia in the aftermath of the cold war, and its role in opposing the homogenising and hegemonising tendencies of globalism and 'new' regionalism. The key question here is whether such a resistance is possible by turning to a geopolitics from below, from a subordinate position as it were, which draws its inspiration from grass-roots-level struggles especially of the indigenous peoples of Asia. Finally, the chapter concludes with an assessment of the desirability as well as feasibility of developing an Asian geopolitics.

Asia in Civilisational Geopolitics

The origins of geopolitics and modern geopolitical imagination – the predominant manner in which global politics has been represented, and acted on geographically, both by major personalities and intellectuals/ institutions of statecraft over the past two centuries – can be traced back to the late nineteenth century, when the Great Powers of Europe embarked upon unprecedented imperial-territorial aggrandisement. It is within this imperialist framework that geopolitics first arose as a concept and practice. According to Ó Tuathail,

> As the Eurocentrically imagined blank spaces on the globe succumbed to the sovereign authority of governmental institutions and imperial science, the surface of the globe appeared for the first time as a system of 'closed space', an almost completely occupied and fully charted geographical order. The dawning of this new order of space, together with the transformative effects of technological change on the exercise of imperial power across space, provoked the emergence of a distinctive genre of geo-power within the capitals of Great Powers; the name this new genre of geo-power acquired was "geopolitics".[6]

By this time, a distinctive geopolitical discourse showing a firm commitment to European uniqueness as a civilisation had also emerged; it was sustained by "a belief that the roots of European distinctiveness were found in its past, a 'sense that though other cultures might have noble pasts with high achievements they had been eclipsed by Europe, and an increasing identification with a particular nation-state as representing the most perfected version of European difference".[7] Ancient Greek geographers were perhaps the first to divide the earth's land area into separate continents – Europe, Asia and Africa – bounded by the Mediterranean Sea and the rivers Nile and Don. But later geographical knowledge established beyond doubt that Europe was a peninsula of Asia. Even at the time of Czarist Russia's expansion, in the sixteenth century, into the vast, thinly populated lands of Eurasia to the north of the steppes, there had been no clear geographical divide in this gigantic land empire between Europe and Asia.[8] As Mark Bassin puts it,

> The basic geographical proposition that Russia divided cleanly and naturally into Asian and European sectors entered into the very foundation of the imperial ideology that was refined in the course of the eighteenth century. It was disseminated in the geography texts that began to appear in even greater numbers after 1750 and by the end of the century it had become a universally accepted truism.[9]

Once the realm of Europe was successfully transformed from a physical-geographical into a coherent social-cultural entity with the help of the enviable material-intellectual resources at the disposal of European powers, the 'differences' between the continents came to be construed on a global scale. Europe, by the first half of the nineteenth century, was shown in some imaginative maps as a queen among the continents, complete with orb and sceptre.[10]

> This illustrates not only a sense of difference but also an emerging sense of superiority. This was reinforced by the European voyages of 'discovery' which demonstrated the self-evident initiative, vision and zeal of Europeans. Over the next centuries, the feeling of superiority gradually hardened into an inflexible conceit that held Europe to be the most civilized and best governed of all the world regions.[11]

Since "geopolitical discourses are inevitably intertwined with economic sources of power", it was in the political-economic context of the period from 1815 to 1875 that civilisational geopolitics was more fully and firmly established.[12] At this stage in the growth of world capitalism, European political elites considered the growth and stability of the British national economy as central not only to their national interest but also to a 'global' interest. The perceived need for 'global stability' often compelled successive British governments to intervene militarily in different parts of the world whenever the status quo was threatened.

In Asia, "the most serious, persistent and planned effort of European nations in the nineteenth century was their missionary activities in India and China, where a large-scale attempt was made to effect a *mental and spiritual conquest* as supplementing the political authority already enjoyed by Europe".[13] In India, for example, in the wake of the English East India Company serially annexing, or else extending its indirect rule over each of the Indian States from 1757 to 1857,[14] "the period of 1860–1870 saw a rapid expansion of what might be thought of as the definition and expropriation of Indian civilization".[15] In British imperial geopolitical imaginations, points out Thomas Metcalf,

> There existed a 'changeless' India inhabiting a past that endured in the present; an India of racial 'decline' marked by the triumph of Dravidianism and the anarchy of the eighteenth century; and an India of a gendered 'effeminacy' which made its women and men alike dependent on a benevolent British 'masculinity'. Each of these descriptions of India's difference had its own theoretical, even 'scientific' rationale; each too was rent with deep contradictions both within itself, and in relation to the others. Above all, race and gender provided explanations of very different sorts for India's plight. The theory of racial decline announced a process of irreversible physical deterioration brought about by the mixing of blood, while the degeneracy defined by effeminacy was one of characters and morals.[16]

The British ethnographic enterprise, despite its inconsistencies and its subordination to the needs of colonial rule, had far-reaching consequences for India because these various categories – of caste and community, of race and sect – informed the ways in which the British, and in time the Indians themselves, conceptualised the basic structure of Indian society.

Naturalised Geopolitics and Asia

The creation of a naturalised geopolitics in the early part of the twentieth century implicitly recognised the importance of Social Darwinism.[17] It represented the human entirely in terms of natural processes and phenomena, comparing the State with a living organism. The transformation and displacement of the more 'primitive' societies of Asia at the hands of the 'civilised' overseas colonial empires of western Europe as well as the Czarist Empire was justified, since Darwin had pronounced that "the variety of man seems to act on each other in the same way as different species of animals – the stronger always extirpating the weak".[18] Geopolitics, rather than a feature of civilisation, to quote Agnew,

> was now largely determined by the natural character of states that could be understood 'scientifically' akin to the new understanding of biological processes that also marked the period. . . .Humanity had lost control of its destiny. Nature ruled in affairs of state. The naturalized geopolitics. . .had a number of tell-tale needs for territory/resources and outlets for enterprise, a 'closed' world in which one state's political economic success was at another's expense (relative ascent and decline), and a world of fixed geographical attributes and environmental conditions that had predictable effects on a state's global status.[19]

The pseudo-scientific justification for colonial expansionism was provided in general by "a stratum of organic intellectuals of empire",[20] many of whom theorised the influence of geography on the social evolution of States and the conduct of foreign policy.[21] Intellectuals like Alfred Thayer Mahan and Nicholas John Spykman in the United States, Friedrich Ratzel and Karl Haushofer in Germany, Rudolf Kjellen in Sweden and Halford John Mackinder in Great Britain all sought to promote an imperialist agenda within, of course, the political culture of their own State.[22]

For Asia, the discursive as well as practical implications of a naturalised geopolitics were numerous, profound and far-reaching. As States came to be seen as powerful political, organic entities, relentlessly engaged in the 'natural' pursuit of a greater *Lebensraum* (living space), yet another pseudo-scientific rationale was added for the imperial scramble for politically valuable territory in Asia. The idea that a State had 'natural boundaries' was used – or rather, misused – by the Swedish conservatives, including Rudolf Kjellen (who coined the term 'Geopolitics' in 1898), "to argue against Norway's independence partly because they claimed that the Scandinavian mountains were not a natural boundary".[23] Even the Nazi concept of Lebensraum justifying German territorial expansion in *Mitteleuropa* (Central Europe) was a logical offshoot of the notion of natural boundaries.[24] But the logic was never extended to the 'stateless' colonised world of Afro-Asia. The scramble for Africa, for example, subsequent to the agreement among the major European powers at Berlin in 1884–1885 to carve out their spheres of influence in the 'dark continent', "produced lines on a map which had little relation to underlying cultural or economic patterns. Elsewhere, the establishment of colonial boundaries was less hasty if often no less arbitrary. These designations continue to haunt these regions to this day.".[25]

German nationalists, smarting under the humiliating provisions of the Treaty of Versailles after the First World War, took stock of Kjellen's concept and grafted on to it what they believed would vindicate the honour and aspirations of Germany. For this purpose, Karl Haushofer and his colleagues selectively synthesised Kjellen's and German nationalist ideas into practically a dogma; the German school of *Geopolitik* thus emerged to hold sway from about the beginning of the 1920s to about the end of the Second World War.[26] Accordingly, Lebensraum automatically became the key concept of Haushofer's Geopolitik, as indeed of the Nazi State. In contrast to Friedrich Ratzel's idea of Lebensraum – which in fact had influenced Haushofer so profoundly as to make him adopt it as the very kernel of his work and mission in life – the new German term was made to mean the space the Germans were entitled to occupy to its natural limits, in accordance with the 'inner laws of development' of the German State. As the new dogma made Geopolitik both a prescription and justification for territorial expansion, *Kampf* (struggle), *Strategie* (strategy) and *Totaler Krieg* (total war) became the instruments and ideology for attaining Lebensraum and *Autarchie* (economic self-sufficiency) – the other vital pillar of the ideological edifice. German Geopolitik also talked of certain 'pan-regions' as being the world powers of the future. For the most part, they consisted of groups of States that were brought together under the domination of one major power. It was envisaged that a future Asian (Far Eastern) pan-region would be dominated by Japan and a European pan-region by Germany.

Outside Germany, Geopolitik found fertile ground only in Japan, a country with which Haushofer had special ties and about which he wrote six books. As shown by Yoriko Fukushama,[27] from the latter half of the 1930s this otherwise questionable geopolitics was Japanised by linking it to the traditional Japanese concept of their land (as a sort of physiocracy, which emphasised the importance of agriculture for the legitimacy and rule of the State), and it began to attract many followers. He reveals that the history of Japanese geopolitics began with the introduction of Kjellen's book *Staten som Lifsform* by a jurist in 1925, after which mainly German geopolitical thought was pursued in Japan. In the 1930s "the Japanese began to believe that a pan-Asian movement under Japanese leadership would liberate Asia from Western imperialism and end the implicit assumption of racial inferiority".[28] Opinions vary as to the relationship between geopolitics and the formative process of the now notorious "Greater East Asia Co-Prosperity Sphere" policy, pronounced on 1 August 1940 by the Japanese foreign minister, Yosuke Matsuoka. The policy embraced East Asia and Southeast Asia and, during the Second World War, India, Australia and New Zealand were also included. According to Fukushama, "[s]ome authors have pointed out that the concept of Lebensraum originating in German geopolitics became an inspiration for Japanese policy".[29] In the end, it appears that geopolitical arguments were abused to justify Japanese imperialist policies. In post–war Japan, however, intellectuals who had been associated with the study of geopolitics were dismissed from public posts because of their alleged contributory role in Japan's war of aggression.

Finally, it was during the period of naturalised geopolitics that Asia came to be enframed in the most enduring bipolar view of the world in the twentieth century, a worldview centred as much on the long-perceived fundamental duality of Europe and Asia as on the newly invented, essential dichotomy of the 'mighty opposites' of land power and sea power.[30]

Alfred Thayer Mahan, a naval historian who eventually reached the rank of admiral in the US navy, argued in his book *The Problems of Asia*, published in 1900, that acquisition of sea power was essential to America's future success as a world class power. In this work, which in many ways was "a part of the agenda of various factions of national ruling elites at the time, namely naval militarism",[31] an area on which Mahan specifically focussed was Asia. Mahan made the future political importance of this area explicable in terms of geographical causation in political history. He identified the unique location of Russia in what he termed "the Debated and Debatable Middle Strip" running from Turkey to China.[32] This was a geopolitical "no man's land", which was "destined" to be a disputed area between Russia and the maritime powers. Mahan not only anticipated a struggle between Russian land power and British sea power, but also predicted (note that he was writing before the turn of the twentieth century) that the containment of Russia and control of China would become the joint concern of the United States, Great Britain, Germany and Japan.

While Mahan emphasised sea power largely in the context of the "the problem of Asia" and the US efforts to create an international 'open door' policy in China, in Britain, Halford John Mackinder propounded a counter-thesis of "global closure": of the world having become a single unified globe of occupied space, where the consequences of events in one part were inevitably felt in all other parts. The geopolitical gaze of Mackinder too was focussed on Asia, but with a difference. Mackinder in his 1904 address to the Royal Geographical Society in London argued that after the maritime powers had expanded their influence throughout the "Columbian Epoch" (1500–1900), until it covered the whole world, the balance of power in the post–Columbian epoch was going to witness the reassertion of the pre-Columbian "Pivot Area" – from where the most mobile, horse-borne societies of Central Asia periodically descended on the coastal regions of Eurasia and decisively changed the course of history. This Eurasian core area, or the pivot area, was later broadened by Mackinder into "Heartland". Mackinder reasoned that in the post–Columbian scene, "the balance of power threatens to swing back to Asia, where railways are transmuting the conditions of land power and threaten to permit the continental resources of the heartland to be used as the basis for an empire of the world".[33]

What lay behind the geopolitical imagination of Mackinder that led to the imperial urge to impose an ethnocentric system of control and intelligibility upon the diversities and complexities of Asia? The answer, from yet another critical perspective, was that the heartland model was no exception to the rule that behind every general model lies a specific case from which it is derived:

> Throughout the second half of the nineteenth century Britain and Russia had been rivals in much of Asia. While Britain was consolidating its hold on India and the route to India, Russia had been expanding eastwards and southwards producing many zones of potential conflict from Turkey through Persia and Afghanistan to Tibet. But instead of war, this became an arena of intrigue, of bluff and counter-bluff, known as the 'Great Game'. . . . Put simply, the heartland model is a codification and globalization of the Great Game; it brings a relatively obscure imperial contest on to the center stage.[34]

Lastly, we may note that Mackinder fully shared organic definitions of national interest as the driving force behind economic growth, and by doing so became an influential spokesman of economic nationalism, under which a State was seen as defining the basic unit for economic transactions. Firms and individuals were held to be subordinate to the greater 'organic' needs of the nation-state.

The impact of the European geopolitical debates on the United States of America was brought sharply into focus at the approach, and during the course, of the Second World War by the views and writings of Nicholas John Spykman, a professor of international relations and the director of the Institute of International Studies at Yale. His open advocacy of stark amorality in politics earned him the title, the 'American Haushofer'.

Spykman's major and better-known geopolitical contribution is that of "Rimland", which is a direct antithesis of Mackinder's heartland theory.[35] He maintained that Mackinder had overestimated the power potential of the heartland: not only were its supposed resources unknown and undeveloped, the area was beset with the formidable problem of internal transportation. It was thus incapable of sustaining the role of world conqueror. Moreover, he contended, Mackinder's other basic premise that land and sea power were in opposition or conflict with each other was not borne out by history. The real power potential of Eurasia, said Spykman, actually lay in the rimland, which was thickly populated, better endowed with resources and had shown better manoeuvrability in history. The Mackinder dictum is false, he said; "[i]f there is to be a slogan for the power politics of the Old World, it must be, Who controls the rimland rules Eurasia; who rules Eurasia controls the destinies of the world".[36]

Ideological Geopolitics: Enframing Asia in the Cold War

The advent of the cold war in the mid-twentieth century saw the fledging discipline of geopolitics mature as both a theory and a practice. The Second World War brought to an end the old order of inter-imperial rivalry and created the conditions for the construction of a new post–war geopolitical face-off, characterised by the break-up of the old colonial empires through the decolonisation process, and the hegemony of the United States in the economic, military and political spheres.[37] Those were the heydays of an 'ideological' geopolitics, which served as a "pseudo-scientific instrument for a war-promoting political propaganda".[38] Cold war geopolitics tried to explain complex spatial and political connections through a monocausal, often environmental, determinist approach; it trivialised the details of human-cultural geography, and subordinated the singular attributes of a particular place to its perceived position in the abstract spaces of the East–West conflict.[39] Geopolitics became an integral part of the world's power-political heritage, a fixture in the Realist tradition of international relations, from the gaze of which no part of the world, including Asia, could remain unseen.[40]

Once subjected to the strategies and counter-strategies of the cold war, the physical as well as human geography of Asia came to be dominated by a militarised geography of strategic alliances, military intervention, civil wars and arms flows. At the ground level, an unprecedented fragmentation of Asia and the Asian took place as a result of US–Soviet depictions of Asian space: 'South' Asia, 'Southeast' Asia (invented perhaps by the

National Geographic magazine in 1945) and 'Central' Asia. 'Middle East' was considered outside Asia. The containment era of the cold war, inspired by the heartland theory of Mackinder, coincided with the beginning of a period in which the geostrategic significance of Eurasia changed dramatically. With the onset of the cold war, the heartland theory formed the geostrategic basis of the nuclear deterrence theory. "The West's nuclear arsenal was originally justified in part as compensation for the USSR's 'natural' strategic advantage as the heartland power."[41] The littoral belt of Asia came to be seen as strategically located within Mackinder's "Inner or Marginal Crescent" (also the area identified around the pivot area in 1904, and the contestable rimland in Spykman's redesign of the heartland model in 1944), and thus geo-historically 'destined' to serve as a vital component in the containment ring against the allegedly expansionist, evil-communist occupant of the heartland. The US-constructed security alliances fought wars in rimlands.

The second cold war period (1979–1985) was characterised by a much more aggressive containment.[42] Many parts of Asia and the Indian Ocean were subjected to a new and highly vigorous phase of militarisation. The aggressive Mahanist belief in maritime strength was brought back and rejuvenated, with both the superpowers and many Asian countries placing great emphasis on the build-up of still more powerful naval capabilities. The hegemonic bipolar conflict left a majority of small States in Asia with very few choices, while forcing them to accept US perceptions of the Soviet threat to their national security. They responded with national variations, which essentially reflected the combination of their perceived core security problems and the individually specific circumstances of geographic location and national politics, but found it hard to escape the eventual entrapment in cold war geopolitics.

The analysis thus far might give the impression that cold war geopolitics was only about strategies and counter-strategies within the heartland–rimland framework. In the early phase of the cold war, the rimland did occupy a critical place in the geostrategic calculations of the US policy makers as bases from where the US nuclear-armed aircraft could attack the Soviet Union if needed. But why did the US persist with the heartland theory, seeking the support and control of rimlands, even after the advent of inter-continental ballistic missiles? One plausible explanation is that the American cold war geopolitical discourse always had an important economic dimension. This only confirms the general rule that, as pointed out earlier, geopolitical compulsions are intricately intertwined with economic motives. As the cold war evolved, the

US economy became not only militarised but also internationalised; "American patterns of trade and investment were transformed, and what had been virtually a self-sufficient economy before the Second World War became locked ever more deeply into the global trading system that was emerging."[43] These intimate links between the domestic economy and the military needs of global powers are explored by Mary Kaldor, who interprets the second cold war period as an American attempt to reinstate the rigid bipolarity of the post–war years in a global economy of multipolarity and pluralism.[44] The US military containment of the Soviet Union was thus driven by economic concerns, which were increasingly being globalised throughout the cold war; the maintenance of US bases and troops was necessitated by a desire to contain the threat to 'market democracies', which also implied containing the rimlands within a US-led capitalist world economy. According to Ó Tuathail, "through exaggeration of the Soviet threat, American intellectuals of statecraft were able to transform the U.S. state from a reluctant isolationist power into a crusading interventionist power dedicated to promoting an open world economy and safeguarding the free enterprise system".[45]

Yet many parts of Asia, such as Vietnam, would become sites of anti-superpower resistance. The Asian Relations Conference at New Delhi in March–April 1947, attended by delegates from twenty-eight countries in Asia, "to meet together, to hold together and to advance together" was one of the earliest attempts by Asian leaders to articulate Asian consciousness against the backdrop of cold war politicking on the one hand, and the process of decolonisation and democratisation of various parts of Afro-Asia on the other. Non-alignment, largely pioneered by India under the stewardship of Jawaharlal Nehru, was the single most significant attempt to resist the cold-war-instigated geopolitical clutches of a polarised world, and to reconcile "the typical realist, unit level concerns of a state's national interest, of which the core is national security however perceived, with larger, more idealist-oriented concerns of system change and transformation".[46]

The role of India in the world was seen in a quite different light by both Nehru and his foreign policy advisor Krishna Menon. According to Geoffrey Parker, "the Third World of which India was to be firmly a part was seen by them [Nehru and Menon] not so much as a third centre of power in the traditional sense but as offering an alternative vision which was cooperative rather than confrontational in stance".[47] This alternative vision – which was deeply rooted in the romantic belief at that time widely held in India that ancient, wise and peaceful Asia, once freed from the colonial yoke of a relatively young, aggressive, violence-prone Europe, would be dedicated to international cooperation for the collective good of Asians, and the benefit of mankind in general – disappeared from Nehru's speeches after the 1955 Bandung Conference of Asian and African Nations.[48] At Bandung, Nehru not only confronted an Asia in its full diversity and range of mutual incompatibilities, but also opposition from countries who saw their security interests better served by strategic alignments with either of the two military blocks. Clearly, the ramifications of Western cold war policies suited the political-economic agenda of the political elites of some of the post–colonial Asian States. This substantiated in a way the Foucauldian view that power is the play of discourses that ensnare and entrap, not by coercion, not by causing pain, but by seduction, by the promise of power and pleasure. A fairly large number of Asian States were seduced by the ideology of cold war geopolitics and its logic of containment. Pakistan's foreign and defence policy orientation towards the West and China was thus fundamentally at odds with the non-aligned posture of India. Pakistan signed the first ever defence cooperation and supplies agreement with the United States in 1954, and joined the Central Treaty Organisation (CENTO) and South East Asia Treaty Organisation (SEATO) immediately thereafter. While Pakistan aimed at buttressing its military strength against India by seeking an alliance with the Western powers, the objective of the United States was to have a sub-continental link in the cold war containment policy against the Soviet Union. In December 1955, Nehru is said to have confessed that Asia was too large an area, and "to talk about it as one entity is to confuse ourselves. . .and to talk of Europe and Asia and America as separate entities is also misleading, for the future at any rate".[49]

The Non-Aligned Movement (NAM), at least in its early, formative stage, showed some promise of posing a serious and systematic challenge to superpower militarism, and made an important, though not entirely successful, attempt at 'deterritorialising' the cold war construction and labelling of Asia. As M. S. Rajan has pointed out, "during the 1950s especially, the policy of nonalignment has had considerable attraction for sections of public opinion in many aligned West European countries, particularly by way of peace and nuclear disarmament and lessening of the Cold War".[50] Not surprisingly, the calls for Asian solidarity were seen as a threat to the power of the political elite within each block to determine geopolitical spheres of influence. Moreover, by attempting to revitalise spaces of public autonomy, NAM challenged the superpowers' ability to militarise the public mind and control public opinion. In fact, one of the earliest anti-geopolitic narratives came from Nehru himself. In his book *The Discovery of India*, published in 1946, especially in the chapter entitled "Realism and Geopolitics, World Conquest or World Association: The U.S.A. and the U.S.S.R.", one finds a critique of the geopolitical theories of Mackinder and Spykman, which, according to Nehru, are pseudo-scientific justifications for "power quest", "power politics" and "world domination". To quote Nehru:

> Geopolitics has now become the anchor of the realist and its jargon of 'heartland' and 'rimland' is supposed to throw light on the mystery of national growth and decay. Originating in England (or was it Scotland?), it became the guiding light of the nazis, fed their dreams and ambitions of world domination, and led them to disaster. . . .And now even the United States of America are told by Professor Spykman, in his last testament, that they are in danger of encirclement, that they should ally themselves with a 'rimland' nation, that in any event they should not prevent the heartland (which means now the USSR) from uniting with the rimland.[51]

But the cold war geopolitics, as preached and practised by the major powers of the time, "submerged the realities of what we now call the Third World",[52] and shattered Nehru's vision of a non-dominant universal order in which hundreds of millions of Asians and Africans could realise their destiny. Perhaps one major weakness of the Non-Aligned Movement was that despite its larger humanist appeal and potential to usher in a non-statist world order, it remained confined to "nothing more or less than a firm assertion of sovereignty by the post-colonial state";[53] which often implied, for a majority of its proponents, compromising the principles of non-alignment for the sake of 'national interest' and 'national security'. According to A. P. Rana, "the contrary pulls of two streams of thought have irreconcilably dominated the NAM: on the one hand, the tenets and framework of action of inter-war Idealism, and on the other, post–World War II Realism; except of course, that while Idealism is plentifully enunciated, Realism is plentifully practiced".[54]

Be that as it may, the discourses and practices of cold war geopolitics had an impact on the indigenous communities throughout Asia, causing great harm to their environment, culture, health and human rights.[55] Militarisation imposed costly and undesired policies, priorities and activities upon indigenous peoples, and undermined their right to self-determination within the boundaries of their homelands. It also increased the dependence of local communities on military installations in terms of employment and services, and provided an additional stimulus for resource extraction and the setting up of megaprojects. Ecological concerns were conspicuous by their total absence or relative neglect in the cold war priorities of the two superpowers and their allies. For example, a large number of military industries were set up in Kazakhstan, and almost all the atomic tests were carried out in that State, with severe repercussions to the environmental health of the area. The largest and most significant test area in Kazakhstan was Semipalatinsk, where as many as 470 atom and hydrogen bomb tests were conducted in an area of 18,000 square km. As a consequence, at least 1.3 million people are reported to be suffering due to radioactive pollution. The magnitude and consequences of nuclear contamination in Kazakhstan are difficult to assess at present, but Central Asia on the whole is in the midst of a major ecological crisis.[56]

Critical Geopolitics and Post–Cold War Asia: An Emerging Research Agenda

Critical geopolitics can be generally described as an ongoing intellectual interrogation of the politics of geographical knowledge in both national and international political arenas.[57] According to Ó Tuathail, "[c]ritical geopolitics. . .is a question not an answer, an approach not a theory, which opens up the messy problematic of geography/global politics to rigorous problematization and investigation".[58] Critical geopolitics seeks to challenge the assumptions and conceptual infrastructure that have historically defined the study of geopolitcs.[59] It begins from the premise that geography as a discourse is a form of power/knowledge. Although often assumed to be an innocent bystander, the geography of the world is not so much a product of nature as a product of the history of struggle between competing authorities over the power to organise, occupy and administer space. As Iver B. Neumann puts it, "Geography, including geopolitics is a matter of social construction. This is not to say that the lands and seas do not exit, or that they have no relevance for politics, but rather that the relevance they are seen to have is a matter of how geography is constructed."[60]

Through its engagement with contemporary theoretical developments, including post–colonialism, geopolitical economy and critical development theory,[61] critical geopolitics has come to emphasise the importance of constructing theoretically informed critiques of the spatialising practices of power; undertaking critical investigations of the power of orthodox geopolitical writing; investigating how geographical reasoning in foreign policy in-sights (enframes in a geography of images), in-cites (enmeshes in a geography of texts), and therefore, in-sites (stabilises, positions, locates) places in global politics, and exploring how this reasoning can be challenged, subverted and resisted.[62]

Accordingly, the epistemic realism of geopolitical representations is questioned and fractured, and a student of critical geopolitics is better positioned to see how the global as well as regional representations of statecraft, including those focussing on Asia, are social and political constructions: how geographical knowledge is transformed into the reductive geopolitical reasoning of the intellectuals and practitioners of statecraft; and how places are reduced to security commodities and geographical abstractions – as various sub-regions of Asia were, for example, during the cold war – which need to be 'domesticated', controlled, invaded or bombed, rather than understood in their complex reality.[63]

'Globalisation' and 'Regionalisation': Asia and the Hegemony of Trans-National Liberalism

In the aftermath of the cold war, and at a time when 'informationalisation' and 'globalisation' are remaking global space, a congruity of geography with governance is also emerging as a result of this space–time compression.[64] What we are witnessing today is the "gradual emergence of financial and trade structures, a virtual system of global economic governance that is at once bypassing, superseding and shaping statist geopolitics".[65] According to John Agnew and Stuart Corbridge, what is being manifested in the facts of globalisation, and in the attendant ideologies of neo-liberalism and market-access economics, is a new "hegemonic regime of transnational liberalism".[66] This new expansionist hegemony is polycentric because economic, cultural and geopolitical power in the modern geopolitical economy is no longer monopolised by nation-states; it is shared unevenly by a network of dominant but internally divided countries, regional groupings, city regions, international institutions and the main circuits and institutions of international production and financial capital. What binds these diverse regions and actors together is "a shared commitment to an ideology of market economics and a growing recognition that territoriality alone is not a secure basis for economic or geopolitical power".[67]

It is precisely in the context of 'globalisation from above' that the long-standing image and reality of many segments of Asia as 'suppliers' of natural resources and 'markets' is currently being reinforced. Central Asia is being reimagined as a geo-economic space awaiting 'development'. While the intellectuals of statecraft are trying to figure out the 'new' Central Asia in all kinds of geo-economic (scramble for resources), geo-strategic (new Great Game) and 'civilisational' (clash of civilisations) equations,[68] the five Central Asian republics of Kazakhstan, Turkmenistan, Uzbekistan, Tajikistan and Kyrgyzstan are coping simultaneously with an array of formidable tasks: State building; seeking and consolidating political legitimacy; national integration and nation building as well as accommodating citizens' pressures for political participation and social and economic justice.[69] These States are also handicapped by their lack of experience in self-government and international relations; fledgling communication networks; insufficient trained indigenous administrative and technical personnel; and ethno-linguistic tensions within and across the geographical region.

At the other end of the spectrum is East Asia, which, after having been integrated into the global economy since the post–war years, seems to have acquired a sudden and unprecedented 'uncertain' status in Western geopolitical calculations.[70] According to some observers,

> The current Asian situation is not unique in historical terms. Many of the region's states – including India, Indonesia, Hong Kong and Singapore – were initially unified or established by private companies. As economic growth is the primary goal of most countries in East Asia today, the current infrastructure of trade and investment is probably adequate to serve the region's needs during the final years of this century. But the sheer pace of economic – and consequently social – change occurring in this region will eventually strain the political framework inherited from the colonial and Cold War eras. There is no way to predict when nationalism, ethnic conflict over income shares, or some other ideological impulse will overwhelm Asia's current obsession with economic growth.[71]

The question is not whether economic development is going to take place in Asia. It most certainly will, but at what further cost, by whom and for whom? In other words, will it lead to ecologically sustainable and socially equitable development for the benefit of Asian communities, especially the indigenous communities, or will it simply repeat the well-known cycle of boom and bust, leaving behind damaged ecosystems, increasingly dependent 'empty' economies and shattered kinships? Questions such as these acquire additional importance in view of the recent crisis faced by the so-called 'Asian tigers'. As Professor Barun De, puts it, "if globalisation is not to be a battering ram but a facilitator of mass progress, if we have to indigenise it and popularly benefit from it in our own culture; then we have to think in terms of co-operative, but also enforceable, processes by means of which the popular will can become the general will".[72]

In recent years, 'global' problems and 'global' security have also become part of the geopolitical lexicon. Many environmental questions have been geopolitically imagined and construed to be a matter of 'global' concern, and in the process a series of new environmental threats such as ozone depletion, biodiversity loss and global climate change have been produced. These new modes of knowledge, points out Simon Dalby, "in which the globe is now the topic for discussion and analysis, and crucially of 'management' by international agreements and agencies set up for the purpose, suggest that a new form of power/knowledge is now part of twentieth-century geopolitics".[73] In other words, the discourses of 'global' environmental threats and 'environmental security' are now a part of the new agenda of the same old imperialist geopolitics.[74] As Ó Tuathail puts it,

> The emergence of a new congealment of geo-power called "environ-mental security" can be interpreted as a response to the problems that decades of environmental degradation are posing for the rich and powerful, planetary-wide dilemmas involving questions of production, technology, sustainable development and consumerism that the rich cannot afford to ignore. Even in their relatively immunised, tame zones, the world's richest peoples and ruling classes will be affected. Thus questions of ozone depletion, rainforest cover, biodiversity, global warming, and production using environmentally hazardous materials are the subject of a new environmental mapping of the global, contemporary acts of geo-power that triangulate global space around the fears and fantasies of the already affluent.[75]

There are no simple answers to the contradictions arising from the desire for economic growth and the imperatives of environmental conservation – often casually compressed into the term 'sustainable development'.[76] There is a fear that the discourse of sustainable development can become a dangerous formulation that allows injustice and environmental degradation to continue as part of the ideologically refurbished process of 'development'.[77] The Western interest in sustainable development may also result in restricting the economic options of the poor countries;[78] so also the sustainable development concerns of the 'modernising' elites in

Asian countries may be part of an imperial system of consumption. Yet alternatives to the dominant paradigm of growth-oriented economic development must be found. The question is: how does one construct an ecological practice that answers the needs of the vast mass of Asian peoples and avoids the trap of imperialist designs? Since most interactions between human activities and the natural environment are best observed, measured and managed at the grass-roots level *in situ,* i.e., by those directly affected, it is vitally important to conceive of sustainability, first and foremost, from the lowest levels: from the experience of those most disadvantaged and vulnerable. This applies equally to coastal communities throughout Asia, considered to be at special risk because of their isolation, fragile resource base, and often, poorer levels of education and health. Community-based development calls for an alternative to State-centred, highly centralised and bureaucratised approaches to economic growth. As Vandana Shiva puts it so aptly,

> the 'global' must bend to the local, since the local exists with nature, while the 'global' exists only in the offices of the World Bank and the IMF and the headquarters of multinational corporations. The local is everywhere. The ecological space of global ecology is the integration of all locals. The 'global' in global reach is a political space, not an ecological one.[79]

How the Asian States would respond to financial liberalisation, the imperatives of economic development and basic needs, resisting at the same time the ecological imperialism of Western economic/cultural powers remains to be seen. Can non-alignment, both as a movement and a foreign policy strategy, play a role in challenging the 'hegemony of trans-national liberalism' and help the peoples of Asia realise an ecologically sustainable and socially just development also remains to be seen. At best, one can hope that, as pointed out by A. P. Rana, the movement will be able to go into a self-introspective sabbatical, re-thinking basics, so that it can emerge stronger for its self-critique. Perhaps it may then conclude that its immediate major agenda should focus on seriously addressing the complexities of its members' intra-State affairs rather than, like Don Quixote, tilting at the windmills of contemporary international relations. Without this 'home-front' effort, the movement will continue to be ill equipped to handle the momentous issues of international change.[80]

Between the two extremes of nation-state and global totality is yet another level, consisting of groups and clusters of States located within particular geographical–geopolitical regions. What kind of geopolitical entities are the regional clusters of this sort in Asia, with the Association of

South East Asian Nations (ASEAN) constituting the most significant and the Indian Ocean Rim-Association for Regional Cooperation (IOR-ARC) being the most recent example, going to become in future?[81] Will they eventually create genuinely trans-national structures, equipped with the necessary will and capability to bypass the hegemonic interests both within the nation-states and in the world at large, thereby serving the interests of the peoples of the region concerned? Or will they simply "replicate many of the spatial characteristics of the nation state at the transnational level" and eventually become some kind of 'Regional States'?[82] What will be the implications of 'regional cooperation' for resource-supplying peripheries within the nation-states that are now going to be integrated into a new 'regional order'? What about the people and their perspectives at the grass-roots level, the ones long marginalised and peripheralised by the dominant centres of power in the name of 'national interests'? Will the emergence of a 'region' ensure ecologically sustainable and socially equitable development for civil society as a whole? Or will it imply further exploitation of natural resources, now in the name of regional interests rather than national interests? As new trans-national corporatist spaces are envisioned for the future, the geopolitical significance of Asia too is likely to change. This change could witness yet another round of the political fragmentation of Asia, this time along regional fault lines.

Emerging 'Terrains of Resistance' in Asian Peripheries: The Promise and Prospects of Anti-Geopolitics

The term 'anti-geopolitics' has been defined by **Paul Routledge** as

> an ethical, political and cultural force within civil society – i.e., those institutions and organizations that are neither part of the processes of material production in the economy, nor part of state-funded or state-controlled organizations (e.g. religious institutions, the media, voluntary organizations, educational institutions and trade unions) – that challenges the notion that the interests of the state's political class are identical to the community's interests.[83]

Anti-geopolitics invites attention to the fact that geopolitical knowledge tends to be wielded by those holding positions of power and privilege. Little surprise therefore that the various histories in the annals of geopolitics have tended to focus upon the actions of the States and their elites. What one finds missing from such histories, however, is an account of how various forms of domination, subjugation and exploitation, which result from such practices, have been met by popular resistance. According to Routledge,

> These histories of resistance can be characterized as a 'geopolitics from below', emanating from subaltern (i.e. dominated) positions within society that challenge the military, political, economic and cultural hegemony of the state and its elites. These challenges are counter-hegemonic struggles in that they articulate resistance to the coercive force of the state—in both domestic and foreign policy—as well as withdrawing popular consent to be ruled "from above".[84]

Routledge argues for (1) locating social movements within a contested web of power/knowledge relations; (2) theoretically analysing social movements as multiplicities explored through the concept of 'terrain of resistance' (a 'terrain of resistance' refers to the sites of contestation and the multiplicity of relations between hegemonic and counter-hegemonic powers and discourses; between political forces of domination, subjection and exploitation and the moral forces of protest, resistance and struggle); and (3) a critical identification with locally-based and single-issue-oriented new social movements (such as ecological, anti-nuclear and indigenous rights struggles) that represent attempts to create political alternatives outside the purview of organised electoral politics.[85]

Applying such critical geopolitical perspectives to peoples' movements, especially to the struggles of indigenous communities across Asia, promises to deflect any Westernised analytical focus away from an exclusive concern with the political machinations of the Asian States towards an investigation into how such social movements challenge State-centred notions of hegemony, consent and power as well as the colonisation of the 'political' in Asian studies.

Defining 'indigenous' and 'tribal' peoples, the issues of collective and individual rights and those of national unity and self-determination are highly sensitive, complex and controversial.[86] While the largest number of tribal and indigenous peoples in the world are in Asia,[87] a majority of them are in India. There is a fair amount of politics involved in defining 'indigenous' at the national as well as the United Nations levels.[88] For example, in any country 'indigenous' can be perceived in two ways: one in terms of the time frame; the other with reference to an earth-bound quality of life with or without reference to a time frame. To most perceptive leaders of indigenous and tribal peoples what matters most is the authentic ground reality of these peoples' peripheral existence, and the manner in which their communities – call them native, aboriginal, indigenous, tribal, etc. – are being further marginalised by the forces of modernisation and globalisation. Definitions notwithstanding, indigenous peoples the world over are under acute pressure today. In practice, very few countries in the world show genuine regard for their cultural or ecological rights or for their rights to proper rehabilitation when dislocation was said to be 'inevitable' in the larger national interest. Governments by and large seem bent upon integrating and assimilating them, and entrepreneurs, trans-national corporations, development agencies and other economic forces are eager to exploit the mineral and other resources located in their habitats. As Christoph von Fürer-Haimendorf puts it,

> There can be no doubt that the establishment of vast industrial enterprises in tribal zones lends urgency to the extensions of protective measures to all tribals whose rights and ways of life have been placed in jeopardy. . . unfortunately for the tribals the original idealism of the politicians and legislators is wearing thin, and while the laws for protecting the tribals are still in existence, their implementation leaves much to be desired. . . .While many may concede that any privileges enjoyed by the tribes were required only for a period of transition, and that within a span of perhaps ten or twenty years the integration of tribes within the mainstream of the populations should be completed, whereupon there would be no more justification for the continuation of scheduled areas and privileges for scheduled tribes. This new trend in public opinion represents as great a threat to the future prospects of the tribals as the greed of land-grabbers does to their present well-being.[89]

'Globalization', says B. K. Roy Burman, "is taking its toll, where it has made massive inroads in many Latin American countries and from this experience it can be predicted that the future will be bleak for the tribals and indigenous peoples in the countries where globalization process is now entering, unless appropriate steps are taken".[90] It is no surprise, therefore, that indigenous peoples everywhere, Asia being no exception, consider the geopolitical imperative of having an effective say in the development and management of their land, water and other resources as integral to any meaningful democratisation. But the ground reality is that the institutional arrangements to ensure indigenous peoples' meaningful participation in political decision-making processes are missing in most of Asia. The Indian experience, points out Roy Burman, is that till now it has not been possible even to initiate a meaningful public debate on these matters:

> For the affected peoples this is a matter of pervasive bitterness; ebb and flow of darkness of varying intensity in their soul, from which they try to run

away through alcoholism, participating in drug trafficking or through collective moral cleansing by participating in or sympathizing with acts of violence and insurgency.[91]

The dominant ethos of the 'globalisation-from-above' market logic, with minimal attentiveness to adverse human and environmental side effects, is being contested in several distinct areas by local grass-roots-level initiatives and trans-national networks created by women and indigenous peoples in support of human-centred and earth-sensitive values and approaches.[92] One of the better known peoples' movements against ecologically destructive mining is in the Doon Valley villages of Nahi-Kala and Thano near Dehra Dun in Uttaranchal, India, where activists of the Chipko movement have been working with local communities to draw attention to the fact that mining of limestone has totally undermined the material basis of the survival of the people.[93] A fairly large number of anti-dam movements in India continue to be led by people facing displacement due to the submergence of large areas upstream of the dam sites.

Indigenous discourses on nature, land use, economic regulation and management offer alternatives to Western theories of development, and propose new perspectives on the issue of sustainable development that can no longer be disregarded. As Franke Wilmer puts it, "Indigenous peoples' demand for inclusion in global civic discourse not only challenges the status quo but it is in some ways an exercise in the deconstruction of meaning attached to international values such as modernization and development."[94] The emerging popularity of indigenous perspectives, evidenced by the growing acceptance of the validity of indigenous peoples' interpretation of events that had heretofore been the exclusive (interpretative) domain of non-indigenous experience and knowledge is becoming less marginalised in the dominant State-centric geopolitical discourse. It remains to be seen, however, whether such counter-discourses of knowledge and resistance will have any meaningful role to play in shaping Asian geopolitics in the twenty-first century.

Perspectives on the Twenty-First Century

I tried to show in this essay that 'Asia' can also be seen as a social construction, one that is located within an essentially imperialist geopolitical framework. Asia has been construed and represented differently in Western geopolitical imaginations at different times in history, and the Western perceptions of, and attitudes to, the continent and its various sub-regions have also changed from one geopolitical phase to another. In each of the three geopolitical epochs, Asian politics has been discursively organised around specific characterisations of space, place and people. Even though the geopolitical perception of each specific 'age' is distinctive in many respects, there are perceptible continuities as old themes are recycled and refurbished in new contexts. Western imperialism defined Asia in ways to suit its own interests, with geopolitics as a discursive field helping to structure a view of Asia that stressed the continent's difference from, and inferiority to, the West and thereby legitimised a pursuit of conquest and domination. The geopolitical legacies of the age of imperial exploration and 'discovery' still persist in many parts of Asia. Geopolitical thinking from the classical period of geopolitics was extended to the cold war period, and Asia was reimagined as a rimland that had to be controlled and made available for Western containment of the heartland power, the Soviet Union. After the end of the cold war a 'new' geopolitics has been formulated that is continuing to classify Asia in ways that fit into the broader strategic vision of the imperial powers, principally the Western. The discourse of transnational liberalism has superseded the realist vision of containment; Asia is once again enmeshed in imperialist designs through the forces of economic globalisation and political fragmentation. Thus globalism and the new regionalisms can be seen as insidious structures which are assimilating Asia or 'segments' of it into a new imperial order. The manner in which 'Asia Pacific' has been discursively carved out of Asia in recent times is one among numerous examples that attest to such assimilation. How a new 'strategic region' can be constructed from the narrow 'national security' and 'national interest' point of view of a hegemonic global power is borne out by the contention that,

a new strategic region may be in the process of emerging. It is an area of the world where Americans have had the fewest contacts, yet where a number of issues of importance to the United States are increasingly evident. *The region is "three Asias" encompassing large portions of South, West and Central Asia.* Here, *American security and non-proliferation interests* reside in the shape of two emergent nuclear weapon states (NWS), India and Pakistan; one acknowledged NWS, Kazakhstan; and at least one incipient NWS, Iran. Here *American interests concerning human rights and democratization* reside in the shape of the experiments in democracy in Pakistan, India and some of the Central Asian states, and in the violation of human rights in countries such as Afghanistan and Iran. Here in the Three Asias, one also finds *the origins of some of the strongest Western fears about the contagion of a radical, politicized brand of Islam.* Here, *American economic and development interests are joined because the region is the source of much of the world's oil reserves, contains many of its poorest people, and yet also has the resources to emerge as a significant market in a global economy.* Finally, and not least, here is *where American counternarcotics interests* reside, within a region responsible for the world's second largest supply of heroin. (Emphasis added.) [95]

It is obvious from the emerging constellations of geo-power at the end of the twentieth century and the beginning of the twenty-first, that just as Halford John Mackinder proclaimed a post–Columbian epoch of closed global space at the turn of the nineteenth century, intellectuals of state-craft – both from within and outside Asia – are tempted "to proclaim at century's end the emergence of an 'unruly epoch' of 'ungovernable', 'turbulent' and 'disorderly' global space".[96] As the State-centric ruling systems and disciplining institutions of statecraft (such as the army, police and bureaucracy) face a challenge to the 'hegemony of trans-national liberalism', the 'new' rules of the world order are likely to be rewritten by the 'old' masters of global space. To cite just one example, the sensational, but ahistorical and ageographic "Clash of Civilizations" thesis of Samuel Huntington shows how deterritorialising geographical space is "to be hardened against foreign civilizations and reterritorialized along the lines of an imaginary Euro-American cultural and political order. The real is to be disciplined to fit the imaginary".[97] Among the many implications inherent in this remarkably simplistic and comprehensively flawed thesis for Asian polities and peoples is not only how the 'West' is rewritten to partially exclude Japan – the United States' traditional cold war ally – but how Asia is fragmented while producing the 'civilised' global scene.

Can there be an Asian geopolitics? Yes, there can be an Asian geopolitics, in the sense of a critical geopolitics that resists the takeover of Asia by globalisation and regionalisation 'from above' – that is, not an 'Asian geopolitics' with the connotation of some native, independent theory of strategic spaces but a forever critical practice *for* and *in* Asia, based also on peoples' struggles and on ecological practices. It is absolutely vital, however, that a critical Asian geopolitics also seeks to construct alternative discourses directed at reconceptualising the notions of sovereignty, security· and development in an increasingly interdependent world, while examining the question of an ecologically sustainable present as well as future at local, regional and global levels in an emerging global society. Obviously, the success of such alternative geopolitical discourses (they may have to compete and even coexist with the hegemonic doctrine) will depend to a large extent upon radical changes in the perceptions, policies and practices of those who speak for and act on behalf of Asian nation-states.

In order to be truly radical, an Asian geopolitics will also have to contest the persistent State-centric and geo-strategic preoccupations of a fairly large number of Asian States and the militarised, geopolitical mindset of their political elites. To cite just a few examples, the mini-cold war in South Asia between India and Pakistan has entered its most aggressive phase after the two traditional rivals decided to 'go nuclear'; Afghanistan and Tajikistan are involved in a bitter conflict; Central Asia is struggling through a geopolitical transition; and Russia continues to search for a new 'strategic' role.[98] Disputes over territorial boundaries exist everywhere in Eurasia. The national security concerns of East Asian countries are being increasingly expressed by a number of observers in reference to a perceived threat from China, "because, only it [China] has the capacity of projecting its power far beyond its borders, and historically this is what it has done. The situation can be summed up in two words: Chung Kuo (Middle Kingdom), which carry with them China's old claim to be the center of a world."[99] With the exception of Vietnam, with which Japan is said to be boosting political and security ties, the other countries of Southeast Asia are said to be extremely fearful of Japanese intentions, since "they were subjected to a very harsh occupation and many atrocities by the Japanese forces during World War II and are wary of the resurgence of Japan as a great military power".[100] Serious differences persist among the South, West and Central Asias on core issues affecting their security and future aspirations.[101]

As Ó Tuathail aptly puts it,

Critical geopolitics is one of the many cultures of resistance to Geography as imperial truth, state-capitalized knowledge, and military weapon. It is a small part of a much larger rainbow struggle to decolonize our inherited geographical imagination so that other geo-graphings and other worlds might be possible.[102]

In the case of the Asian societies the key issue for an alternative normative geographical discourse is to articulate its geographical vision of an Asian order in which space and ecology is reclaimed for people, especially indigenous communities; the 'inevitability' of mastering space and resources by either States or markets under the banner of 'globalisation' and 'regionalisation' is effectively contested and rejected; and peaceful diplomatic solutions are found for resolving outstanding bilateral and multilateral disputes. As new geographies in Asia are being written and as new geopolitical narratives continue to emerge, it will be vital to ensure that the sights and sounds of 'anti-geopolitics' at the grass-roots level are not ignored. Herein lies the challenge for both scholars and practitioners of the new Asian geopolitics in the late twentieth century and beyond.

Frontiers and Borders: Spaces of Sharing, Spaces of Conflict

PAULA BANERJEE

Introduction

> Just beyond the perimeter of what nationalism constructs as the nation, at the frontiers separating us from the alien, is the perilous territory . . .
>
> — Edward Said, *Mind in Winter: Reflections on Life in Exile*

This chapter is an attempt to explore the concept of borders in recent history. The occupation of territory is fundamental to a State's sovereignty. An exclusive command over a territory, however, also implies an unwillingness to share it with 'others'. The State creates its own markers within which its 'self' disengages from the 'alien'. Terms indicating the proclivity of social groups to engage with others, or to disengage 'us' from 'them', serve as markers of that engagement/disengagement and are as old as human history. At certain historical junctures these markers came to be called 'frontiers', 'boundaries' and 'borders'. However, the three words have different meanings and historical significances. To further compound the problem, etymologically related words such as the French *'frontiere'* and English 'frontier' have widely different connotations. Furthermore, while western Europe uses terms such as 'boundaries' and 'borderlands' to describe borders, 'frontier' is widely used in the United States. Thus the task of defining the subtle differences between frontiers, boundaries and borders is a complex one.

In Europe, the history of frontiers and borders is ancient and varied. Malcolm Anderson in his book *Frontiers: Territory and State Formation in the Modern World* traces this history back to the Roman Empire. The density of population within the empire meant a lack of uninhabited spaces; as a consequence, the Romans were compelled to mark out discrete territories. When the Romans extended their empire into Gaul (France) and Britain, they took this practice of demarcating boundaries with them.[1] One such marker is Hadrian's Wall, which separated Roman Britain from the wilds of ancient Scotland. Later on, newly discovered trade routes during the Middle Ages necessitated a clear assertion of political control over them; routes were thus divided into zones of control. But political control did not necessarily mean economic control. The city or the league in which the route was located, for instance, could have controlled the trade in a zone, while politically the area may have been under a feudal lord. This ambiguity often led to demarcations that were not distinctly marked or completely accepted. Emperor Charlemagne, for example, was confronted with the problem of maintaining control over the marches of his empire; although he employed *missi dominici* (government agents) for this purpose, the periphery often remained under the jurisdiction of the local counts. This state of affairs continued until the twelfth century, when the descendants of Hugh Capet consolidated their power under centralised monarchies in France, thus leading to the creation of political boundaries for the first time. When cartography became popular during the Renaissance maps came to be used as a further aid to the centralisation of power. The colonial period in the nineteenth century, however, elevated maps into a weapon of statecraft: without setting foot on the mountains and rivers of the present Afro-Asian States, the imperial powers used the topographical features on maps as bargaining tools among themselves. In this context, Liberals and Marxists alike agree that boundaries are made to manipulate a certain distribution of power, and that there is a clear connection between imperialism and the demarcation of a State's borders.

The preceding paragraph describes how borders evolved in western Europe; circumstances in eastern Europe lead to borders being formed in a different way, which is not pertinent to this article. This chapter will show how the west European concept of borders was imposed on, and subsequently internalised, in South Asia, with very definite repercussions on State formation in that region.

In contrast, the Great Wall of China epitomises East Asian boundaries. The wall was built as an essential precaution against the 'barbarians' of Central Asia, though the actual frontier lay further west in a region that contained important trade routes. In South Asia however, the concept of borders differed in many respects from the European version. Seas and oceans largely bordered the Indian sub-continent, and there were no centralised regimes that ruled over the entire land area; thus there seemed to be no need for a marker of frontiers. The pillar inscriptions found in many parts of India were usually meant to spread the message of a ruler throughout his land; they were not constructed to mark frontiers. Further, unlike the Russian monarchs, the rulers of South Asia had no ambitions of controlling the oceans, for it was the land routes that had decisively influenced the history of the region before the advent of the Europeans. One of the reasons why the South Asian political system did not concern itself particularly about political boundaries was that, traditionally, the unit of administration was not the ruler but often the village. The rulers largely confined their jurisdiction to within the capital and the adjacent provinces. The village, which was primarily composed of kinsmen, was governed, according to the ancient Indian political commentator Sukracharya's work, the *Nititsara*, by the panchayat, an elected body that was treated with the greatest respect by the ruler's officers. The panchayat collected taxes and paid the government its share. It was very difficult for an outsider to recognise where one village ended and another began without some knowledge of the kinship ties between these villages. Recent researches show how difficult it was to locate the boundaries of each village. Frontiers, on the other hand, were regions where claims of ownership were often contested. In the South Asian context, rulers did not concern themselves too much about these regions as long as they did not overtly disturb the peace of the land. Such a state of affairs continued until the British took charge of 'rationalising' the South Asian administrative system after they brought the whole of the region under a centralised authority.[2] Thus, while the local political systems before the advent of the British did concern themselves with frontiers (which were largely areas impossible to govern), they did not attach the same degree of importance to borders and boundaries in the west European way.

To understand this dichotomy, it is necessary to comprehend the differences in meaning between frontiers, boundaries and borders.

Internationally, the first efforts to differentiate between frontiers, as distinct from boundaries and borders, came from political geographers. In 1947, A. E. Moodie wrote that "frontiers are areal, boundaries are linear.... The former may be correctly described as natural....The latter are artificial."[3] A border, he argued, is a boundary line, and frontiers are boundary regions. In common usage they are synonymous, because in many cases, until very recently, the limits of a State were ill-defined. This was largely due to a lack of detailed knowledge of its outlying terrain and the absence of its exact cartographic representation. Even to a present-day scholar of geopolitics, frontiers and borders are differentiated in similar terms. Frontiers are, to such a scholar, regions "of varying widths, which were common features of the political landscape centuries ago. By the beginning of the twentieth century most remaining frontiers had disappeared, replaced by boundaries which are lines", and the State made these boundary lines its borders.[4] Frontiers, then, are zones at the periphery of a political division that have been slowly replaced in the last two centuries by boundaries or lines of political control, which have subsequently become borders. A differentiation of frontiers and borders is crucial for the argument that a border has a political connotation that was acquired as the result of a historical specificity, which necessitated its formation. In western Europe, borders had resulted from political developments over the last three centuries, as a result of which demarcation of States became a necessity. But if borders were simply lines to demarcate the limits of States, why then do they appear as constructs that bedevil the given history of States? Is a border a problematic in itself? It is necessary to sift through the existing histories of borders to answer this conundrum.

Classical Works on Frontiers and Borders

> The space accessible to humankind is continuous, yet there is a compulsion to control access and create partition.
>
> –Jean Gottman, *The Significance of Territory*

The philosopher Michael Berube once said about canons in literature that they are "at once the location, the index, and the record of the struggle for [cultural] representation; like any other hegemonic formation, they must be continually reproduced anew and are continually contested".[5] Seminal works become classics in the histories of their fields, and they become canons when their authenticity is repeatedly reaffirmed.

After having established that frontiers and borders are two different entities with their own, though not very distinct, histories, classical studies in geopolitics begin with frontiers – the psychology of an expansive push. Traditionally, frontiers referred to the territorial expansion of States into 'empty' areas. Such an expansionist view of frontiers was voiced by the American scholar, Frederick Jackson Turner, in his paper *The Significance of the Frontier in American History* at the annual conference of the American Historical Association in 1893.[6] This was a time of turmoil in America, with, in the East, the Populists leading an agrarian revolt, and a similar revolt of farmers, which was to culminate in the Bryan Campaign, growing in the West. There were also signs of a growing revolt in the West against the cultural dominance of the East. Although the paper failed to create an immediate stir, according to American historian Richard

Hofstadter, it has become "the most famous and influential paper in the history of American historical writing".[7] Turner in his paper argued that it was the frontier that had produced American democracy and individualism: the frontier stripped the European of most of his "cultural baggage" and subordinated him to the "disciplines of wilderness". He ascribed much of the impact of the frontier to the fact that it symbolised a process of perpetual rebirth: the vast, empty expanses of the frontier brought men close to the fundamentals of existence and forced them to rebuild social structures from the bare basics. American social development, to him, had begun time and again on the frontier.[8] These assertions in the Turner thesis were not to be confined to the United States alone; historians, in most cases quite unsuccessfully, tried to test the applicability of Turner's thesis in other parts of the world, forgetting that Turner was inspired by certain specific historical developments in the United States alone. D. W. Treadgold's portrayal of the great drift of Russian immigrants into Siberia as a similar movement is a case in point.[9] Others found a relevance to Turner's views in Latin America, particularly in Brazil, where frontier policies were markedly similar to those in the United States. Indeed, Brazilian history is replete with a number of sequential frontier pushes. It has been argued that

> The epitome of mobility were the *bandeirantes* [expeditionary groups]. Brazilian historians have regarded them as their frontiersmen par excellence, exploring the interior, discovering gold and staking out political claims for the Portuguese crown.[10]

Comparisons with Turner's thesis, in which the search for new spaces was seen essentially as individually motivated, could give rise to the question of whether frontier expansion under authoritarian military rule was any different from that under democratic governments, with which these movements were equated. There seems to be no clear answer to this, and present-day social scientists and historians are still debating the issue.[11] In the 1990s, an interesting variant on the Turner thesis was produced by David A. Chappell, who argued that frontiers were zones of transformative interaction between systems. Whereas Turner referred only to the transformation of the European man, Chappell stressed that "any frontier is really dual". It affected both the "intruders" and the "indigenous people".[12] Despite some similar recent studies on the issue of frontiers, social scientists in the United States are increasingly shifting the focus of their attention to borders and borderlands.[13] This shift is largely in response to the need for utilitarian solutions to the problems arising from cross-border migrations and drug trafficking as a result of infiltration into the US from Mexico and Canada.

The psychology of an expansive push associated with frontiers is, ironically enough, only a step away from the delimiting line – the boundary. The German geographer Friedrich Ratzel made the first determined efforts to produce a set of laws that could allow for boundaries to be predicted. Ratzel believed that each State had some idea of the possible limits of its territorial dominion, which he called "space conception". Ratzel's book, written during the reign of Emperor Wilhelm II, reflected the transformation of Germany from an amalgamation of small kingdoms and principalities into the greater German Empire by the 1870s. Ratzel's geopolitical reasoning followed logically from his belief that a country was like a living organism; the boundary and its adjacent territory, which he termed the border, were dynamic, and if they were fixed in position, that position was purely temporary, pending a further political expansion. He argued that a political balance between countries was dependent on the characteristics of the borders they shared. [14]

Students of *Geopolitik*, about thirty years later, again popularised the view that a border was the area within which the growth and decline of a State originated. Karl Haushofer, the geographer who founded the Geopolitik school, held in the 1930s that attention to geography in policy making would help Germany become strong again after her defeat in the First World War. In a reflection of his times, he proposed, significantly, that a homogenous population should have a cultural periphery beyond which should lie the military boundary. However, German aggression and the Second World War led to Geopolitik being discredited in the post–war years. Moreover, German geopoliticians lost much of their prominence when it became clear that occupation of territory was not the only form of dominance. Between 1945 and 1989, most changes in the balance of power between adjoining States were not accompanied by changes in international boundaries. Having said this, however, it has to be kept in mind that the post–war boundaries were to change again within fifty years in Central and eastern Europe, and that physical determination of new borders became necessary once again.

The French social scientists took up the mantle of boundary and border studies from the German geopoliticians in the late 1930s and '40s. The French were discovering connections between geography and history around this time, and a lot of creative work on boundaries and borders was undertaken. P. de Lapradelle, a lawyer by profession, was the first to identify a series of stages in the evolution of a boundary. These were, 'preparation', 'delimitation' and 'execution'. The process of preparation preceded delimitation: the boundary was first debated at the political and then at the technical – map-marking – levels. Thereafter, the process of execution consisted of the demarcation of a boundary on the ground. Lapradelle propounded the view that laws were required to facilitate boundary changes.[15]

Just before the Second World War, in 1938, J. Ancel, another French social scientist, theorised that boundaries were temporary lines where the opposing power of neighbouring States was neutralised. He referred to these international boundaries as 'Isobars'.[16] The theories of the Frenchman, Norman J. G. Pounds, published in 1951, acquired prominence at a time when the French were trying to revive a sense of pride and identity after the fall of the Maginot Line – their supposedly infallible eastern border – and their psychologically crushing defeat and occupation by the Germans. He explored the concept of *les limites naturelles* (natural boundaries) with respect to France, and established that, for much of history after the sixteenth century, successive French rulers had regarded France's desirable boundaries as coinciding with the Mediterranean Sea, the Alpine watershed, the Pyrenees and the Rhine. He not only put the question of boundaries in a historical context but also made the concept of "natural boundaries" fashionable.[17] His assumption was that although France may not have natural boundaries which extended up to those regions, French political influence, by virtue of its history, should certainly spread that far.

Thus, from a review of the classics on frontiers and boundaries it is clear that American writers concentrated largely on the development of frontiers, while west European scholars expounded mainly on boundaries and borders. This is not surprising, since the difference in the political realities of the two regions encouraged this divergence in ideas. It was during the cold war and the ever-increasing influence of the Realists in geopolitics that borders acquired a whole new political significance.

Space and State

What the word for space, *Raum, Rum*, designates is said by its ancient meaning. *Raum* means a place cleared or freed for settlement and lodging. A space is something that has been made room for, something that is cleared and free, namely within a boundary . . .

Martin Heidegger, *Building, Dwelling, Thinking*

The Second World War revolutionised the understanding of the State as a territorial phenomenon, and necessitated the examination of political space such as boundaries and borderlands in relation to less tangible but readily identifiable ethnic and cultural elements, particularly in what came to be known as the Third World. Between the late 1940s and early 1960s, borders the world over became a crucial issue for newly emergent States. Borders became markers of political control and an expression of the consolidation of territorial gains. In most countries in the Third World national borders were in large measure determined by the economic, military and diplomatic policies of the imperial powers that had colonised those countries. Erstwhile European colonies in this region were carved up with little regard for tribal boundaries, and even less for the requirements of a viable nation-state. On the one hand, for instance, the division of their land into Belgian Congo and Portuguese Angola split up great tribes such as the Bakongo in Africa; the Somalis were similarly divided among five States. On the other hand, Western imperialism enclosed peoples of different religions, languages and levels of development into colonies that later became independent. The new theories on border demarcation that were being propounded in Western Europe were completely disregarded when it came to the creation of new boundaries in the Third World. The State elites within these newly created countries then hardened these lines when they tried to legitimise their hegemony by imposing a firm control over these borders. According to Michiel Baud and Willem Van Schendel, by "taking possession of disputed or unclaimed areas, state elites tried to resolve the problem of loosely defined border regions to which two or even more states might lay claim. In this way, they drew sharper lines between citizens, invested with certain rights and duties, and 'aliens' or 'foreigners'."[18] Thus it was that by colluding with their former colonisers, the State elites formalised the borders of the Third World at a time when control over space by cold war antagonists became crucial for political hegemony. The border, as distinct from space, seemed to be fast losing its significance. Paradoxically, what was increasingly considered redundant in the West was becoming vitally important for the Third World. Mapping borders now became essential for the establishment of clear-cut territorial, and hence political, jurisdiction.

Mapping necessarily meant that conflicting claims of control could no longer be ignored;[19] thus, precision in cartography led to the emergence of fully-demarcated territorial States.[20] According to Stephen B. Jones' well-known study, the mapping of borders went through three stages: establishment, demarcation and control.[21] This study acquired enormous significance during the period of decolonisation and it was therefore in the former colonies that the relevance of these ideas was closely scrutinised.[22]

Mapping facilitates the constructing of morphological models for States by modern political geographers. These models impart cultural attributes to certain spatial structures such as core regions and frontiers. Such models have been the basis for theorisation both on the morphology of States as well as the spatial processes connected with it. These theorisations have led to a redefinition of territoriality as a means to some end, such as material survival or political control. Some scholars argue that territoriality is an attempt by an individual or a group to affect, influence or control people, phenomena and relationships by delimiting and asserting control over geographical areas. Territory then becomes a justification for claims, as opposed to occupation, though the latter may be a prerequisite for the former.[23] Other theorists describe territoriality as a phenomenon occurring when a bounded geographical space is ruled by an elite that wants to dominate not only within but also beyond its limits.[24] Boundaries and borders thus become markers of the power that States wield over people. This has been particularly true of those post–colonial States that had to negotiate not only their borders but also, more importantly, inter- and intracommunity demarcating lines with their neighbouring States.[25]

Classical works on frontiers and borderlands thus show us how borders become markers of sovereignty – an essential characteristic for modern State formation. Recent discourses on borders, however, based largely on African and Latin American experiences, deal with this marker of territoriality and power from a different perspective. These discourses reveal that borders have constantly to be renegotiated between communities; new identities then evolve through these processes of negotiation. In their study, Astrid Suhrke and Lela Garner emphasise that the 'external' presence influences internal issues in border making: they believe that the paramount question of identity is leading to a collapse of other sub-categories, making borders and borderlands the homesteading ground for "cultural determinism". There is a growing emphasis on how socially-constructed "fine lines" determine to a great extent who we are and what kind of identities we evolve.[26] Border studies, as a result, have shifted away from a simple focus on territory to an examination of the influence of borders on the identities of people, be they political, cultural or any other. The border thus becomes a cultural zone shared by co-ethnics who may or may not be co-citizens.[27] A study by W. F. S. Miles and D. A. Rochefort portrays how this has given rise to irredentism and cross-border conflicts in sub-Saharan Africa.[28] The well-known African social scientist, A. I. Asiwaju, focusses on the human factor in the formation of borders in Africa, which transforms the received colonial status quo into an evolving border where none previously existed. In effect, borders in these areas are products of a partition from above, often accepted by the State elites, but constantly challenged by ethnic resistance from below. This is how many Third World borders have acquired a unique non-Western characteristic. [29]

Borderlands in South Asia

> Frontiers are indeed the razor's edge on which hang suspended the modern
> issues of war or peace, of life or death for nations. . .
>
>   Lord Curzon, *The Romanes Lecture*

History books on South Asia suggest that South Asian borders had remained undemarcated for centuries, evoking little interest from the British colonialists and almost none from the indigenous inhabitants themselves. Merchants, traders and religious men were able to cross its frontiers at will because there was no rigidly demarcated border. The "frontier idea was introduced when the East India Company's expansion up to, and then beyond the Himalayas precipitated rivalries between Britain, China and Russia" in the nineteenth century.[30] The Durand Line, set up in 1893, separating present-day Pakistan from Afghanistan, and the McMahon Line between India and China were constituted within ten years of one another. These demarcations, however, were in virtually inaccessible regions, which meant that frontiers were quickly reduced to lines on maps, with little knowledge of what this actually entailed on the ground. Thus, South Asia probably had one of the first borderlands in the world, and commentaries on the border soon followed. British administrators like Sir Mortimer Durand and Sir Thomas Holdich, who was, at the end of the nineteenth century, the Surveyor-General of India, conducted the initial mapping of South Asia's borders. Holdich's study of the Himalayas led him to remark that the mountain range was the finest "combination of boundary and barrier that exists in the world".[31] While Turner in America was expounding on the philosophical aspect of frontiers, the British were shrewdly demarcating South Asian borders with essentially political intentions.

British interest in South Asian border studies had commenced with George Nathaniel Curzon, later Marquis of Kedleston, when, as a member of Parliament with colonial interests, he had explored the Pamirs and the Karakorams. Awake to the possibility that Tibet as a frontier region could in future become a field of play for the Great Game between Russia and Britain, he encouraged Francis Younghusband's path-breaking mission to Lhasa in 1904. He was fully aware that, as far as Asia was concerned, the idea of a demarcated frontier did not exist. Thus demarcation had to take place under "European pressure and by the intervention of European agents". Curzon had very definite views about the sort of frontiers that he wanted for the British Empire: he advocated a scientific frontier that "unites natural and strategic strength".[32] Curzon coupled an innate strategic sense with practical geographic knowledge, but the politically sensitive nature of India's newly-defined borders at that time caused him to cast a cloak of secrecy over all matters pertaining to those regions, accessible only to government agents, military personnel and secret service agents. Curzon's influence can well be gauged by the realisation that even today many South Asian States continue to deny their own citizens access to maps of the border regions, even outdated ones.

The next major stage in border commentaries was during the 1940s. The Second World War regenerated an interest in borders not just in Europe but also in Asia. When the Southeast Asian States fell to Japan one after another during the war, the Assam frontier in India assumed enormous importance as the easternmost British–Indian outpost. After the war, the decision by the British government to partition the Indian sub-continent led to an interest in not only the natural frontiers of the region but also in the people who inhabited those areas. Among the various studies undertaken by government officials, a classic study by Sir Robert Reid in 1941 entitled "Future of the Present Excluded, Partially Excluded and Tribal areas of Assam" noted that the British had at best only "the most shadowy control" over this whole area but that the importance of this region from the point of view of strategy and politics could not be overlooked.[33] Thus treatises on borders in South Asia were, in effect, being written by those who created them, while at the same time tying them in neatly with the 'might is right' concept of power, in much the same way as the Germans were doing in Europe. Literature in a similar vein continued even during the partition of South Asia; following colonial tradition, borders were legitimised on maps with great enthusiasm by the out-going British. However, the very people legitimising these borders soon realised their unworkability: Sir Cyril Radcliffe, the official in charge of demarcating partitioned India's new borders, confessed to the impos-sibility of trying to construct a contiguous boundary between eastern India and East Pakistan.[34] As a result, maps were drawn that were both too static and too simple. The South Asian nation-states thus came into being, or to use a more current word, were 'constructed', on the basis of these maps and an admixture of territorialism, cartographic absoluteness and outright frontierism.

Frontiers rapidly harden into borders, and those at the centre of power often vehemently deny the fact that there are two sides to a border. Many historians too have subscribed to this myopic viewpoint. Some historians, both Indian and European, have tried to understand the dynamics behind the formation of borders during the Great Game period in the late nineteenth and early twentieth centuries, but such efforts have clearly been inadequate. In the Bharatiya Vidya Bhavan series on history entitled *History and Culture of the Indian People*, for instance, the creation of the northeast and northwest frontiers of India have been dealt with in such a manner as to show that State formation followed the European imperialist urge to be the "mistress of the East".[35] Other Indian historians have also analysed the frontiers, borders and borderlands of South Asia in a similar, shallow fashion.[36] On the other hand, a British historian observed that they examined the creation of these frontiers "from [a] practical point of view, i.e., India's defence".[37] This is not surprising, since the standard histories of India by British historians depend a great deal for their source material on the accounts of government personnel serving in India at that time, who were not aware, or chose not to be aware, of the 'other side' to the issues surrounding the emergence of these borders.

While the Great Game converted frontiers into borderlands in the late nineteenth and early twentieth centuries, it was the partition of India in 1947 that changed borderlands into borders. Despite being represented as a continuation of the Great Game, partition had a substantial role to play in the post-colonial State formation of South Asia.[38] However, the post–colonial borders of South Asia have not been of much interest to scholars. One reason for this disinterest is perhaps that the new boundaries were immediately ratified by the States' elites; what was lost in the process was the understanding that borders are not some innate traits of sovereignty, but merely human constructs built on an amalgamation of geography, cartography, theories of sovereignty and the prevalent system of power. By refusing to contextualise the history of border formation in South Asia, historians have lost sight of the fact that borders take different forms in different political and historical circumstances. It is important that historians unearth the specific historical context of border formation to evolve such an understanding of circumstances. In the fifty years since partition there has been some, if not enough, interest in the process.[39]

Whither South Asian Discourses on Borders?

In the borderlands/ You are the battleground
Where enemies are kin to each other. . .

Gloria Anzaldua, *Borderlands/La Frontera: The New Mestiza*

The emphasis in this chapter on classical, imperial and largely Atlanticist discourses on frontiers and borderlands and then a probe into the historiography of South Asian borders may seem antithetical; but there is, I believe, a thematic coherence to this analysis. As South Asians, we have inherited our discourses on borders from the Western powers: there is an overlapping of the Atlanticist version of border history and historiography with our own writings that we cannot ignore. Do we as South Asians lack a sense of borders? South Asians historically have had more of an affinity with the local than the national. Under strong emperors like the Great Mughals South Asians briefly enjoyed a centralised form of government, even though such empires were not marked by a precise demarcation of borders. The region subsequently reverted to a basic level of social organisation in the absence of other strong emperors. Village economies became localised, and "communities tended to develop into self-sufficient centres. This was to become the prototype of Britain's picture of India. . . ."[40] South Asians did not have a sharply demarcated political border before the advent of the British. The leaders of India's nationalist movement, even as late as the pre-partition days, had no precise understanding of political borders: in his book *The Discovery of India* Jawaharlal Nehru envisaged India to be within a regional network of States from Iran to Thailand. Nehru himself was against geopolitics as a discipline influencing policies of governance, since geopolitics aided most of all the Realist school.[41] Although there was a growing sense of belonging to the region among Indian leaders in the early twentieth century, they were not particularly enamoured then of the idea of a politically demarcated South Asia. It is ironic that the British not only gave us our borders, but also the tools with which to study them. Instead of understanding our own historical specificity, we have tried to emulate the Western style of border studies. There remains much to be done beyond such a historical legacy.

Indian historiography is replete with interesting works on State formation that deal implicitly, but never explicitly, with borders. In *Politics in India,* political scientist Rajni Kothari describes how the Congress party created a system that married dominance by the centre and resistance from the peripheries into a consensus politics.[42] Marxist historians have done a better job of portraying the State as a site for power wielding by the dominant classes for whom centralisation is a way of acquiring political hegemony.[43] None of these studies however, explains the core/periphery dichotomy in South Asia. M. S. A. Rao and Francine Frankel view Indian politics as a clash between the rising power of formerly low-status groups and the established elites. Although this study does deal by extension with the resistance to centrist politics from the borders, this linkage is at best tenuous.[44] A number of monographs on political dominance and resistance have also been written, but none that deal exclusively with resistance from the borders as a phenomenon resulting from partition and ongoing State formations in South Asia, just as there is nothing that deals with the history that these borders have created.

By ignoring this phenomenon, we have missed an opportunity to understand the historical forces that shaped our borderlands and the complex realities of the state-systems in South Asia. This is borne out by studies on the wars fought by India against neighbouring States, particularly the 1962 Sino-Indian border war which generated a lot of interest in borders. Sadly, most of these studies were meant either to apportion blame or justify a position; the issue of the border itself appears to be only incidental. A typical example of such a study is British historian Alastair Lamb's work on the China–India border in which he finds India's stated position untenable, since China had never accepted the McMohan Line drawn by the British in the first place.[45] Neville Maxwell's study on the same subject is also along similar lines.[46] The Indian point of view is largely represented in the memoirs of Indian generals like B. M. Kaul's, in which he tries to legitimise his own campaign decisions, and that of India's then foreign minister, Krishna Menon's, whose book is an attempt to legitimise the position taken by his country in the conflict.[47] That the South Asian borders have prompted a specific kind of State formation and a resultant pattern of diplomacy is not apparent from these studies.

Dorothy Woodman's account of India's Himalayan frontiers also falls within the same genre. Woodman argues that it is the overwhelming geographical presence of the Himalayas that has shaped relations between Britain, Russia, China and India. Although the much acclaimed study has an international thrust, rather than a focus on a single country, the author tries to justify the British predatory action in the Himalayas by stating that Russia and China had similar intentions on the region, and that they actively supported Britain's policy of aggrandisement when it suited them. Thus Britain could not be blamed for the situation that India and China faced in the 1950s and '60s.[48] Such studies duplicate the tools used by the

Atlanticist powers in understanding their borders. Imposing the same parameters for understanding South Asia denies a recognition that the region shares a long history of cross-border movements that existed much before the East India Company was born.

The last two decades in the twentieth century have witnessed the formulation of policies to make South Asian borders even more rigid.[49] Yet a glance at the history of the region will show that the concept of demarcated borders, both inter- and intrastate, was not considered viable. It still remains to be seen whether it is wrong to contend that South Asian frontiers cannot be dissected into rigid boundaries, but can at best be organised as borderlands. The concept of strategic frontiers is a mainly imperial and Western one. When the British carved up South Asia they did it largely on paper; the ruling classes in the States thus created then ossified those borders due to power considerations. This goes against the social, cultural and economic traditions of the region. As South Asians, we are yet to come to grips with border studies, and are producing Western imitations only because we have not been able to formulate a South Asian concept of borders. To us, borders remain 'rimlands', difficult to govern, and Western hegemony, even in the realm of ideas, has made it imperative that for the purposes of 'sovereignty' these borders be converted into watertight lines. A close study of Indian efforts at a total demarcation of borders cannot be considered a success story. Such rigid demarcations will work against topography, economy, kinship networks and other linkages; in an effort to serve the political demands of the received theory of sovereignty, we are breaking 'utilitarian complementaries' and denying recognition to the history of the region.

The repeated changes in borders, whether in Central and eastern Europe, in the Eurasian region or in the heartland of Africa, have their own histories that have contributed to the politics of those regions. If anything, a historiographical review of borders in South Asia suggests that a fresh outlook is needed to understand the complex histories of space and politics, realities and ideologies. Mahnaz Z. Ispahani's account of the politics of access in the borderlands of Asia is an example of such a study: it is an analysis of the amalgamation of the forces that shaped events in South, Central and West Asia, and on the major land routes through these regions. She observes that in an effort to gain control over these routes, countries converted "zones of transitions", or peripheries, into borderlands and then demarcated them. Technological innovations notwithstanding, the primary role of land routes in this region has historically shaped relationships and alignments between Afghanistan, Pakistan, India and

China. The 1963 Sino-Pakistani friendship treaty, signed immediately after the China–India war, which resulted in the reopening of the ancient 'Silk Routes', is a case in point.[50] Ispahani's work, far from showcasing geographical determinism, offers a fresh perspective on the border studies of the region.

As mentioned earlier, scholars are now undertaking studies on Latin American and African borders, with an interest in the sociological dimensions of the field. At a 'sub-regional dialogue' held in Dhaka in February 1997, efforts along similar lines were made to understand the India–Bangladesh borderland. Such efforts will go a long way in providing fresh insights into core/periphery problems, as well as understanding cross-border linkages, or, to use a more fashionable phrase, the 'external compulsions' of South Asia today. A subsequent comparison of South Asian experiences with that of other contentious regions such as sub-Saharan Africa, Central and eastern Europe, to see how they have faced partition, post–colonialism and experiences in 'State making' and 'State breaking' is essential. Such studies would entail an appreciation of comparative historical perspectives. I admit that this is not an easy task, but definitely one worth taking on for historians.

Empires, Kingdoms and Mobile Frontiers in Central Asia

SUCHANDANA CHATTERJEE

Introduction: Changing Perceptions of the Great Game

For nearly a century, Czarist Russia and Britain had been engaged in a struggle for territorial supremacy in the lonely passes and deserts of Central Asia. Later immortalised by Rudyard Kipling in *Kim* as the "Great Game", this colonial tussle over territories in the nineteenth century brought the borders of the two empires within a few miles of each other. It began with the southward march of Russian troops through the Caucasus into Central Asia, which was perceived as a threat to India, the 'Jewel in the Crown' of the British Empire. The threat never materialised, but a shadowy struggle ensued, leaving behind a genre of literature that depicted the region itself as a pawn in a game over which the antagonists had little control. Nearly a century later, with the sudden 're-emergence' of the Central Asian region as a separate entity in the wake of the dissolution of the Soviet Union, concern over the continuing presence of numerous new 'little games' across the region has emerged, fuelled both by the perceived political 'vacuum' in the region and its rich oil and natural gas resources.

The Great Game genre, which was principally constituted of the travel writings of men who braved the unknown dangers of the region to gather information, began a tradition of perceiving the region from an onlooker's perspective, thus failing to emphasise certain crucial aspects of Central Asian reality. The imperial struggle over territory portrayed in these writings represented space as an issue of territorial control; in geopolitical terms, 'control' was viewed as crucial. But such a perception did not reckon with the feelings of the local populace that frontiers were essentially mobile. An imperial viewpoint on this issue has continued to this day. Today, the Great Game has given way to numerous little games that have reinforced the dominant image of the area as one destined to be the subject of competing foreign interests. However, new scholarship on the region is now cognisant of the need for an alternative vision – one that revises this imperial historiography to take into account the indigenous perceptions of territoriality at that time.

This essay is thus an enquiry into the mechanism of geopolitics as it evolved over the past two centuries in the Central Asian region of erstwhile Czarist Russia and, subsequently, the Soviet Union. This region, bounded in the east by China and in the west by Persia, stretched from the taiga regions of Siberia in the north to a string of oases cities in the south. It comprised of an expanse of oases, deserts, steppes and mountains, and was traditionally regarded as central to the colonising tussle over territories in the nineteenth century. In the current phase of 'transition', the same area is identified as the bone of contention among States competing with each other for its principal sources of commerce, oil and gas. The crux of all geopolitical debates on Central Asia is that contending powers get drawn into conflict by initially gaining access to routes that are used for commercial transportation. This essay examines how perceptions of routes, central to the Great Games debates, changed over time, and thus moves on to the related question of violations of territoriality, frontiers and borders in Central Asia.

In the nineteenth century, the Great Game pertained to issues of territoriality, zones of influence and buffer zones. It entailed wide-scale diplomatic exercises by the Russians and the British, who sought to legitimise their predatory missions in the Persia–Afghanistan–Bukhara–China sector by charting out new routes of access to warm-water ports in the Persian Gulf and the Caspian, Aral and Black seas. The opening-up of these new routes constituted an important excuse in the rationale of diplomats, military administrators and 'men-on-the-spot' who formed a vital link in the chain of events that were to follow, which ultimately led to the diminished independence, in one way or another, of the lands explored. These men were sponsored either by the Royal Geographical Society in London or the Imperial Russian Geographical Society in St. Petersburg. Testimonies of British reconnoitring agents and men-on-the-spot claimed that they were undertaking high-risk missions in the uncharted terrain of Central Asia solely to secure safe passage for men, money and trade.[1] These accounts vindicate the argument posited recently by a scholar that "depending upon priorities, states created or used routes".[2]

The entire gamut of colonial literature indicates that these shadowy operations acquired more complex features when the imperial administrators used local powers as pawns in a gigantic colonising enterprise; the perfidious inter-principality links of the local *emirs*, *shahs*, *khans* and *ambans* (governors) were utilised by both Britain and Russia to foment tension in the region.

Recent discourses on 'decolonisation' tend to focus particularly on the region that was affected by the Great Game. There is an increasing awareness of 'interlocked histories', wherein regional and international politics determined the context within which the local rulers tried to preserve their authority;[3] new scholarship is now taking into account the compulsions of the indigenous rulers by 'recontextualising' imperial visions, conquests and enterprises.[4] At the same time, there is an increasing focus on other factors that were crucial to the region in more ways than one. In the opinion of an Uzbek scholar, for instance, it is simplistic to analyse the history of Turkestan exclusively from the angle of Russian military imperatives, which dated back to as early as the fifteenth century, without taking into account the various aspects of Turkic society, ethos and economy in the history of the region.[5] Colonial historiography also seems to indicate that the Great Game was the outcome of a voluntary submission by the local rulers to their colonial masters.[6] But the present day volatility of the region suggests that the Great Game not only forcibly fragmented the region, but also had the effect of imbuing it with a consciousness that was antipathetic, if not absolutely belligerent, towards colonial rule.[7]

Despite the resurgence in scholarship on the region, however, certain issues still remain unclear. For instance, there was no determination of actual frontiers by the Great Game arrangements. The emergent disputes over territoriality indicate that military conquests, protectorate arrangements and the delimitation of inaccessible terrains (mountains, lakes and deserts) were only stop-gap arrangements. In the present situation, they have proved to be both unrealistic and unfeasible, as these arrangements took no account of close-knit identities of community and clan. The need at that time to distinguish one community of people from another, solely to suit imperial compulsions, has generated complications today; and the ad hoc territorial demarcations in Central Asia have added complexities to a region in which identities are not always clearly defined. Thus the need to re-examine the term 'border' in the context of the endless hustling among imperial powers for the preservation of their territorial integrity in the frontier regions has been outlined in this essay.[8] The question that emerges is, whose territorial integrity was at stake? It is therefore crucial to understand the 'space' within which the Great Game was played.

Identifying 'Space': Areas of the Great Game

The Great Game was located primarily in two areas: The Perso-Afghan sector and the Chinese sector.

From the beginning of the nineteenth century, the Perso-Afghan sector became the bone of contention between the major powers – France, Britain and Russia. The British wanted to stop the French and the Russians from reaching the open sea via the Persian Gulf. The British interest in the Persian province of Khorasan, which encompassed the principalities of Merv, Khiva, Herat and Kandahar, was indicated in a statement by the imperial visionary, Lord Curzon, that Turkestan, Afghanistan, Trans-Caspia and Persia were "pieces on a chessboard upon which is being played out a game for dominion over the world".[9] He was keen to expand British knowledge of the Seistan frontier, particularly after the Russian general A. N. Annenkov tried to reach beyond the Caspian littoral with the Trans-Caspian railway project. His gaze was fixed on new trade routes in the Persian Gulf sector through Bandar Abbas, Shiraz, Bushire and Teheran, across which British and Indian merchandise could be transported.[10] Curzon's intention was to connect the Caspian littoral with western Turkestan and Khorasan through telegraphic connections, arterial roads and rail links. He was confident that Britain would then have a political edge over Russia, as these routes would eventually connect India via Afghanistan, touching Herat and Kandahar on the way.

Herat's geographical position was enviable: it was situated at the junction of all the overland commercial routes in Asia, and all the riverine routes converged on its main river, the Hari Rud. Merchants from Persia, Turkestan, Afghanistan, India and Seistan came to Herat to trade; their commodities included wheat, barley, rice, saffron, tobacco and tea. The combination of geographical location and commercial hub made Herat especially attractive to all the contending powers.

Apart from wooing the local governor of the border principality of Herat, the British and the French also found it convenient to capitalise on the traditional rivalries of the two feuding principalities of Herat and Kandahar. It is apparent from the accounts of the French armyman J. P. Ferrier (who had served in Shah Fateh Ali's government in Persia in the early nineteenth century), that these rebellious, self-styled rulers were courted so as to suit British interests in getting access through India's western frontier into the Hazarah country in Afghanistan and up into the Pamirs. Given the fact that the Russians had established military bases in this sector and along the Amu Darya (Oxus) by the middle of the nineteenth century, it was imperative for the British to get access to information about troop movements in this region. The control of this route, which touched Herat and ran through Khulm, Chardzhou, Merv and Kandahar, could also serve as an important artery of trade for British merchants. For this, the British counted largely on the military help of the *Wazir* (ruler) of Herat. As far as British frontier policy was concerned, control of the Perso-Afghan region was a careful balancing act between diplomatic understandings and a subtle manipulation of inter-tribal relations in the Herat province.[11]

British designs in the Perso-Afghan sector were effectively matched by Russian oriental missions in western Turkestan. An 'academic' interest in the Orient became the vehicle for consolidating Russian control over areas that were of vital strategic importance. Nikolai V. Khanykov, a prominent orientalist, was a diplomat in the Russian Ministry of Internal Affairs in the 1830s. As a member of the two Russian missions, to Khiva in 1839 and Bukhara in 1841, Khanykov noted that the political situation in the Bukharan Emirate had deteriorated, particularly after the espionage activities of two British officers, Colonel Charles Stoddart and Captain Arthur Connolly. He advocated caution in Russia's deliberations with Bukhara, but Persia and Afghanistan were to be directly converted into military outposts to prevent British expansion in those areas. Khanykov's views were to be adopted in their entirety by Russia in her relations with her Muslim neighbours to the south, and particularly in Bukhara and Khiva.[12]

The Chinese sector, including eastern Turkestan, contained the traditional route of pilgrims and traders between China and India, romanticised in literature as the Silk Route. A thriving intraregional trade was monopolised by the Kokandi merchants of Kashgar, who had considerable commercial links with the Bukharan and Khivan merchants. Local trade and economy experienced a major boom with the entry of Russian merchant capital into eastern Turkestan from the late 1850s onwards. Both Kashgar and Kulja became important entrepôts in the entire route between Russia and Chinese Turkestan. The Russian policy of carrying trade to Chinese Turkestan was enumerated in the accounts of the Kazakh orientalist, Chokan Valikhanov.[13]

The economic imperative of opening up new trade routes in the eastern sector of Central Asia was also reflected in the accounts of the British–Indian tea trader, Robert Shaw. To thwart Russian exploratory missions in the area, the British utilised the ambitions of the local merchants and their protector, Yaqub Beg of Kashgar, who was encouraged by them to challenge Russian commercial interests in the region.[14] The British initiative in Kashgar was motivated by their traditional commercial interest in carrying British tea, tobacco and calicoes into Chinese territory. It began initially with the geographical explorations of William Moorcroft in the early nineteenth century,[15] and the survey missions undertaken by the Trigonometrical Survey of India and the Royal Geographical Society of London in the mid-nineteenth century. The British subsequently resorted to travelling in disguise as local traders to dispel the fears of the Chinese – who were wary of foreign intrusion into their territory – and the Russians, who wanted to combat all foreign trade competition in the Chinese sector. Robert Shaw and George Hayward were two of the earliest travellers in disguise to chart the Yarkandi and Kashgari terrains of the local ambans.[16] Others were to follow, for the economic imperatives of carrying Indian trade beyond the Hindu Kush soon turned into a relentless pursuit by British political agents and men-on-the-spot to protect their Indian colony on the eastern side. The mountain ranges of the Hindu Kush, Karakoram and Pamirs were targetted as strategic posts of defence; British officers were deputed to the entire region extending from eastern Turkestan to Herat in the west to woo a plethora of local tribes whose domains would be subsequently carved out as 'protective buffer zones'.[17]

Although the process began with the trading pursuits of Robert Shaw, subsequent work of surveying and reporting was taken up by Ney Elias, who was dispatched by the British–Indian government to report on the land on the Afghan side of the Amu Darya.[18] Sir Francis Younghusband extended Elias's work into China, actively encouraged by Lord Curzon, who was anxious to establish a safe, contiguous border between the two empires, Britain and Russia.[19]

Having located the principal areas of the Great Game, I will now explore Russia's territorial ambitions in Central Asia. Depending upon various imperatives, territories were either conquered or colonised, or turned into protectorates by Czarist Russia.

Russian Conquests: Re-Examining the Determination of Borders and Frontiers in Central Asia

Conquered Terrains

Although Russia's Asian frontiers were an enigma to European intellectuals in the nineteenth century, scholars today are focussing on the long process of *kolonizatsiya* (colonisation) and *zavoevaniya* (conquest) that expanded the territorial limits of Russia from the fifteenth to the nineteenth centuries, in an effort to find continuities in the border policies of Czarist Russia and the Soviet Union.

Czarist Russia's borders in the Kazakh Steppe and Turkestan were created through a process of 'demarcation' of territories, a word that acquired different meanings at different stages in the late nineteenth and early twentieth centuries. *Razgranichenie* (border demarcation) in the 1880s and the 1890s was very different from *raionirovanie* (delimitation of territories) between 1917 and 1924. While razgranichenie was the result of imperial adjustments that led to the creation of buffer zones in China, Afghanistan and northwest India, raionirovanie was worked out by Soviet administrators between 1924 and 1936 on the basis of the ethnic composition of the region. The absorption of Kazakh territories through military conquest from the 1820s to the 1840s was due to the need for the construction of defence posts that consolidated Russia's defence lines throughout the vast reaches of the Steppe. But the precise character of political authority in this region was never established by the Russians, and delimitation of territory was vague at best. The sense of border was "vague and protean, shaped by the constellation of power on its frontiers at any given moment".[20] Spheres of influence were delineated along frontiers that were ill-defined and elastic.[21]

Although the initial motives for Russian advances in the three regions of western Siberia, Kazakhstan and Turkestan were almost always of a commercial or political nature, the Ministry of War invariably had a subsequent role to play. For example, Kazakh territory was considered to be an effective entry point for trade not only with Central Asia but also with the markets of Persia and India. To safeguard their fur trade in western Siberia, and to defuse the tensions that were caused by tribal clashes between the Kazakhs and the Kalmyks in the eighteenth century, the Russians felt that they had no recourse but to step into the political and military 'vacuum' thus created south of the Kazakh Steppe.[22]   The Ministry of War soon set up fortified lines: the Orenburg Line enclosed the Bashkirs, and the Irtish and Ishim Lines contained the Kazakhs. For Russia, populating the region with Russians now became crucial to sustain its ability to dominate it. Military outposts and a long line of forts were supplanted from 1861 onwards by peasant settlements that extended from the north to the south of the Urals, and the indigenous nomads were pushed deeper and deeper back into the Steppe. [23]

Russia's move into Central Asia was bound to clash with the interests of the khans of Kokand and Khiva, who had already absorbed large chunks of the Elder Horde's possessions.[24] Khiva had watched with growing disquiet the gradual Russian expansion into the Steppe, with the Syr Darya as the intended frontier. The Khivan Khanate's expansionist aims across the Syr Darya northwestward to the Caspian Sea and beyond the

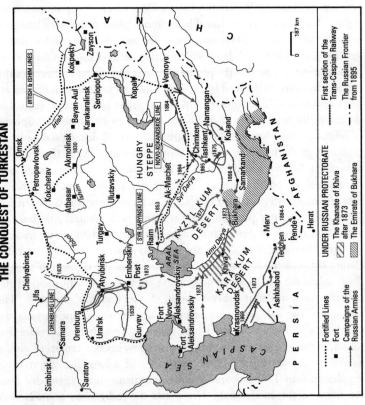

THE CONQUEST OF TURKESTAN

IRTISH & ISHIM LINES

NOVO-KOKANDSKE LINE

SYR DARYNSKI LINE

ORENBURG LINE

HUNGRY STEPPE

KYZYLKUM DESERT

KARA KUM DESERT

ARAL SEA

CASPIAN SEA

C H I N A

AFGHANISTAN

PERSIA

Omsk
Petropavlovsk
Kokchetav
Atbasar
Ishim
Akmolinsk 1830
Ulutavskiy
Kokpekty
Zaysoñ
Bayan-Aul
Karakaralinsk
Sergiopol
Kopal
Vernoye 1864
Chimkent
Tashkent/ Namangan
Kokand
Samarkand
Bukhara
Khiva
Merv
Pende 1884-5
Herat
Tedzhen
Ashkhabad
Krasnovodsk 1869
Fort Aleksandrovskiy
Fort Novo-Aleksandrovskiy
Guryev
Ural'sk
Atyubinsk
Embenskiy Post 1873
Raim 1853
Ak-Machet 1864
Turgay
Simbirsk
Saratov
Samara
Orenburg
Ufa
Chelyabinsk
Irtish
Tobol
Torgay
Syr Darya
Amu Darya

1835
1839
1873
1865
1866-8
1875
1873
1873
1873
1873

Fortified Lines
Fort
Campaigns of the Russian Armies

UNDER RUSSIAN PROTECTORATE
The Khanate of Khiva after 1873
The Emirate of Bukhara

First section of the Trans-Caspian Railway
The Russian Frontier from 1895

0   187 km

river Emba were to clash with Russian designs in the west. Khiva was not ready to lose control of its self-acclaimed right to levy duties on caravans that passed through its land, which was bound to happen as Russia pushed farther east and south. Russia soon alleged that caravans were being pillaged and plundered by Khivan feudals. On the plea of slavery and brigandage, they sent a punitive expedition under General Count V. A. Perovsky in 1839, which was repulsed by Khiva.

Subsequent expeditions were successful, however, and the establishment of Russian military authority over the entire caravan route from Orenburg to the outposts of Kokand and the merging of the Russian fortified lines – the Syr Daryinski and the Semirech'e with that of the Novo-Kokandskoe – led to an eventuality that was not envisaged earlier. The Kazakhs became the colonial brethren of the Kyrgyz, who were an integral element of the Kokand Khanate. The conquest of Kokand in 1864 and the formation of the Turkestan Oblast' in 1865 subsequently created dual elements of unity and conflict among peoples with diverse identities and histories.

Territorial Management of the Steppe and Oases

There were innumerable frontier zones in inner Asia where Russian and non-Russian people mingled or clashed over expanding spheres of authority. To try and delineate spheres of control and carve out regions of common identities, the Russian authorities undertook territorial adjustments in the principalities of Bukhara, Khiva and Kokand and the militarisation and colonisation of the Steppe.

In the early nineteenth century, however, the Steppe was excluded from Russia's initial plans for expansion in the region. They were more interested in establishing a firm grip over the Aral Sea, which was essential for Russian water transport. The riverine routes along the Amu Darya and the Syr Darya were their first choice, since the Steppe was trackless and the deserts were teeming with robbers.[25] In time, however, the 'unruly' features of the Steppe themselves became the imperative for exercising control over the nomad Kazakhs and Kyrgyz. The Russian foreign minister Prince A. M. Gorchakov in 1864, and subsequently the war minister General A. N. Kuropatkin in 1897, conveniently appropriated the notion of *mission civilastrice* (modernisation),[26] which constituted a backdrop to the military conquest of the land between China and the Aral Sea and extending south to the Issyk Kul.

The question of border security for the Russians did not become a crucial one until the 1870s, as the Central Asian principalities did not have a sense of boundary prior to that date. The accounts of travellers suggest that the Russians, as well as the indigenous rulers, were actually more concerned with guarding their trade monopolies than with protecting their frontiers or borders from nomadic raids. Prior to the 1870s political jurisdiction over mountains, rivers, lakes, deserts and the Steppe, where ownership was unclear and debatable, had almost no meaning in the modern sense of the term 'border' or 'frontier'. The emirs, khans and *begs* (chiefs) in the oases and the Steppe were, with their weak sense of territorial understanding, more interested in protectorate arrangements whereby their right to levy tributes was not disturbed. With the introduction of railroads in the 1880s however, access to the Caspian Sea assumed prime importance. The term 'border' was redefined at this time. Territorial inviolability henceforth became essential; for Russia, buffer zones and client states in Central Asia assumed significance as a means of control in disputed territories. Actual disputes were settled through mutually amicable arrangements, while the border itself became a mere geographical determinant in maps.

In the 1890s, therefore, the policy of the Russian government was one of diplomatic territorial adjustments with the settled population of Turkestan on the one hand and Britain on the other. These diplomatic negotiations, rather than military encounters, were pragmatic solutions for dealing with whoever challenged Russia's expansionist goals.

Displacement of Nomads

Although the Russians had occupied vast stretches of the Steppe by the 1820s, it is unjust and inaccurate to allege that they had transgressed the 'territories' of the Kazakh and Kyrgyz nomads. These nomads were always on the move in this region, either for grazing cattle or in search of newer pastures. They inhabited what may be best described as common land, whose frontiers were not very easy to define; it is incorrect, therefore, to speak of a violation of 'nomadic territory'. But there are other aspects of this invasion that have been accorded little importance so far: the political authority of the Kazakh sultans and Khivan emirs *vis-à-vis* the Russians; and the social structure of the Steppe dwellers that was badly affected by the Russian military presence.

The nomad rulers had enormous control over vast tracts of land by virtue of the tributes they levied on caravans. The Russians defined them as exactions, though in most cases they were bargains struck between the *caravanbashi* (leader of caravans) and the *ziaketchik* (customs collector). The centralised structure of the Czarist Russian government clashed with that of the local authorities, who derived their power from clan ties and religious and regional affinities. Disaffection among the local rulers grew from 'core/periphery' disparities, wherein the 'core' was empowered and the 'periphery' was not in a position to counteract it. Of greater import were the rude shocks rendered to the social unit of the nomad as a whole. The Russian military presence challenged the social structure of the Steppe nomads, and as a result of Russian settlement policies, the Kazakhs lost their social cohesiveness. Pastoral nomadism[27] was evacuated in the real sense of the term as Siberian villages appeared on Kazakh winter pastures.[28]

Further, the economic fabric of the region came under increasing strain with the steadily rising numbers of Russian settlers in the Kazakh pastures. The attempts by the Russians to sedentarise the Kazakhs by urging them to combine farming with breeding livestock automatically created competition between the indigenous farmers and the new immigrants. As a result, rivalries erupted among clans and groups for better lands and pastures. Moreover, the Kazakhs were culturally completely dissociated from the settled Russians, and were constrained to cope with a dual kind of existence.[29] Not only were some of them displaced from the best pastures but they also became economically subservient to the Russians by being forced to patrol the grasslands now used by the them. All these changes led to a transformation in the Kazakh lifestyle: those Kazakhs who raised cattle and goats and had surplus grain to sell in Russian markets became moderately successful, while others fell prey to unscrupulous Russian and Tartar middlemen. This led to their cultural dissociation from the rest of the population. The Russians also levied taxes on Kazakh households and on native occupations such as timber-cutting and salt-gathering.

Disruption of nomadic life also took place through administrative 'reforms' that took no heed of tribal relationships. An example of such reforms was the appointment of a *sultan pravitel* (the local ruler of the Kazakh nomadic groups) for each of the three divisions of the nomadic Horde – western, central and eastern – and its thirty-two territorial *distansii* (sub-divisions), all of whom were responsible to the Governor-General of Orenburg.

The entry of the Russian military in the Kazakh Steppe introduced a strong element of conflict in Russia's relations with the local powers. The presence of Russian military officers acted as a restriction on the liberty of the princes while the territorial divisions imposed by them cut across nomadic family ties. Territorial restructuring of the Kazakh Steppe started in 1822 with its annexation and addition to the Omsk Oblast'. The four *oblasts* (provinces) of the Kazakh Steppe – Ural, Turgay, Akmolinsk and

TURKESTAN REDEFINED: POLITICAL DELINEATION AND SLAVIC SETTLEMENTS AFTER 1858

Empire
Protectorate
Oblast'
Railway

RURAL
Cossack Lands and Settlements
Peasant Lands and Settlements

URBAN
Settlement Point
Citadel or Fort
Capital of Russian Turkestan

OTHER
Capital of Protectorates

SLAVIC SETTLEMENTS

SEMIRECH'E

Sergiopol
Lepsinsk
Kopal
Dzharkent
Przheyalsk
Vernyy
Tokmak
Pishpek
Skobelev
FERGANA
Turkestan
Chimkeni
Tashkent
SAMARKAND
Samarkand
SYR DARYA
Perovsk
Bukhara
ARAL SEA
Amu Darya
Khiva
Merv
TRANS-CASPIA
Ashkhabad
Tedzhen
Kushka
Krasnovodsk
Fort Aleksandrovskiy

N – Namangan
A – Andizhan
K – Kokand
O – Osh

Semipalatinsk – were sub-divided according to the Russian pattern of territorial divisions into *uezd*s (districts), *volost*s (sub-divisions of a district) and *aul*s (peasant villages). Speransky's reforms then tried to represent the Kazakhs as just a clan in a council composed of regional rulers who were responsible to the Russian commanding officer of the Siberian Defence Line at Omsk. This was a serious challenge to the sultan's hegemony. By defining the boundaries of each volost, named after a clan it contained, the reforms restricted the clan's range of movement. The *okrug* (territorial administrative unit in a province), administered by a team of Russian officers and the Kazakh sultans, in effect became a Russian garrison. Moreover, Siberian Cossacks were commissioned to consolidate Russian military control over the region. The Cossack *stanitsy* (settlements) along those newly defined boundaries traversed the entire Kazakh upland, thus enclosing the Steppe and constraining the nomads' free movement across pastures.[30]

Secured Frontiers

The Russian policy of converting Central Asia into a political appendage continued until the 1860s, but from then on territorial security in that region came to be viewed as crucial by the Ministry of War and the Asiatic Department in the Ministry of Foreign Affairs. This security issue was highlighted in the Gorchakov Circular of 1864:

> The position of Russia in Central Asia is that of all civilized states which are brought into contact with half savage, nomad populations, possessing no fixed social organization. In such cases it always happens that the more civilized state is forced, in the interests of the security of its frontier and its commercial relations, to exercise a certain ascendancy over those whom their turbulent and unsettled character make most undesirable neighbours. First there are the raids and the acts of pillage to be put down. To put a stop to them the tribes on the frontier have to be reduced to a more or less perfect submission.[31]

Gorchakov argued in favour of a safe and stable border in Central Asia, and was supportive of Russia's territorial conquests since 1858. The first outcome of this support was the creation of a single fortified border along the various nomadic territories already indicated above. The emphasis by the Ministry of War on 'frontier security' was due to concerns that Russia's steady inroads into nomadic territory were bound to arouse the wrath of the local population. This aggrandisement would also expose Russia to the difficulties of managing a far-flung empire – from Orenburg in the west to

SLAVIC RURAL SETTLEMENTS OF NORTHERN KAZAKHSTAN BY 1905 AND 1915

Novonikolayevsk

Barnaul

Zaysan

Semipalatinsk

Kokpekty

Slavgorod

Barabinsk

Pavlodar

Karakaralinsk

Omsk

Akmolinsk

Petropavlovsk

Kokchetav

Kurgan

Atbasar

Kustanay

Chelyabinsk

Ufa

Aktyubinsk

Samara

ARAL SEA

CASPIAN SEA

0   147 km

| Cossack Allotments |
| Railroads by 1915 |

| Peasant Allotments by 1905 |
| Railroads by 1907 |

| Peasant Allotments by 1915 |
| 200 mm Annual Precipitation |

Turkestan in the east – that was controlled by a single administrative unit. The Governor-General of Turkestan was Konstantin Petrovich fon Kaufman, whose respect for the "prestige, honour and rights" of Russian territorial gains in Turkestan called for a separation of the Turkestan Governor-Generalate.[32] As a pragmatic solution to the administrative problem he proposed that the Governor-Generalship of Turkestan be clearly divided along a north–south axis, whereby the commercially viable Zeravshan province would be separated from the Syr Darya and the Semirech'e provinces that lay further to the east. The Kazakh Steppe and its two provinces were to become part of the Turkestan Oblast'.

As a result, a system of regional administration was introduced, dividing the entire Turkestan Oblast' into two provinces with two entirely different sets of governors and provincial boards. The provinces were subdivided into districts, each of which was under a military commander. The cities were to be further governed by city commandants, while the local inhabitants were allowed to govern their own villages or rural districts. Kaufman as Governor-General of Turkestan became directly responsible for the management of the two provinces of the Kazakh Steppe – Syr Darya and the Semirech'e – while the remaining areas of the Steppe were divided into six provinces governed by Russian military governors responsible to the Governor-General of Turkestan, who was helped by local Kazakhs in the administration of the various districts within these provinces.

Commercial prospects for the Russians in the Zeravshan province in the Bukharan Emirate led to a series of diplomatic-cum-military manoeuvres that culminated in the Russo-Bukharan Commercial Convention of 1868. This opened the gates of Bukharan commerce to Russian merchants who were granted the right to trade, establish caravanserais and to maintain commercial agents throughout the emirate. 'Territoriality' for Bukhara was defined strictly in terms of its control over merchandise that was transported by Bukharan and Russian merchants along the caravan and riverine routes; while Russia stationed military garrisons at strategic locations within the emirate, thus maintaining a watch on the administration of the emir. At the same time the Russian Political Agent in Bukhara acted as an ambassador on behalf of the Ministry of Foreign Affairs.

But all this did not signify an intrinsic loss of authority of the Bukharan Emir. The 'reduction' of Bukhara is open to question because the religious–social, military–feudal hierarchy in the emirate continued to exist even after the accord. The sovereign was accorded immense respect by Russian dignitaries, who took care to address him variously as *Vysokostepenstvo* (Highest Honour), *Vysokoprevoskodichelstvo* (His

Highness), *Svetlost* (Illustrious) and *Vysochestvo* (Highness).[33] The emir was also in full possession of his sovereignty in domestic affairs, though subject to Russian authority in external matters. As Bukhara's guarantor in external matters, Russia became involved in numerous agreements not only with her trade rivals Britain and China, but also with her local protectorates.

Bukhara's hegemony in commercial matters become more apparent when Russia's expanding railway network in the Zeravshan plain connected the entire Bukharan Emirate through main lines and branch lines. The *Tamozhennoe Uchrezhdenie* (Department of Customs) incorporated Bukharan frontier outposts on the Afghan border along the upper reaches of the Oxus into its system. The old caravan routes from Bukhara to Orenburg and the frontier outposts on the Persian and Afghan borders were colonised with Russian settlers. The Russian banking system allied with local manufacturers, viz., the Tartars, Jews and Persians, to expand the highly lucrative cotton market.

Bukhara's economic prosperity was in striking contrast to its 'reduced' political status, while gaining geographically by the subsequent territorial readjustments – addition of the Trans-Caspian, Ferghana and Samarkand provinces and the Oxus *otdel* (division) to the Governor-Generalate of Turkestan – which led to a sharing of the riverine territories lying between Russian Turkestan, Afghanistan and the Bukharan Emirate. In the west, Khal At, Gugertlia and Mesheklya along the right bank of the Amu Darya became part of the Bukharan Emirate after 1874.[34]

However, Bukhara's border with Afghanistan in the south continued to remain undefined.[35]

Afghan and Bukharan Frontiers: Inaccessible and Undefined

The undefined nature of the Afghan–Bukharan frontier led to imperial tensions in the latter half of the nineteenth century. Was Russia alone in provoking Britain to consider serious military intervention in the lands in the border areas? Grown powerful by its strategy of domination, Russia had a territorial edge over Britain and China in the east;[36] this was manifest in its control over local authorities in the frontier regions and the semi-autonomous mountain kingdoms in the Hindu Kush and the Pamirs. As a result, the rapprochement in 1873 between Britain and Russia, which delineated their respective northwestern, southern and eastern dominions, came under strain and finally ended in 1875.[37] According to this agreement, Russia was to have considered Afghanistan (including Wakhan and

Badakhshan) as outside Russia's sphere of influence, and Afghanistan was to have been treated effectively as a British protectorate. The Afghan Emir on his part was to promise not to extend his frontiers further northward; the British were to give their assurance that the area "beyond Afghanistan" was outside the British sphere of influence. Russia's clean sweep, therefore, over the Kokand Khanate and the formation of the Trans-Caspian military division caused alarm in the British foreign office. In their minds, Russia's borders with Persia and Afghanistan were open to question, and thus the delimitation of the Afghan boundary became essential.

The Hindu Kush, and the Afghan-occupied districts in the Pamirs that bordered the upper Amu Darya (river Pyandzh), became the bone of contention between the Russians and the British. Since the 1873 Anglo-Russian agreement, the British had realised the strategic importance of this river. Its meandering course had rendered the fixing of a boundary difficult, since it flowed through the shared geographical space of the Bukharan and Afghan domains. Principal among the lands under dispute were Chardzhou, Kerki and Merv in Bukhara and Badakhshan in Afghanistan.

The Russians alleged in the 1880s that, in violation of the 1873 Anglo-Russian accord, the British had instigated the Afghan Emir to lay claim to Shugnan and Roshan, which were enclaves within the autonomous kingdom of Badakhshan.[38] Under the auspices of the Imperial Russian Geographical Society of St. Petersburg, Russian military missions were dispatched to keep a watch on whatever was happening in these enclaves. The crucial question here centred on who owned the unexplored regions around the source of the river Pyandzh. The region was thus transformed into a disputed territory not only by the British and the Russians, but also by the Afghan and Bukharan Emirs, who were their respective clients.

Matters became further complicated when China extended her control over Taghdumbash Pamir, which was inhabited by Kyrgyz fugitives from Afghanistan. China's control over the local Kyrgyz in the eastern Pamirs around the Rangkul district meant that Russia would probably consider expanding south of Rangkul. This would bring her straight to the Muztagh range, in the Kunlun Shan mountains, with its passes into British India. As the Russians posted military garrisons all along the Amu Darya, the strategic importance of the river (repeatedly stressed by the Russophobic Lord Curzon) was brought home to the British. While Curzon argued that Britain's pre-eminence would decline as a consequence of Russia's new outlets in the Persian Gulf, Francis Young-husband and his colleagues in the British intelligence department in Simla saw that British commercial prospects for tea in eastern Turkestan would be thwarted by both the Russians and the Chinese.[39]

On their part, the Russians saw that there was the twin danger of antagonising the Chinese by encroaching on their territory, and alarming the British into making territorial moves of their own. Their respective apprehensions drove both the imperial powers to discuss the question of territorial integrity, and specifically of those regions that were largely inaccessible. They both saw the need to legitimise zones of influence through a demarcation of borders in Afghanistan and the Pamirs. However, the imperial joint commissions of 1885–1886 and 1895 ended in a fiasco, as they failed to agree on any one formula for the demarcation of this lonely region. Although both parties came to some sort of 'understanding', the future course of events indicated that these did not resolve the issue of disputed borders.

Curzon was clearly at odds with the views of his own foreign office, which held that the Pamirs were a wilderness, a barren tract of land, and therefore impossible to determine as a boundary. What bothered him was the contiguity of the borders of Afghanistan, China and Russia, all of which converged on eight glacial valleys in the Pamirs. The narrow corridor of Wakhan became the bone of contention between Russia-backed Bukhara and Britain-backed Afghanistan. The demilitarisation of contiguous borders in Afghanistan seemed to the British to be the only way to dispel tensions over the region for the time being. But by conceding to Bukhara's claims over Roshan, Shugnan and Wakhan, the 'legitimate territorial settlement' of 1895, mediated by Lord Curzon, in a way bartered away the interests of Afghanistan.

Conclusion

The insubstantial nature of the nineteenth century 'agreements' over borders in Central Asia became apparent in the twentieth century. Said Alim Khan, the Emir of Bukhara and Amir-Amanullah Khan, the Emir of Afghanistan, consistently challenged or flouted all the conditions of the imperial accords. The latter particularly tried to undo all the pro-British policies of his predecessors, Emir Abd ur Rahman and Emir Habibullah, which pertained to the transfer of Afghanistan's territories to Bukhara in the 1890s.

Anglo-Russian tensions over colonial territories and friendly buffer States eased somewhat after the Anglo-Russian Convention of 1907. Soon afterwards, however, the Russian foreign office once again became suspicious as to whether Britain was abiding by the 1907 Convention in relation to her northwest frontier, i.e., in Afghanistan and the Pamirs.[40]

Subsequent events in the context of the First World War and Russia's friendly overtures to Germany, Turkey and revolutionaries in India compelled the British to rethink their diplomatic strategies in this region. Conceding that the earlier territorial arrangements between the imperial powers were no longer tenable, the British now relied more upon manipulating regional politics. Britain and Russia once again tried to create a neutral Afghanistan, but the means by which they were to do so was to change; they now had to depend on the support and reliability of their allies, whether in Bukhara, Khiva or Afghanistan. Those who had deified the Great Game, wherein territorial destinies were shaped at the whims or needs of the imperial powers, now had to deal on a more equal footing with the indigenous rulers.

The debates that surfaced in official circles from 1917 onwards challenged the earlier perceptions of territoriality and the grounds on which territorially demarcated boundaries of a sovereign State were created or recreated by imperialists.[41] There is an increasing emphasis among scholars of international relations today, on the importance of 'shared' spaces everywhere, in which individuals coexist, cohabit and interact – or conflict – with each other. In the Central Asian context this argument is especially valid because the fluidity of borders was an integral part of Central Asia's chequered geopolitical history. Furthermore, there is a serious attempt to recontextualise the events of the imperial period and take into account the geostrategic significance of Central Asia. Consequently, increasing attention has been paid to Central Asia as the 'pivot' and not the 'periphery' of Great Game politics, since the region played an important role as a 'borderland' between the competing security interests of larger powers. Three centuries of relative isolation has brought the same territories of inner Asia within the scope of world politics today.

Apart from security reasons, inner Asia also became important for the contributions of its intellectuals in the realm of social reform. Reformism, often dubbed as modernisation, swept through Central Asia at the turn of the twentieth century. Modernisation is viewed today in terms of the societal development of the region. Advancement of knowledge, development of expertise, economic growth, social mobilisation and changes in social environment cannot even remotely be explained by the unidimensional Great Game discourse. G. A. Akhmedjanov, among other Uzbek historians, contends that the tunnel-vision perception of Central Asia, solely in terms of imperial geopolitical compulsions, must now give ground to other issues. The emergence of a cultural awareness among Central Asian intellectuals in the early twentieth century, and the region's cultural contacts with its neighbours, are now the subject of recent debates. Central Asia, therefore, has re-emerged on the world map and is regaining its centrality in the newly discovered aspects of its historic cultural contacts, civilisational links and intellectual life.

This study has attempted to show that the 'centrality' of Central Asia lies in examining not only the geopolitical compulsions of the Great Game players of the late nineteenth century but also in indicating the atmosphere of conflict and cooperation in the region. Although territorial aggrandisement in Central Asia undoubtedly baited the interests of regional powers like Afghanistan and the Khanate of Kokand, others like the Kazakhs and the Emirate of Bukhara were sucked into its maw by imperial political exigencies. Despite this, the latter was hardly subservient to imperial policies, and there were attempts to solve differences through commercial negotiations and territorial adjustments. Similarly, territorial readjustments and administrative restructuring in the Steppe resulted in cooperation.

In a way, the underlying aspect of this study is also that one cannot ignore the strength of imperialist historiography. The resurgence of Great Game literature for the understanding of the motives for territorial conquest and colonisation, and the questioning of the relevance of treaties and agreements regarding demarcation of territories and borders in Central Asia, is something that is worth taking note of.

FOUR

Territory and Identity: Slaves during the Age of Imperial Frontier Management

INDRANI CHATTERJEE

Introduction

Recent theorists of the State in South Asia have asserted that the post–colonial State has as its *raison d'etre* the production, maintenance and reproduction of the concept and apparatus of national security.[1] According to this perspective, the ideology of territoriality has been a singular device in the service of the security-conscious State. This ideology of territoriality compresses the representation of multiple and conflicting processes among people living on the lands under discussion into a single frame, that of 'spatial borders', and validates events in terms of their spatial properties only. In this chapter, I shall try to indicate the antecedents of such a territorially-minded State by examining a particular moment in the history of the British–Indian State. This history revolves around the efforts to manumit some slaves in Xinjiang (historically Sinkiang, a province in the southwest of present-day China) who were believed to be 'originally' of British–Indian territories. It will show that British colonial officials manipulated ideologies of territoriality in order to limit governmental responsibility for those who were emancipated.

At the same time, this essay will show that the ideology of territoriality expressed in official British reports, while strong enough to obliterate the possibilities of other affiliations – of religious denomination, ethnicity or even gender and age – that might have been enacted by the very human beings who were the subjects of these inter-government diplomacies, was defeated by another alternative ideology, that of 'space'. This alternate spatial idiom was familial, in that the homeland was where one had kin. The fact that a majority of slaves after emancipation did not tamely return to, or embrace, their territorially defined identities, is a possibility that complicated statism's conception of freedom itself.

The larger issues which conditioned the nature and chronology of freedom and the emancipation of slaves in the Western Hemisphere in the first half of the nineteenth century are well known. Much water has flowed under the bridge since Eric Williams first argued that it was the rise of capitalism in England that led to the general growth of abolitionism as a movement, and to the realisation of slave labour as a costly encumbrance.[2] Seymour Drescher, Roger Anstey and David Eltis, who re-examined this thesis, found that slavery was a successful and expansive economic system in the early nineteenth century, and that emerging industrial capitalists were not the force behind antislavery politics in Britain.[3] This debate is important in order to locate the time frame for the manumission project in inner Asia in the latter half of the nineteenth century. Although historians on slavery, and the abolition of it, have drawn our attention to the complex international and diplomatic agendas that were tied up with these issues in Africa and the Gulf States, they have yet to address these questions in the inner Asian context.[4] Antislavery in the West was historically associated with liberalism; in the later nineteenth century, this liberalism was often hostile to territorial expansion. However, protagonists of imperial expansion then used the emotive issue of the suppression of slavery to justify an active 'forward' policy. Thus, as Suzanne Miers has pointed out, the antislavery movement was made to coincide with the imperialist drives of various European nations in Africa and the Indian Ocean littoral.[5]

In Xinjiang too, it may be argued, antislavery was part of the expansion of extraterritorial jurisdictions that Western powers were keen to establish vis-à-vis the Chinese Empire. Yet, while it is true that for a brief while in the 1860s the Government of India was keen to secure trading privileges, lowered octroi and greater sales of Indian tea and shawls in this region, it had reconciled itself to the impossibility of achieving this in any substantial measure after the reconquest of Xinjiang by the Imperial Chinese forces by the 1880s.[6] Furthermore, while abolition and antislavery had become an extremely popular cause within Britain, there is very little at the moment to indicate that slavery in Central Asia attracted anything like the attention that African slavery commanded in Britain. While various Christian missions and unofficial organisations were the major buttresses of anti-slavery work in Africa, these appear to have been either nonexistent or quiescent in the southwestern provinces of China, mainly Xinjiang, with which this chapter is concerned. Though this region was not under the direct control of any European power at this time, it is possible that British efforts at the suppression of slaving and manumission could have been a part of the project of conquest and expansion in the north and northwest of their Indian Empire – which was directed against Russia – and not primarily concerned with Xinjiang or the welfare of all slaves.

Slavery in Interior Asia

The procurement and selling of slaves was apparently a well-known and established feature in Central Asia, at least until the nineteenth century.[7] The 10,000 slaves reported from Samarkand in mid-nineteenth-century Bukhara were mainly Persians captured from Khorasan by Turki raiders; a sprinkling of Kalmyks, Afghans, inhabitants of Kafiristan and the other regions near the Pamirs; and Russians captured on the Kazakh Steppe and the fishing grounds of the Caspian Sea.[8] Young Russian males seized by the Kyrgyz fetched the highest prices in the Khivan slave markets, while Persian males were considerably less expensive and the Kurds least of all.[9]

However, the long-established practice of slaving across this region should not suggest an uninterrupted and ahistorical continuity of tradition. When Russia had conquered Bukhara and suppressed slaving there,[10] the withering-up of a major market is said to have led to changed patterns in slave holding by Turki slave catchers, who earlier would have disposed of their victims to brokers within three days.[11] Occasional and contemporary critics of the Government of India, like the ethnologist G. W. Leitner, were quick to point to the discontinuities and differences in slaving patterns between regions at the end of the nineteenth century. Referring to the region between Kashmir and Kabul, where slave raiding and sales existed prior to 1866, dropped off after 1867, and picked up again after 1886, Leitner asserted that it was the aggressive frontier policies of both the Great Powers that had caused this fresh spurt in slave dealing.[12] Indeed, he urged,

the recrudescence of kidnapping is largely due to the state of insecurity and confusion caused by our desire to render the Afghan and Chinese frontiers conterminous with our own, in the vain belief that the outposts of three large and distant kingdoms, acting in concert, will keep Russia more effectively out of India than a number of small independent republics or principalities...[13]

It is possible that the closure of the northern markets in Khiva and Bukhara after 1870 had realigned the sellers to a more easterly direction. It is equally possible that raiding was becoming more vital to some economies of the landlocked and mountainous regions of upper South

Asia and inner Central Asia (where earlier travellers had not noticed it). Perhaps this was a consequence of the gifting of arms to the people of the region by British and Russian officials, as Leitner argued; or perhaps it was a consequence of the shattering of other sources of income. Certainly Chitral's ruby mines were yielding little profit by the end of the century, and the Dard wars with Kashmir between 1856 and 1864 had dislocated many semisedentary populations, along with their cattle.[14] As Safdar Ali, the *Mir* (chief) of Hunza bluntly informed the British explorer and government agent Francis Younghusband, the profits obtained from slave raids formed his principal revenue; should the Government of India wish to stop such raids, it would have to compensate Hunza for the loss in revenues.[15] Turdi Kol, the leader of the Kyrgyz herdsmen, recounted to Younghusband the story of how the Kanjutis (men of Hunza and Nagar)

> lay hid on the cliffs overhanging the river, and as a man called Khoja Mohammad was passing through with his family and a large party, they fired down on them...killing all the men, and taking the women and children captive....[16]

Apart from merchants of Kashmiri and Afghan origin whose caravans on the trading routes between Leh and Yarkand were vulnerable to such raids, there appear to have been other, less-prosperous groups that were prone to being thus captured. Poor Muslims from Baltistan (alternatively referred to as Little Tibet or Iskardol in some travellers' accounts) – who worked mainly as coolies or baggage porters in the mountainous terrains of Kashmir and India – presumably badly affected by the famine of 1877, were sold by their Kanjuti neighbours.[17] While the Kyrgyz herdsmen were similarly raided by the Kanjutis, an example of which were the 21men and women carried off from Shahidula in 1888,[18] the Astor Valley was the particular 'raiding-ground' of the Chilas tribesmen, who singled out crops, cattle, children and women to carry off.[19]

Many of the slaves, both male and female, thus began as prisoners of raids and wars conducted between neighbours (like Hunza and Nagar) or between landlocked feudatories and their suzerains (Hunza and Kashmir); or even between neighbouring valleys (Kam and Presungul in old Kafiristan, or present Nuristan), who were generally transported to Sarikul in Central Asia and sold there.[20] Sarikulis in turn transported their purchases to Yarkand and the neighbouring province of Xinjiang. In fact, according to Sarda, the British trader and explorer Robert Shaw's personal servant, who talked with some of these male slaves in Kashgar and Yarkand in 1868–1869, the captives were first sold to traders in

RELIGION OF SLAVE TRADE IN INNER ASIA

TRANS-CASPIA
Amu Darya
KYZYLKUM DESERT
Tashkent
Syr Darya
ALTAI RANGE
XINJIANG
(CHINESE TURKESTAN)
Khiva
Petro-Aleksandrovsk
Kokand
FERGANA
KARAKUM DESERT
Ashkhabad
Merv
Bukhara
Samarkand
BUKHARA
Kashgar
KASHGAR
Lake Lob Nor
ROSHAN
DARWAZ
SHUGNAN
Somatash
SARIKOL
Yangi Hissar
Yarkand
Karghallik
Khotan
CHINA
Penjdeh
Balkh
BADAKHSHAN
PAMIRS
WAKHAN
CHITRAL
HUNZA
NAGAR
GILGIT
BALTISTAN
KARAKORAM
Karakoram Pass
PERSIA
Meshed
Bala Murghab
Sangbost
Herat
Kabul
KAFIRISTAN
HINDUKUSH
KASHMIR
Indus
LADAKH RANGE
Leh
Peshawar
Khyber Pass
LADAKH
AFGHANISTAN
Gartok
SEISTAN
Kerman
Kandahar
Bolan Pass
Quetta
PUNJAB
Simla
HIMALAYAS
TIBET
BALUCHISTAN
INDIA
NEPAL
Tashilhumpo
Lhasa
Gyantse
SIKKIM
Chambi Valley
BHUTAN
Darjeeling
Gangtok
0
184 km

Badakhshan by the Kanjuti inhabitants of Hunza and Nagar. Their purchasers then brought them over from Badakhshan into eastern Turkestan and offered them for sale to the ruler there.[21]

According to this account, the journey from Badakhshan to eastern Turkestan was truly horrific. Three Badakshi merchants and their servants on horseback herded the unshod and barely clothed slaves on foot through snow in which they sank up to their thighs. At every camp of a nomadic transhument community like the Kyrgyz, small numbers of these captives were sold off at prices ranging from 1 *koor* and 2 to 5 *tillah*s (between Rs. 170 and Rs. 210 in the 1860s and 1870s).[22]

Clearly, many among these were soldiers – young, presumably fit men – from various groups alternately listed as Rajputs of Guler, or *Gujar* (Jat/ Punjabi) sepoys in the army of the Maharaja of Kashmir. For instance, of the 100 Kashmiri soldiers captured by their opponents in the 1850s, about 70 were handed over by victorious locals to the Chitrali general for selling to the Tajiks and thus compensating for "the blood of Chitralis" shed by these soldiers.[23] It is clear from this account that the Tajiks were meant to act as intermediaries and brokers in the trade. In fact, the existence of middlemen means that sufficient profits accrued from this trade to warrant the existence of this group; certainly, Shaw had met an old Kyrgyz man who claimed to have traded in slaves, buying between 10 and 30 slaves in Chitral and selling them at Kashgar.[24]

The subsequent deployment of such male slaves as *sarbaz* (infantry-men) and herdsmen in the surrounding regions were the visible signs of wealth and power of the acquiring parties.[25] The institution of slavery also provided for a degree of continuity in social and administrative traditions, even when political regimes changed. Lashkar Beklarbegi, "the slave from Chitral", who served in the Kokand administration till 1841, was reputed to have established the dominance of Kokand over Kazakhstan.[26] Arminius Vambery, the Hungarian orientalist who travelled in inner Asia between 1863 and 1868, remembered a Persian slave who had become the *topchibashi* (commandant of artillery) in the fortress of Kerki in 1863.[27] Another such slave, of the Khojas in Kokand, a dancing-boy who rose to the post of *kilaochi* (fort commander) and eventually established control over Kashgar as its *Ataliq Ghazi* (Guardian Warrior) was Yaqub Beg.[28]

It is an anomalous feature of the English accounts of this region that though the prohibition of slave raids was offered as the main justification for the takeover of provinces like Hunza, very little personal notice was taken of the characteristics (religious denominations, linguistic or cultural affiliations) or subsequent destinies of those captured in a raid. Leitner had indicated that, in Gilgit before 1866, "women and weak men" were preferred as slaves, since it "was difficult for them to escape once they have reached their destinations". Moreover, in the war between Kashmir and Yasin, 1000 of the 3000 captives were women, and a few were children and old men.[29] But in addition to capture by raiding, women and children could also be acquired as slaves through more mundane methods. A certain number of "beautiful girls", along with a promise to hand over all prisoners, was often the price one feuding group had to pay for the military assistance of a third party, like that which the *Mehtar* (ruler) of Chitral extracted from Kam in Kafiristan for assistance in the intermittent inter-valley feuds.[30] Were the females and children acquired by the raiders themselves? It would appear not, since most of the booty had to be surrendered to the chief: whether he redistributed them as largesse, or converted them into ready goods by means of sales elsewhere is difficult to say. For the moment, we will have to accept that those captured in raids were also driven across the mountains to be sold either directly to buyers in Chinese Turkestan, or to Kyrgyz dealers who served as middlemen in this trade.[31]

However, within Xinjiang, slaves were transferred on by other transactions such as inheritance and presentations, like the one witnessed by Shaw, which involved a gift of horses by a subordinate provincial governor to his chief; each horse was ridden by a male slave (who was presumably also gifted alongside). Not surprisingly, reports like these rarely noticed female slaves; in Shaw's narrative there is only one report of a female slave, a maid-of-all-work in the house of a *pansadbashi* (commander of five hundred), who was originally Sinic but spoke Turki.[32]

The manumission of such slaves in Central Asia had been an important aspect of the rivalry between European powers in the early nineteenth century, as well as later. Peter Hopkirk devotes an entire chapter to explaining how the freeing of 416 Russian slaves from Khiva by a British officer in 1840–1841 was motivated by the Anglo-Russian rivalry in this region.[33] Lieutenant Richmond Shakespear, says Hopkirk, was "less concerned with introducing Christian civilization to Central Asia than with keeping the Russians out – not to mention advancing his own career".[34] Certainly, the selective nature of the manumission – the release of Russian rather than Persian slaves or all slaves held by the Khivans – would tend to lend weight to this perspective.[35] It would appear to have been a coup in political terms: a lone British officer "achieved single-handed what a heavily armed Russian force had so abysmally and humiliatingly failed to do" ever since 1819. It removed any excuse St. Petersburg might have had for moving into Khiva, a stepping stone on the path to India. It was all the more remarkable for having never been attempted in British India itself, where the government moved towards a hazy de-legalisation of slavery after 1843. It never attempted either an outright manumission of slaves or even a proclamation of freedom for slaves in India.

Though Hopkirk's own work is completely silent on the manumission projects undertaken by the British in Central Asia later, others have paid some attention to the process initiated by George Macartney, an intelligence officer and British representative in Xinjiang, in 1893--1895.[36] It is the latter phase that concerns us in this chapter. The truly intriguing aspect of the matter was that in the most active period of the manu-missions, Macartney had no official position or brief on the basis of which he began to parley with the Chinese administration for the release of the slaves. There is very little in the biographical literature on Macartney that gives clues to his particular abolitionist bent, unless it is that the very lack of an official brief made this half-Chinese British officer keener to establish one through the project, like Richmond Shakespear before him. Perhaps the timing of these efforts offers a clue: the Brussels Conference of 1890 had resolved to stop slave trading in all areas of Africa under European control, and the resolution had come into effect in 1892.[37]

Between Governments: Costs of Manumission

In their analysis of the economics of emancipation in the West, Robert W. Fogel and Stanley L. Engerman have argued that three potential groups could have borne the costs of emancipation: the slaves, the non-slave-holding freemen and the slave holders. In the northern United States, a process of "gradual emancipation" ensured that the last group bore a minimal burden and the first the maximum; in the British colonies, however, non-slave holders bore a significant share of the cost of emancipation.[38] However, in the case of Chinese Turkestan, the potential bearers of costs were governments – Chinese, British–Indian and Kashmiri. Interestingly, the largest share of the financial burden never seemed to be borne by the Government of India.

Initially, in 1892, Macartney felt that the Government of India should pay no ransom to the slave holders, and that the ransom was to be "settled between the local authorities and the slave owners", i.e., between the Chinese administrators and the largely Muslim and Turki-speaking slave holders. However, the sanctity of property rights was undeniable for most officers of the Government of India, for whom it was unthinkable that slaves could be released without compensation to their holders, with the latter having to forfeit their purchase money.[39] The solicitousness towards slave holders was actually conditioned by a larger anxiety among the British officials: in 1891–1892, when the ever-present Russian threat from the northwest was uppermost in their minds, any scheme which caused discontent among slave holders, and set them against their Chinese administrators, was thought to be both unwise and inexpedient. As George S. Robertson, a doctor-turned-political officer, put it,

> To let owners run the risk of having a portion of their property taken away from them for an inadequate sum of money paid as compensation... might cause a feeling of tension between the ruling authorities and the subject peoples, and particularly if such a plan were likely to lead to the idea that the resulting trouble, perplexity, and irritation caused by it, were directly due to the fact that a British Agent had been permitted to reside in Kashgar.[40]

Since this was the view also taken by the foreign secretary, H. Mortimer Durand, in his instructions to Macartney, it was presumably an influential one in the British–Indian bureaucracy. However, if honouring the idea of the inviolable rights of slave holders in their property required that the Government of India would have to dig into its own pockets, or worse still into Parliament's pockets, manumissions would become an unaffordable extravagance. A way around this difficulty was to make the Kashmir *darbar* (government) liable for these payments on the grounds that the slaves to be liberated were its subjects. In 1890, when 16 Balti captives had been released in Yarkand, the Kashmir darbar had been called upon to pay their ransoms; by 1893, this was considered a precedent to be followed for all slaves to be ransomed.[41]

In a directive that required some clever tightrope walking from Macartney, Durand instructed him a) not to press ransom matters "to the point where relations between the Chinese authorities and their subjects became bad"; and b) to accept only a minimal British fiscal responsibility for the ransoms by ensuring that slave holders did not make large claims, and by preventing the Chinese administration from throwing a greater share of the burden of payments onto the Government of India. The aim, as one official note succinctly stated, was "to make political capital out of this slave manumission as well as to do a work of philanthropy" but to do both cheaply.[42] Macartney's task then was to secure for his government "the *maximum* advantage at the *minimum* costs".[43]

Calculations of ransom and costs were, however, related to a whole host of factors. One was the number of slaves to be released. Macartney's initial information put the figure at 500 slaves in Yarkand, and another 100 dispersed in the towns of Aqsu, Khotan and Kashgar.[44] At the monetary level, the price at purchase of each slave had to be converted into appropriate currency terms. But there were many hidden factors that went into such a simple affair, for the price of a slave was a highly individualised thing. A skilled male adult's price was different from an unskilled but reproductive female's price, as well as from an unskilled male child's price. Moreover, the price of a second or third generation slave was different from that of a first generation slave. Thus, right at the outset, all calculations on ransom stumbled on the classification of slaves on two apparently discrete but fundamentally interrelated issues – their political 'nationality' and the length of time spent in slavery.

According to Macartney, the slaves hailed from "the feudatory states of Kashmir and Afghanistan" and were chiefly Shignis, Wakhis, Chitralis, Gilgitis, Nagaris and Kanjutis, and also 5 or 6 Punjabis, some of whom had been at least thirty years or more in bondage in Xinjiang, and yet others who had been born in slavery and spoke only Turki.[45] In another letter, Macartney wrote that these slaves owed their lot to the Kanjuti wars at "the time of the Kashmir Rajas Gulab Singh and Ranbir Singh".[46] Since these wars are dateable to 1847–1852 and 1860–1868, there were clearly large numbers of old first-generation slaves among those to be liberated, alongside younger, slave-born second or third generation slaves. The former were likely to have been of little commercial value while the latter, though considerably more valuable, were presumably less clearly identifiable in political or cultural terms, since the identity of a child of a slave father and a non-slave mother depended upon the culture in which it was born.

In an often overlooked, but critical, section of his seminal work *Slavery and Social Death* Orlando Patterson has argued that sizeable non-slave populations existed in every slave society. The rules of status inheritance for the two sections of the same society condition the social reproduction of slavery. Accordingly, most slave-holding societies can be understood as falling under either one of two categories: a) a group of societies in which rules determining the inheritance of status for children of free parents *differed* from those determining the inheritance of slave or freedmen status; and b) a group of societies in which the rules of status determination in both slave and free populations were *identical*. In societies where there was a high incidence of mixed unions (between free individuals and slaves), it made a huge difference to the progeny of such unions whether the rules of determination were similar or different.[47] According to Patterson's classification, both the late-Imperial Chinese and British–Indian patterns of status determination were those of group a), in which the status-reckoning systems for the free/free were different from the status reckoning systems for the 'slave/free unions. However, the population of Xinjiang was predominantly Sunni Muslim, of the Uighur Turkic and Hui clans, who were administered by a handful of provincial administrators from among the Han Chinese.[48] Apart from the fact that they came from a broad swathe of Islamic cultures, there is very little in the archival records on the religious affiliations of the slaves of this region. For instance, slaves from the southern valleys (like Chilas) might have been Sunnis by faith; those from the northeastern valleys of Hunza, Nagar and Baltistan might have been Shias; while the Wakhis and Shignis from the northwestern valleys could have been Ismailis.[49] Precisely because other documentation of such groups in the sub-continent indicate such a likelihood,[50] denominational affiliations may have had a significant role in determining methods of status reckoning. For this reason, though we have no way of knowing right now how non-slave Sunni Muslims in Xinjiang reckoned the status of their slaves' progeny, either of slave/slave unions or of slave/free unions, it is likely that they belonged to group b).

Rather than adopt these finer socio-cultural frames for distinguishing between slaves, the Government of India adopted a strictly secular and territorial mode of reckoning the status of those eligible for emancipation. Political and fiscal imperatives indicated that only the most recent captives who had been subjects of the Kashmir darbar (and therefore of British India after 1889) be emancipated. However, for a slave captured in the 1860s, when the territorial jurisdiction of the rulers of Kashmir over their neighbours caused little concern to British–Indian officials, the ascription of citizenship or 'political identity' was a conundrum. This was so particularly in the case of the regions referred to by the British Resident in Kashmir, Charles Prideaux, namely Hunza and Nagar, whose formal allegiances to China and Kashmir fluctuated throughout the nineteenth century. The chiefs of Hunza, for instance, paid formal tribute to the Chinese emperor and acknowledged him as suzerain in the first half of the century. Though the Chinese exercised no administrative control in Hunza, its chief had a hereditary landholding in the Yarkand district, and was authorised to collect grazing polls from the Kyrgyz.

However, in 1866, when Yaqub Beg of Kashgar wrested control over the Xinjiang provinces from his former masters and their Chinese overlords, the chiefs of Hunza and Nagar had turned to Kashmir. In return for an annual subsidy, these chiefs had acknowledged Kashmir as their suzerain, allowed the Maharaja's troops to occupy the fort of Chalt, and pledged never to raid Kashmiri soil.[51] But in 1885, Safdar Ali, the chief of Hunza, ejected the Kashmiri garrison from Chalt and appealed to China for support; he also received a Russian scientific delegation led by Gromchevsky in 1888, and resumed raiding sorties for caravans and slaves.

All this proved too threatening for the Government of India, which promptly deposed Pratap Singh, the ruler of Kashmir, reorganised his army, reactivated the Gilgit Agency which had been withdrawn in 1881, and initiated a road-building programme between Gilgit, which had been hitherto virtually inaccessible, and Srinagar.[52] By 1891, Hunza had been attacked and captured by the British, and Safdar Ali had escaped into Chinese territory. Hence, in 1892–1893, when negotiations over slave manumissions had to be undertaken, the political problem of slave identities was a loaded one, both in terms of the enormous disparities within catch-all categories like 'Gilgitis', and because of the administrative difficulties in ascertaining the 'original' identities of slaves. The first problem can be understood if we consider that the Gilgit Agency was an umbrella entity covering a vast area: the region it encompassed was a mosaic of independent valleys and principalities, of which the southern ones (like Chilas) had no centralised political authority, whereas the northern ones (like Hunza, Nagar and Baltistan) did. The southern regions used the Dari (Persian) language, whereas the roving Gujar herdsmen spoke an archaic Punjabi; while the northern regions used the "remaining liguistic puzzle", Burushaski, and Balti, a Tibetan language.[53] The second, and administrative, problem of the statist ascription of identity can be thus illustrated: a slave hailing from erstwhile Hunza (now part of the Gilgit Agency) counted as an old Kashmiri subject and hence newly-made British subject; however, the status of slaves hailing from regions whose rulers were not (yet) subject to British authority, like Chitral, did not merit the attentions of the manumitters.

In terms of purely diplomatic logic, too, this was inconsistent. The Mehtar of Chitral, Aman-ul-Mulk, had accepted the suzerainty and alliance of Kashmir in 1879; he had proven his fealty by sending a contingent against his nephew and son-in-law, Pehlwan Singh of Yasin, who had attacked Kashmir-held outposts.[54] Till Aman-ul-Mulk's death in 1892, Chitral did not cave in to the consistent pressure exerted by Afghanistan upon Chitral (as also upon Dir, Swat and Bajaur), and had renewed its agreements with the British Agency at Gilgit in 1889 to improve road communications and fortifications. Hence the Government of India's decision in 1893 to exclude Chitrali slaves from their emancipation efforts appeared politically incomprehensible even to the Chinese officials with whom Macartney was negotiating.[55]

Nor, if manumission was a straightforward issue of abolitionism, was Chitral disqualified for the 'humanitarian' effort, for the British-Indian government had adequate information on various Chitrali nobles bringing slave girls from Chitral to Peshawar, as well as on Afghan slave keeping and slave importing activities.[56] The advice of Robertson, who had stayed for a year between 1890 and 1891 in these regions, seems to have been invaluable to the opinions formed by the foreign secretary of the Government of India. Robertson had urged that if the Wakhis, Shignis and Chitralis were released and permitted to return to their places of birth, they would in all probability be promptly sold again, while some (such as the Chitralis), might even be killed as a warning to slaves against running away, or to show the good faith of the individuals who had originally sold them to their buyers.[57]

To be sure, in the period between 1892 and 1895, Chitral was in the grip of a disputed succession to the mehtarship, and the consequent clan warfare affected the outlying peoples and borders as well. However, the Government of India's decision to exclude the Chitralis and Afghans made excellent financial sense, principally because of an underlying assumption that the ruler who claimed back his subjects also had to pay for their ransom. According to an estimate submitted of Chitrali slaves, and descendants thereof, there were approximately 150 such slaves, and their emancipation would have cost around Rs. 8,500. Hence, while the financially well-off Kashmir darbar could be pressed to pay, Chitral in 1893 could not, or would not. Even when the war of succession in Chitral came to an end in 1895, the obstacle to a general emancipation of Chitrali slaves in Xinjiang remained, as did the institution of slavery within Chitral. For instance, when the war of succession ended, and the Government of India sent Robertson to install an infant as the mehtar "in the name of the Maharaja of Kashmir as his suzerain", it did not demand the manumission of slaves held *within* Chitral by the ruling groups. Robertson had written to the Government of India that though the sales of slaves out of Chitral should be prohibited, it was not politic to

interfere with domestic slaves or with field slaves already in the possession of the upper classes of the country. They constitute a valuable form

of property which it might or might not be thought advisable to deprive their owners of. It is nearly certain that if slavery were entirely abolished, the power of the *Adamzad* [ruling clan] class would be irretrievably lost.[58]

The Government of India had accordingly allowed Robertson to proclaim the illegality of "buying and selling slaves" but had complied with the argument he had given, i.e.,

It has been often held to be impolitic, especially when there is no intention of assuming the direct administration of that country, to interfere too rigorously and too soon with domestic institutions sanctioned by custom and religion....Bondsmen such as these have so long been regarded in Chitral as constituting a valuable form of property that it may not be advisable to move at once in the direction of freeing them from the status in which they have been born and brought up.[59]

Thus while concern for the power of the rulers prevented manumission of domestic slaves in Chitral, concern about costs prevented manumission of Chitrali slaves outside their land in 1893. There was absolutely no doubt in British official minds that slaves of Chitrali origin in Xinjiang were to be beyond the pale. Citing the influential Robertson as his authority, the officiating Resident in Kashmir urged that the Mehtar of Chitral "would never pay a rupee except on compulsion", and "owing to recent events in Chitral, there is no prospect, at any rate for the present, that funds for the release of the Chitrali slaves will be forthcoming".[60] Hence Chitrali and Afghan slaves were to be left where they were, at least for the time being.

The decision to manumit only the most recent captives was further qualified by the fact that only those among them that had no "family ties" in Chinese Turkestan were to be manumitted. Since the oldest slaves had either assimilated into the kin and client groups of their holders, and the slave-born in turn had family ties in Chinese Turkestan, those with kinships in the region constituted the largest number of slaves, including most female slaves.[61] The Government of India's decision meant that the freedom envisaged by British officials was to be limited only to a few adult men. According to a statement submitted regarding slaves of British–Indian origin, this number would be exactly 28 (see table below).

Identity of slave	Captives (Recent)	Children of slaves alive	Children of dead slaves
Kanjutis	4	2	–
Nagaris	–	–	–
Gilgitis	24	54	46
Kashmiris	–	–	–
Indians	–	–	–
Baltis	–	–	–

Source: Statement by George Macartney, 18 December 1893, Foreign Secret F, July 1894, no. 595, NAI.

In Yarkand city and surrounding villages alone, there were 107 slaves who had been imported into the country (first generation), and 316 slaves who had inherited their status (second generation); those among the first who had not established any family ties numbered 28 persons, of whom more than ten were Chitralis. In short, the British Government of India would have to bear responsibility for less than 18 slaves.[62]

Chinese Responses

The principle of classifying slaves according to family ties was not a British administrative invention but a Chinese one. All governments did not necessarily share the same sense of geography as the British officials in the Government of India. Chinese officials, both at the town and provincial levels, appeared to be operating from within a landscape of affective geography, which allowed for the articulation of identities beyond the simply territorial. In the process, Chinese officials seemed to have forced Macartney and the Government of India to extend themselves beyond their initial territorially limited and secularly dictated programme of emancipating slaves.

For the Chinese governor of Xinjiang, segregating according to the presence or absence of family ties was the only meaningful way of classifying slaves and endowing them with a post–emancipation identity. Those without family ties, ransomed by the British Agent, would be repatriated to the lands they had come from, but the far greater number of slaves who had been born in the country and had inherited their slave status were to be ransomed by the Chinese officials. "Without reference to the foreign countries" of their origin, they were to become "Chinese subjects".[63] In devising this plan, the provincial governor displayed a subtle aspect of political ideology that differentiated Western concepts of abolitionism from its non-Western counterparts. Where slavery itself was a condition of original kinlessness and deracination, the British-style reckoning of territorial and ethnic identities, based on issues of origin, were impossible to implement. Hence the Chinese administrator's emphasis that the larger number of slave-descended persons would count as subjects within the Qing Empire, with lands allotted to them, made sense in a context where many slaves "only know that they were originally of foreign descent but now neither themselves nor their owners can say from what tribe they claim such descent".[64] This threatened to destroy the *raison d'etre* of the British–Indian government's manumission efforts. The latter could hardly welcome emancipation if slaves, who were to be emancipated because they were 'British subjects' in the first place, were to become Chinese subjects as freemen.

The Chinese provincial administration's insistence regarding post-emancipation identity, and his own fears that the disproportionate financial burden on the Chinese authorities would effectively stymie the whole manumission process, impelled Macartney to override the instructions of his superiors in the Government of India and to offer to pay half the ransom for each British–Indian slave; this was also partly to ensure his own participation in, and control of, the procedures involved.[65] Moreover, since the Yarkand district authorities were responsible for the allocation of lands to the emancipated, Macartney also verbally assured them that the British–Indian government would not insist on the ex-slaves returning to their countries of origin.

Since the number of slaves Macartney was offering to ransom was so small (less than 18), the district authorities of Yarkand, as well as the provincial governor, recommended that the ransom of all the slaves, of first or subsequent generations, be paid by the Chinese administration, and formulated a set of regulations to this effect.[66] According to these regulations, all slaves, regardless of origin, generation and time spent in slavery, were to be ransomed at 20 *seers* of silver per head (approximately Rs. 61); the ransom of children (those below sixteen years of age) being half the amount. However, slaves who had been given lands for cultivation or money for trading purposes by their masters would be required to pay their own ransom. Respective owners were to bring their slaves before the local authorities, along with certificates prepared by the headmen of the villages to which the owners and slaves belonged, stating that there was no collusion between the slaves and the owners. Upon examination of this certificate by the Chinese and British officers, the slave owners would receive the ransoms, give up their deeds of purchase and liberate the slaves.

All liberated slaves would receive a certificate of freedom; those among them who wished to return to their homes would exchange their certificates for passports, and those who wished to remain with their masters could also do so upon the understanding that they would be free to move away at will.

However, the disproportionate financial burden of redemption that the provincial Chinese authorities had committed themselves to (approximately 4,000 or 5,000 seers of silver, or between Rs. 13,000 and Rs. 16,000) proved a stumbling block for the Chinese government at the centre. The *Tsungli Yamen* (Foreign Office) could neither stop the initiative already taken by its local offices, nor willingly pay up the whole of the compensation to the owners of 423 slaves. It was in this context that it tried to curb the efforts of the provincial authorities, instructing them to "take action only on a small scale, the smaller being the better".[67] Hence, only the first generation slaves and their spouses and children in Yarkand were to be emancipated. Despite this retreat, the local Chinese authorities were still to bear the cost entirely. A substantial improvement over the British scheme was that among the 107 slaves to be released, little heed was to be paid to the region of origin, whether Kashmir or Afghanistan.[68]

Indeed, local administrative officials in Xinjiang appeared to have been quite willing to expend their private funds as well as use the Imperial machinery for ransoming slaves. The most remarkable of them was Tseng ta lao Yieh, the sub-prefect of Karghallik, who addressed his superior officers for permission to ransom the one thousand-odd slaves who were not of Kashmiri, Gilgiti, Nagari, Kanjuti, Balti or Indian origin.[69] This particular official had found that the numbers of slaves hailing from the stipulated "six tribes" constituted only a fraction of the slaves under his jurisdiction. Arguing that "all slaves are equally entitled to pity", and that it was unjust that slaves from other areas should continue from generation to generation in their "mean condition", he ordered all the slaves in his sub-prefecture to be summoned, took their evidence, and inspected the certificates of purchase. Those who complained of illtreatment, "even if they did not belong to tribes under British jurisdiction", were ransomed and had their purchase bonds destroyed.[70] Due to the initiative of this local official, approximately 231 slaves were released in Karghallik alone; of this number, 157 were either Kashmiri subjects or their offspring, and were ransomed jointly by Macartney and Tseng ta lao Yieh, while 74 of "doubtful origin" were liberated on the basis of their own complaints. Subsequently, this local officer's efforts were responsible for the release of another 602 slaves, among whom 143 were of Chitrali origin.[71]

Such local Chinese magnanimity must be seen as a key determinant in the success of the emancipation project, for the British–Indian government was becoming increasingly insolvent. Though there were many slaves left in Maralbashi, Yangi Hissar and Khotan in western Xinjiang, the inability of the official Chinese hierarchy to contribute towards the ransom meant that the Government of India had to undertake the whole payment or coerce Kashmir to pay. Though the latter paid the bill for the ransom of slaves in Yarkand and Karghallik,[72] we have no means of knowing whether the cost of the other emancipations was also borne by them.

Beyond Governments: Slave Action in Emancipation Scenarios

The limited scope of British official policy was shown up by the more holistic nature of the local Chinese administrative efforts; both these in turn fade into the background in the context of the slaves' own initiatives. Just as in the Western Hemisphere, where intense political and military struggles within and between the leading Atlantic powers created conditions in which slavery could be challenged successfully, geo-political rivalry in Central Asia also created conditions within which slaves could undermine the structures in which they were enmeshed. The agency of slaves themselves to plead, cajole and threaten matters so that manumission became an urgent and pressing political issue must be highlighted, as must, indeed, older or non-Western efforts at regulating the trade and transfer of slaves. There is a statement, for instance, in Shaw's account that the Ataliq Ghazi had abolished slave trading in his dominions by 1869:

> Formerly there were regular markets where you could go and buy a boy or a girl or a grown-up slave; some sold for debt, some the prize of forays made against the neighbouring Sheeah Tribes. Now household slaves still exist, but the trade is done away with and the markets closed.[73]

The proclamation may have induced some of the passersby or spectators in the market at Kashgar to intervene directly to liberate the slaves put up for sale. There was the instance of a *Haji* who informed the *jamadar dad-khwah* (chief of the artillery) about their presence, and who probably induced the latter into issuing a proclamation prohibiting slave resales.[74] The jamadar apparently give the slaves a "paper of freedom and protection" with his own and the *wazir*'s (ruler's) seal, but had to accede to the slave merchants' representations against this arbitrary manumission. The matter was finally decided by the Ataliq Ghazi who ransomed the slaves for "twenty tillahs" (approximately Rs. 5) and appointed them as soldiers in his service, where they were "well treated and well fed, but not allowed to go to our homes".

Why had Yaqub Beg prohibited slave sales in his newly acquired kingdom? Was his action also rooted in geopolitics, or were there larger issues involved? Though we can do no more than speculate at the moment, it is clear that the moral injunctions of the 'New Religion', and the reinterpretation of the Quran in the light of this, may have had as much to do with prohibiting slave sales as the secular, timocratic concerns of an enlightened elite.[75]

More significantly, the slaves' own desires and efforts at escape seems to have had a considerable impact upon contemporary geopolitical strategies. Captain Nikolai Muraviev, sent to Khiva in 1819 to secure a commercial and political treaty with the khan, wrote of the Russian slaves there who "begged me in whispers to try and obtain their release", smuggled their pleas to him in the barrel of a gun and ran alongside his horse beseeching him not to "forget us poor people"; and of one elderly Russian slave's determination to flee with several others across the Kyrgyz Steppe.[76] The desperation of 3000 Russian and 30,000 Persian and Kurd slaves in Khiva convinced Muraviev that a Russian invasion would rally support from within the khanate: these people, with nothing to lose but their chains, would welcome the overthrow of the khan. In 1873, the British consul at Resht reported that large numbers of Persian slaves in the Khivan army at Urgunj had been "instrumental in guiding their [the Russian army's] steps to the city gates" and actively participated in the smashing of their own chains.[77]

Slaves held in Xinjiang, too, impressed upon visitors in the 1860s their determination to escape. Shaw, the first Englishman to visit the province after Yaqub Beg's rise to dominance, had described at length how some of these slaves tried to make contact with him and his entourage to plead for emancipation.[78] An enslaved Punjabi sepoy from Kashmir told Shaw's servant, Sarda, to convey to his employer that

> their only hope of escape lay in a rising...there were many thousands of natives of the surrounding countries thus detained at Kashgar, who would all side against the Atalik Ghazee in any commotion, in order to effect their escape. He added that they only wanted a leader![79]

Though Shaw cautioned his servant against expressing any opinions in this matter, his own were clear: the slaves' hope of escape lay in upsetting the rule of Yaqub Beg; if this occurred, however, it could upset the Government of India's plans of maintaining a buffer State between itself and the Russian Empire. Thus the only possible way of keeping the imperial rivals apart was by procuring the freedom of the slaves.

An identical moment of truth appears to have preceded Macartney's efforts in Xinjiang. Two of the impressed Balti labourers who accompanied Sir William Lockhart's mission to Hunza as baggage porters fell ill there, and were left behind to be sent back when they recovered.[80] Shortly afterwards, the Mir of Hunza was killed by his son, who sent the two Baltis to be sold at Sirikul for 970 *tangas* (Rs. 140). Purchased and brought to Yarkand, one of the slaves was eventually ransomed by subscriptions raised by resident non-slave Baltis of Shagar and Braldu; the other slave was not so fortunate, being sent off to his master's farm some thirty miles from Yarkand. It was the ransomed slave who rushed in on the trader Dalgliesh one morning "with all the wildness of a forlorn highlander", imploring the Englishman to take him back to his family. A petition, countersigned by the *aksaqal* (representative) of the Baltis, pleaded for freedom for both the slaves.[81] Though in this instance the Government of India appears to have accepted its responsibility for the fate of these two porters, other accounts speak of private manumissions of such slaves in these two regions. Younghusbsand, for instance, refers to "three Baltis" who had been captured by Kanjuti horsemen, sold into slavery, and ransomed and released at Yarkand by the Englishman who accompanied him through the Mustagh Pass in 1887.[82] There were also precedents for the manumission of slaves in Chinese Turkestan well before Macartney arrived there, and it would appear that the impetus for manumission came from both slaves and non-slaves within Xinjiang.

Undeniably, liberation meant something for the slaves, since those freed often tried to ensure the release of slaves left behind: Rajab Bai, for instance, a released Gilgiti slave at Posgam, reported that another slave from Gilgit called Nazar had not been freed at the same time from the possession of his master at Yarkand.[83] Slaves who had heard of manumission or abolition in contiguous regions and towns tried to invoke the help of the British Agent, either by running away from their masters and seeking refuge in his house, or by appealing to him directly for money to ransom their families.[84] Even ex-slaves who continued to reside with their masters had a keen sense of the irrevocability of emancipation, as is revealed by an ex-slave in Karghallik, who complained when his ex-master took away his freedom certificate and tried to re-enslave him.[85]

Alternate Affiliations and Homelands

Given this keenness, it appears puzzling that after their release in the 1890s only a fraction of the slaves tried to return to their native lands. The accounts of the Kashmir darbar show that only 38 slaves returned from Tashkurgan to Hunza and another 13 from Yarkand to Hunza, a total of 51 emancipated slaves.[86] Why did so few return to their older homelands? This is where a closer look at the gender/age profiles of manumitted slaves is particularly revealing. Though we do not have these profiles for all the manumitted slaves, we do have one list of 122 slaves manumitted in Karghallik in 1894, and another of 7 manumitted from Yarkand.[87] Of the 122 slaves manumitted in Karghallik alone in November 1894, 62 were male and 60 were female. 29 of the males released were children under the age of sixteen, and 34 were adults. Of the females manumitted, a larger number (42) were adult and 18 were children. This profile can be explained only by elaborating on the two different kinds of family formations that involved the slaves. One was that formed by the union of slave/slave, and the progeny born thereof (like the thirty-seven-year-old woman slave Tokhta Bibi, the forty-eight-year-old male slave Khush Kadam, and their two infant daughters), of which there were at least 10 such families in one list alone.

A second kind of union, between slave and non-slave, is hinted at by the fact that most of the adult women were listed along with their children. The possibility that the male owners of all the slaves were also the fathers of the children of these female slaves cannot be ruled out (as in the case of the thirty-one-year-old female slave Almakiz with her three boy-children, or the forty-year-old female slave Nazak, with her four children). There were at least 15 such female-slave heads of family units in the list from Karghallik alone. In addition, there were female slaves who were listed as mothers of children with freemen who were not their owners (like Daulat, a twenty-four-year-old female slave who had two children with Khas Muhammad, a freeman). Both kinds of families may then have included adult males from local Sinic and/or Turki populations, as owner-fathers, non-owner fathers and slave-fathers, as suggested by the listing of a Chinese slave Allah Vardi, shown as the husband of a female slave of Gilgiti origin, the twenty-six-year-old Makhmal, and father of their three infant children.

It is clear, from the above-mentioned list at least, that very few adult slaves were without any affective kinships of any sort. In the case of men, it is more than likely that their original levels of subsistence either through soldiering or porterage had been precarious, as in the case of the Balti coolies, so that some means of livelihood in agricultural occupations might have been a more attractive alternative to the system of *begar* (obligatory porterage) which continued as a practical, unofficial policy within Kashmir up till the twentieth century. Though British officers asserted that most of the ex-slaves lived on with their former owners as servants, some may indeed have exercised a choice in desiring, or trying, to become small cultivators on the lands promised to them by the Chinese authorities.

However, while British officers only conjectured about the occupational destinies of manumitted males, other considerations may have been more important to the slaves themselves. An obvious consideration would appear to be familial, particularly since most adult women slaves were inserted into kinship and social structures. But even for adult male slaves in the list from Karghallik alone, it is clear that a majority of such slaves had been born locally; their parents, even though originating from areas under Kashmiri-British suzerainty in the 1890s, had grown old in slavery. For instance, Ramzan was a sixty-three-year-old Gilgiti male slave in 1894, whose adult daughters, in turn, had borne children in the houses of their owners. Or there was the sixty-five-year-old female slave, Sultan Bakht, one of whose adult daughters had married a male slave, and another (Daulat, referred to above) had married a freeman. Similarly, there was a thirty-five-year-old Kanjuti male slave who was the son of a female, and presumably much older, released slave. Particularly where second or third generation slaves existed, there were aged parents or grandparents. The older generations could not have been expected to undertake the enormous physical difficulties of the journey back to their original homelands. Leaving them behind, or leaving behind siblings, may not have been an option too many ex-slaves would have liked to take. Hence, children who had been born in Xinjiang may have had a difficult life at the margins of their owners' societies, but emotional and material relationships in their current situations may have been much more significant determinants for these people's acknowledgement of a 'homeland'.

Certainly, officially inscribed 'original' and territorial homelands did not always evince a desire to reclaim their lost ones. For each brother who might have wished to take his sister back with him – as, for instance, the agent of the Mir of Hunza who brought the customary tribute to Kashgar in 1894 and expressed a desire to return home with his long-estranged sister, the newly-released female slave at Karghallik called Gulbegi – there were many others not so cherished.[88] Manumitted slaves might have understood that once ejected from their respective villages and kin-groups, they were probably seen as 'outsiders', of whom many travellers reported a great fear in these regions. Younghusband's account was the clearest on this score: when he returned with the three emancipated Baltis to the valley of Astor from which they had originated, they found a very hostile reception awaiting them; two of them subsequently elected to return to Yarkand with the British officer. The question, therefore, regarding all these manumitted groups would nowadays be posed in terms of ethnicity; whether they chose to assimilate with Chinese cultural and political identities, whether they chose to enact cultures of 'difference' or whether they managed to maintain a bit of both must remain unanswered for the present.[89] What is easier to resolve, however, is a methodological concern for scholars working on identity politics conducted by territorially defined States. If most of the slaves chose to negotiate their way within their new homelands, then the official myths of primordial origins and territorially fixed identities that came to dominate both Chinese and British–Indian historiography in the early twentieth century could perhaps be recontextualised from the ex-slaves' perspective. In other words, variegated popular experiences, practices and imaginings of territory and home need to be foregrounded in all discussions of State-endowed identities.

Conclusion

The story of the intersecting politics of the post–Brussels antislavery drive and the imperialist Great Game compulsions has a great deal to offer to historians of the South Asia of this period. The limited manumissions that were sought to be effected in Xinjiang were not part of colonial policy in the sub-continent. The case of Chitral, which I have mentioned earlier, was precisely the parallel that was followed with regard to the princely States within the sub-continent. If British imperialist interests required that slavery as an institution be perpetuated within a 'frontier' region in order to maintain the social and political hegemony of its elites, and that State itself as a buffer against Russian imperialism, a similar argument could be made for the preservation of slavery as an institution within the princely States in India. A case in point was Bhopal where, in 1881, the commercial representatives of the ruling house were caught importing African child slaves.[90] A mild note of 'censure' was passed on the *begum* (lady).[91] Nothing was said of emancipating the slaves already present in the household and petty administration. Since the Government of India needed these princely States as buffers against the burgeoning nationalist movements in the sub-continent, efforts to manumit slaves in these States were not even considered in the late nineteenth century. In this respect, the imperialist State in the later nineteenth and early twentieth centuries proved to be both *administratively flexible,* tempering the ideological and moral agendas of international politics to specific and changing strategies of rule, and *socially reactionary* or *reformist* according to such changing local exigencies. For historians of the Indian State in post–colonial conditions, it is this complex nature of the State that is at the heart of current debates. The conjunction of humanitarian rhetoric with imperialist agendas of rule, practiced by an imperial government in the 1890s, can be said to have been subsequently replicated by the post-colonial State in many arenas. If a critical disaggregation of such conjunctions is to be undertaken, there is a pressing need to collapse other boundaries as well – especially those institutional and disciplinary boundaries between 'intellectual history', 'social history' and 'foreign policy' – boundaries which have bedevilled our critical imaginations. Only if we forsake such bounded and fragmented enquiries can we hope to historicise the making of 'identity' politics in the context of nation-states. The historical evidence of slaves from diverse origins and locations (Africa, Afghanistan and Turkey, as much as from Myanmar (Burma), Southeast Asia and Nepal) within an 'Indian' society in the eighteenth and nineteenth centuries could perhaps offer a perspective other than the territorial or linguistic in the current controversies over 'immigrants'. We certainly need to foreground the experiences of ex-slaves in order to understand the mutability of all identities in the politics and economics of survival. But we also need to envisage alternative forms of geography that go beyond territorial limits, for instance in terms of the social and cultural spaces that people inhabit, not always coherently or self-consciously, as the sources of their identities.

Delimitation, Borders and the Unsolved Questions of State Formation in Central Asia

A N I T A   S E N G U P T A

Borders and States

The recent proliferation of independent States in Eurasia has created an interest in the rationale on which these States have come into existence. It has also generated debate on attributes that, after the Versailles Treaty in 1919 and then after 1945, were designated as crucial to the definition of a State. It was generally accepted that the idea of space, as central to the concept of sovereign, bounded communities, was paramount. All contemporary political authorities and jurisdictions were to be given physical limits. The location of these borders, and the purposes they would serve, became significant to the lives of the people separated by these lines.[1]

What has not been adequately observed, however, is that these lines, today appearing as sacrosanct, have a history of their own, and mostly a disputed one. This is particularly true of areas where the construction of these lines required the prior assumption and deliberation of some underlying principles for their demarcation; involving, in effect, the imputation of group identities. As new historical imperatives call for the reconstitution of boundaries, the unsolved questions of a previous era assume great significance. One such region that is re-examining the rationality of its frontiers today is Central Asia.

Independence in regions like Central Asia has meant a reconfiguring of the concept of borders in a region where they were already porous to begin with. The national-territorial divisions of the post–1917 period in the region, that were established on principles determined by Soviet power, were not without their problems, many of which emanated from the nature of the pre-Soviet boundaries in the region. Here, the evidence of disputed frontiers and approximate boundaries bring into question the 'objective reality' of borders across the vast expanse of Turkestan. They also

raise questions about whether potential States of homogeneous populations were cut across by State intervention to create units that, in fact, had
no viability before Soviet 'creation'.

A study of the viability or otherwise of State structures as they exist
today cannot be attempted without an examination of these interrelated
issues. Do the seeds of some of the present territorial discords among the
States have their roots in some creation which was artificial enough not to
have stood the test of time? In order to attempt an answer to this question,
which is crucial before any examination of the reality as it exists today can
be undertaken, it would perhaps be best to look back in time to see to what
extent modern frontiers are grounded in history, for it is inevitable that
these historical legacies will shape the politics of the new States of Eurasia.

It is also important to examine notions of territoriality in the region
prior to the final drawing of the lines in the post–revolution period. What
emerges clearly is the fact that unambiguously demarcated boundaries are
of recent origin in the region, barely over half a century old. The borders of
the present States in Central Asia have no pre-Russian heritage; Russian
and Soviet administrators demarcated them and then set about building
nations to fit States. It is also clear that well up to the second half of the
nineteenth century, on the eve of the Russian advance, all lines on the
map of the region were mere approximations, which were frequently
transgressed, and a further shifting of boundaries ensued after
colonisation. This historical legacy of political ambiguity was inherited
by the new political entities in the Soviet era, as also by the post–Soviet
successor States.

Thus this chapter is an attempt to briefly examine:

(a) the basis on which the borders were finally drawn in the years after
    the revolution;
(b) whether these borders had any historical basis, through a brief
    examination of the nature of the 'early State' in the region;
(c) an illustration of the nature of boundaries just prior to the Russian
    takeover, through an examination of the frontiers of the Emirate of
    Bukhara; and
(d) the problems that were left unsolved by this attempt at State formation
    on ethno-territorial lines.

Basis of Borders

The principal decision adopted by the Seventh All Russian Conference of
the Russian Social Democratic Workers Party (RSDRP) in 1917 reflected a

desire for self-determination as the basis on which the new units were to operate, and decisions were taken accordingly. It pointed out that

> The right of all nations forming part of Russia to freely secede and form independent states shall be recognized. To negate this right or to fail to take measures guaranteeing its practical realization is equivalent to supporting a policy of seizure and annexation.
>
> The party demands wide regional autonomy, the abolition of tutelage from above, the abolition of compulsory state language and determination of boundaries of self government and autonomous regions by the local population itself based on economic and social conditions, national composition, etc.[2]

However, the Central Asian story of delimitation and consequent State formation is a confused one. The Soviet claim of complete support from the people who were disillusioned with the feudal system of the Czars and the tyranny of the local *emirs* (chiefs) clashed with the contradictory evidence of the numerous short-lived alliances between local entities during this time, which assumed shapes crucial enough to warrant attention from the power that was establishing itself in the region. It is therefore necessary to examine the basis of the policy on which this delimitation was implemented – a modern basis of identity largely unknown in the earlier political history of Central Asia.

The importance accorded to the 'national question' in the region was not only in conformity with the ideology of Marxism but also with the multiethnic reality of Central Asia. The decision was thus a solution in terms of a politico-cultural autonomy within the framework of a decentralised, multinational socialist State. In the Central Asian situation of social and national oppression, the Bolsheviks sought the possibility of linking the social and national revolutions together.[3]

As the leader of the Bolshevik Party, V. I. Lenin, though acutely aware of the dangers of nationalism, especially since this was an important factor retarding the development of social consciousness, condemned the view that cultural-national autonomy would democratise relations among nations. He was also opposed to the view, held by the German revolutionary Rosa Luxembourg, that State creation along ethnic lines was a bourgeois charade.[4] More to his liking was the viewpoint of the Austrian Social Democrats, proposed in the 1890s, that people of the same nationality no matter in what part of the country they resided should form an autonomous national union, under whose jurisdiction the State placed all branches of culture. This, in fact, was an option that had appeared at the conference of the RSDRP, in the course of the demands for autonomy in the region. It would be interesting to examine what this could have meant in the Central Asian context, given the scattered nature of the population in the region.

I. V. Stalin elaborated on these ideas in *Marxism and the National Question*, and defined the nation as "a historically constituted, stable community of people, formed on the basis of a common language, territory, economic life and psychological make-up manifested in a common culture", a definition wherein ethnicity, territory and culture occupy important positions.[5] He rejected earlier definitions of the nation by the Austrian Social Democrats Karl "Springer" Renner and Otto Bauer as ignoring objective characteristics of nationhood. Also, according to Stalin, a nation was not just a historical category in isolation, but one belonging to the epoch of rising capitalism. A decisive element in Stalin's nationality policy was his conception of the State. He viewed the State not as an organised form of power but as a framework for the nation's development, thus reintroducing the concept of State sovereignty and, by implication, the right to self-determination. However, it was stressed that the right to secede did not mean actual support to secession.

To Lenin, the national question was irreducibly an issue of self-determination. He defined self-determination as the "political separation of nations from alien national bodies and the formation of an independent national state".[6] He was explicit in pointing out that self-determination cannot have any other meaning but that of State independence and the formation of a national State. Though recognising that this was irreconcilable with the internationalism inherent in Marxism, Lenin accepted the legitimacy of national movements and pointed out that the bourgeois nationalism of every oppressed nation had a democratic content. Also, in order to break away from the legacy of imperial Russian chauvinism, it was necessary to ensure the equality of nations. He also believed that a formal right of secession would make the actual separation unnecessary. The support given to the right to self-determination would depend upon the level of social development of the nation seeking political separation, and on a consideration of which of its classes expressed its will. The recognition accorded to nationalism, however, did not prevent him from proclaiming the primacy of socialism over the claims of nationalism. On the other hand, it did not lead to a repudiation of the right to self-determination but rendered its exercise possible only under certain conditions. In the Seventh Conference in April 1917, Stalin and others turned against self-determination. However, Lenin's arguments led to the acceptance of the right of all the nations that composed Russia to separate and form independent States if they so desired, and far-reaching regional autonomy for those who did not desire self-determination. In the post–1917 period this was expressed in the Declaration of the Rights of the People of Russia and subsequently in the Declaration to All the Toiling Masses of Russia and the East.[7]

R. A. Tuzmuhamedov, in his analysis of how the national problem was solved in the Central Asian region, points out that from a situation in which the administrative-cum-territorial divisions did not reflect national-ethnic boundaries, the Soviet system transformed these divisions to establish a system wherein groups of people formed compact majorities. The change over from the older system was said to have been at the behest of the people of the region who wished to throw off the colonial–feudal yoke of imperial Russian colonialism.[8]

Tuzmuhamedov goes on to describe what he considers noteworthy of delimitation in Central Asia, which, he says, differed from that in Europe. Two of his observations are important enough to be examined in detail. The first is that self-determination took place within the territorial boundaries established in the colonial period, which had split up the national-ethnic groups of the region's population. Secondly, the subject of self-determination was (at first) not a formed nation or even a nationality on its way towards consolidation into a nation, but a multi-national population comprising numerous ethnic groups united in their efforts to eliminate colonial rule from without and social oppression from within.[9]

Thus territorial delimitation and the multi-national character of the population being decolonised were the two major aspects of the process of self-determination. Significant to the character of delimitation in Central Asia was the socio-economic aspect of the transition from colonialism to socialism. As in the rest of the colonised world, the multi-ethnic character of the population created a multiplicity of problems for the post–colonial stage. It was not unnatural, therefore, that there was a carry-over of these problems into the later phase, as many of them had not been adequately addressed earlier.

According to most Soviet scholars writing on this period of transition, the victory of self-determination was accompanied by the formation of national territories as an essential prerequisite for the development of the people towards socialism. Within the RSDRP, and in the writings of its leaders, the problem of identifying the correct and most rational basis for the reorganisation of the people was being addressed. In common with all colonial administrations, the Czarist system had been involved in organising territorial divisions according to administrative convenience. There was no one system of governance for the whole of the region. While Turkestan was organised as a Governor-Generalship, the Khanate of Khiva and the Emirate of Bukhara retained most of their control over domestic affairs and agreed only to abolish slavery and partially change their trade laws in favour of the Russians. The view that the Czarist system was a centrally established 'imperial policy' adapted when necessary to local circumstances has now been largely discarded in favour of the view that Russia ruled her empire through a series of ad hoc arrangements arising directly from contact with the diverse local principalities.[10] Russia's imperial policy was not clearly defined, neither were the institutions it created. It is true that with the gradual recognition of the shortcomings of the administrative system there were efforts to rectify the problems by, for instance, the Palen Commission, which made a detailed study of the legal and administrative structures in the outlying provinces in order to make the system compatible with the requirements of the region.[11] However, problems persisted within the structure of the administration, especially the complex problem of rationally reorganising the peoples in the region, which remained unaddressed. The Soviet approach to the problem was in identifying language as the criteria for determining nationality and making it the rational basis for governance.

The thesis on the national and colonial question that was adopted by the Second Comintern Congress in 1920 pointed out that the party should not advance "abstract and formal principles on the national question but should undertake first of all a precise analysis of the given environment".[12] Lenin was thus faced with the practical problem of the establishment of socialism in a region that lacked a proletariat and was totally different from the rest of Russia; a problem that had to be solved keeping the peculiar characteristics of the region in mind. While one alternative was to superimpose political institutions onto existing ethnographic divisions, determining the true ethnographic contours of the region was a problem. The possibility of uniting the entire region, including the Khanate of Khiva and the Emirate of Bukhara, under one Turkestan seemed to be most compatible with the Soviet plan for converting the region to socialism. It was with this idea in mind that the Turkestan Autonomous Soviet Republic was proclaimed in 1920. In the period between the Bolshevik Revolution and the division of the region in 1924, the people of the region were treated as one nation. But as apprehensions over Turkestan nationalism gained ground in the early 1920s with the appearance of such leaders as Sultan Galiev, Mustafa Chokaev, Zeki Velidi Togan and Enver Pasha, the need for smaller units to retard pan-Turkic sentiments was increasingly felt. This was one of the reasons why the party changed tack, and the delimitation of the region into national republics was agreed upon.

According to most Soviet scholars, delimitation was conducted in the region to fulfill the aspirations for power among the people, to realise Bolshevik principles of self-determination of nations and to create a counterweight against pan-Turkism. More specifically, delimitation was resorted to in order to: (1) adjust the administrative boundaries in line with the settlement of the main nationalities and nations of Russian Central Asia; (2) ensure their territorial integrity; (3) move towards the creation of a statehood for these nationalities and nations; (4) ensure fuller national sovereignty for the Central Asian peoples; and (5) enable the Central Asian peoples to play an effective role in carrying through the political, economic and cultural measures designed to promote a socialist and communist ethos nationwide. The process of delimitation was expected to grant political autonomy to major ethnic groups in line with the policy stated in the Declaration of the Rights of the People of Russia, the degree of formal autonomy granted depending on the degree of political development in that region.[13]

It is necessary to look into the process of delimitation in Central Asia and examine how the official policy was applied to the Central Asian situation, in order to correctly assess the complexities involved in the process of delimitation.[14]

In 1924, Russian Central Asia was divided into five national areas: the more advanced and more numerous peoples – the Uzbeks and Turkmen – were formed into Soviet Socialist Republics (SSR), while the smaller and less advanced were formed into Autonomous Soviet Socialist Republics (ASSR) (the Tajiks), and Autonomous *Oblasts*' (provinces) (the Kyrgyz and the Kara-Kalpaks). Subsequently, the Tajiks were promoted as an SSR in 1929, the Kara-Kalpaks become an ASSR in 1932 and the Kyrgyz rose to the level of an ASSR in 1926 and subsequently into an SSR in 1936.

As early as 1913, the Central Committee of the RSDRP had included a provision in their manifesto that ensured wide autonomy for these national minorities and ethnic groups who did not opt to secede from Russia. The provision also included a clause for the demarcation of old boundaries. This was restated by the Seventh Conference of the RSDRP in April 1917, and the Peoples Commissariat for Nationality Affairs gave shape to this provision when it established separate State formations. In 1920, the Bolshevik government decided to break up the multi-national State structure of the Turkestan ASSR and to redraw its administrative boundaries in conformity with ethnographic divisions. This decision was clearly reflected in the degree promulgated by the Turkestan Commission in January 1920, and in the instructions given by Lenin to the Turkestan Commission in July 1920.

At the time of the revolution in 1917, Russian Central Asia consisted of three political divisions that cut across national boundaries – Russian Turkestan, the Khanate of Khiva and the Emirate of Bukhara. The first was directly administered by the Russian government, and the other two were internally independent but acknowledged Russian suzerainty. In November 1917, Russian Turkestan fell under Soviet rule, but remained isolated from the rest of Russia until late 1919. During this time, Khiva and Bukhara remained isolated Muslim States. The revolution in February 1917 was followed by the establishment of a provincial government in Turkestan. The idea of territorial autonomy for Turkestan was first expressed at the Kazakh–Kyrgyz Congress in April 1917. Shortly thereafter, on 1 May 1917, at the First All Russian Muslim Congress, it was agreed that the need of the hour was for a democratic republic based on national, territorial and federal principles, with national-cultural autonomy for the nationalities that lacked distinct territories.

Between 1917 and 1920, Turkestan was ruled from Tashkent by a government of Bolsheviks and Left SSRs who were non-natives and carried out a policy of repression against the native population. In the meantime, an extraordinary All Russian Muslim Congress was convened at Tashkent, which demanded Muslim autonomy for Turkestan within a Russian federation. In December, the Fourth Extraordinary Regional Muslim Congress met in Kokand and declared its autonomy. At first the demands of the Kokand government under Mustafa Chokaev were considered to be reasonable, but at the Fourth Regional Congress of the Soviets in January 1919 the Chairman of the Council of Peoples' Commissars, F. Kolesov, pronounced the government to be counter-revolutionary. As a result, the Tashkent Soviet disbanded its rival government at Kokand with the help of the Red Army; this in turn gave rise to the Basmachi Movement, in which the followers of the deposed rulers of Bukhara and Khiva threatened to overthrow the then precariously existing government. At this time, Turar Ryskulov of the Turkestan Central Executive Committee put forward a plan for a Turkic Republic, to be governed by the Turkic Communist Party.

At the end of 1919, communications were reestablished between Turkestan and Moscow. A powerful *Turkkommissia* (Turkestan Commission) was dispatched to the east, which dismissed the Tashkent government, drafted a constitution for the Republic of Turkestan and made serious efforts to win over the native population.[15] Under the new constitution, Turkestan was proclaimed an Autonomous Republic within the Russian Socialist Federated Soviet Republic (RSFSR), though it comprised of the same territory as the former Turkestan Governor-Generalship. The constitution of March 1920 declared that Turkestan was to be self-governing in all matters except defence and foreign relations, and that the RSFSR would have a say in budget matters.

One of the first tasks of the new Turkic government was to attack Khiva and Bukhara and establish revolutionary governments. Internal problems had plagued both Bukhara and Khiva, and in both there were small, modernist groups who appealed to the Soviet government for help. The first attempt at a revolt by the Young Bukharans, with the help of the Red Guards had failed, and the emir, who had offered limited reforms, now withdrew them. In 1920 the emir was overthrown and the Peoples Republic of Bukhara was established. The Peoples Republics of Bukhara and Khiva (also set up in 1920) soon came within the political and economic sphere of the RSFSR and Turkestan, despite the fact that they had been granted independence and exclusion from the Soviet Union when it was established at the end of 1922. That the support extended to the Soviets was still conditional becomes evident from a remark made by a delegate from Turkestan, who had said, "Comrade, the Muslims will not desert the Soviets, but on condition that the peculiarities of the Eastern people are recognized".[16]

At the end of 1920, the Central Committee of the Turkestan Communist Party established three national departments – Uzbek, Kyrgyz and Turkmen – for work among the native population. Concurrently, the Central Executive Committee formed Kazakh, Uzbek, Turkmen and Kyrgyz national departments. There was no separate Tajik section, a fact that was resented by the Tajiks. In August 1921, the government of the RSFSR decreed that in principle Turkestan should be administratively divided by nationality. Significant steps were taken between 1920 and 1923 to draw the Peoples Republics into the political and economic orbit of Turkestan and the RSFSR. In February 1922, the Bukharan and Khivan Communist Parties were merged into the Russian Communist Party, and in May the *Turkbyuro* (Turkestan Bureau) was transformed into the *Sredazbyuro* (Central Asian Bureau) and given authority over all communist organisations in Turkestan, Bukhara and Khiva. In March 1923, the economies of Turkestan, Bukhara and Khiva were unified and a Central Asian Economic Council was established, which had authority over all three areas.

By the end of 1923 it had become evident to the party that the existing political divisions of Central Asia were no longer adequate. The notion of abolishing the Turkestan ASSR and the Peoples Republics and of substituting national republics for them was first considered by the party in January 1924. A federation was considered unsuitable for Central Asia, though the region was inhabited by people who, while differing in language and nationality, were united by their Muslim faith and Islamic way of life. The pan-Islamic and pan-Turkic nature of the region was the main reason against the formation of a unified, federal Turkestan. There was a strong strand of thinking in the Soviet government that the best means of welding the borderlands to the Soviet State was by denying them their cultural unity. This was to be done by creating national units, despite the fact that it affected a people to whom the concept of nationality had been historically unimportant. On 31 January 1924, the *Orgbyuro* (Organisational Bureau of the Central Committee of the Turkestan Commission) appointed Ia. E. Rudzutak, a member of the Commission, to examine the problem. In April, the decision to demarcate the region was approved by the Politburo of the Russian Communist Party. Opposition came from the Khivan Party, who proposed the inclusion of Khiva as a whole in the USSR; from local nationalists who demanded a "Great Uzbek State" or a "Great Kazakh State"; and from pan-Turkics who stood for the formation of a Turkic State. The Communist Parties of Turkestan and Bukhara were reconstituted by nationality; and at the end of June the Sredazbyuro appointed a territorial commission and various national commissions to draw up the territorial divisions for the new administrations. By November of the same year, the new boundaries had been determined.

However, it remained a fact that none of the divisions from which the new States were reconstituted had any one ethnic group in a clear majority, though there remained a debate on the figures for each ethnic group in the various States, given the fact that the 1917 and 1920 censuses on which the figures were based were partial and differed from the figures given by the Commission for Economic Unification. The population distribution of the region was clearly mixed: according to census figures, in Bukhara the Uzbeks were in a majority with 50.7%, followed by Tajiks at 31.65% and Turkmen at 10.3%. In addition there were Kazakhs, Kyrgyz, Kara-Kalpaks,

Arabs and Jews. In Turkestan, Uzbeks constituted 41.4%, Kazakhs 19.4%, Kyrgyz 10.7%, Russians 9.5% and Tajiks 7.7%. The Uzbeks, Kazakhs and Turkmen inhabited all the republics. More important was the fact that barring the Uzbeks, no other group constituted a distinct majority in any particular area.[17]

The 1924 national delimitation restructured local boundaries, erasing Soviet Turkestan and the Peoples Republics of Bukhara and Khiva. It gave territorial shape to each of the major nations with a clearly demarcated boundary. The official Soviet policy was to give each of the new States its own language; thus the Soviet regime acted as a catalyst for the creation of a nation out of a group of nomadic or semi-nomadic people, and at the same time gave shape to local aspirations for a separate identity, as among the Turkmen.

The eminent Sovietologist A. A. Gordiyenko has justified the delimitation exercise of that time by pointing out the uneven rates of development in Turkestan, Bukhara and Khiva, and the impossibility of carrying on the demarcation in Turkestan alone due to the mixed nature of the population and the shortage of trained administrative personnel. He also asserts that the necessity for demarcation had become evident in the very first years after the revolution; while rejecting Ryskulov's plan for a Turkic Republic, Lenin had ordered the Turkkommissia to draw up an ethnographic map of the region in the period just after the revolution.[18] The fact that delimitation was delayed by a number of years when discussions on it had already begun immediately after the revolution is significant. It is tempting to see the 'march of reason and rationality' in the reversal of Lenin's dismissal of the ethnic principle for national sub-division to its later application in the region in the following years.

If delimitation along ethno-territorial lines is to be meaningfully critiqued, it is essential to examine the nature of the pre-Russian and pre-Soviet boundaries in Central Asia.

Boundaries and the Early State

It is often pointed out today that the borders of the present States in Central Asia have no pre-Russian heritage. It was Russian and Soviet administrators who demarcated boundaries and then set about building nations to fit States. Frontiers, an entirely new phenomenon to the people of the region, were formulated and established not on a 'national' basis but on imperial and military considerations. Russian and Soviet involvement in nation building is said to have been particularly strong among the

Kazakh and Kyrgyz nomadic groups. With Russian help written languages were created, historic sagas were transformed into national myths and territory was designated as rightful property. To those like Mustafa Chokaev, who subscribed to the view that Turkestan was "nationally and linguistically homogeneous", the division of Turkestan was an attempt to counter the unification of all Turkic tribes around the nucleus of Soviet Turkestan.[19]

The October Revolution ushered in an intense period of debate regarding autonomy in Turkestan. It was during the First All Russian Muslim Congress that demands for political autonomy on national–territorial lines were made. It was also here that Zeki Velidi Togan, a Bashkir, exploded the myth of the 'Muslim Nation' within Russia. He argued that Muslims in Russia were not racially or linguistically homogeneous. Though essentially a romantic who occasionally dreamt of a united Turkestan, he was enough of a realist to appreciate that strictly as a political force pan-Turkism was unfeasible. He was clear that "if we want national autonomy and not merely a national fiction we must organize our self-government on historic and ethnic bases bearing in mind the national-geographical boundaries of these Turkic peoples".[20] National-territorial dreams in the years following the October Revolution, however, also meant that occasionally a Bashkiria leader arose to threaten neat divisions, or a Basmachi Movement threatened to throw the existing government into disarray. It also meant the necessity of a division of the region into innumerable parts. As Geoffrey Wheeler pointed out, "the natural process of nation formation, although discouraged by the Russians who now filled the political vacuum, did not entirely cease".[21]

A study of the nature of boundaries will be attempted by first examining how epic and language boundaries cut across today's frontiers; it will also show that such cross-cutting should not be interpreted as absence of the notion of territory or even of an 'early State'. Here, an examination of pre-Soviet ethnographic material becomes important in the light of the absence of alternative documentary evidence of the times. The study will then move on to the decades just prior to the Russian advance in the region, and will briefly examine the case of the Emirate of Bukhara to see how the emir's boundaries were often severely questioned and frequently transgressed, both by other kingdoms and by its own dependencies. Information on Bukhara becomes crucial for an interpretation of the times, not only because of the extent of its territories or political influence but also because of its strategic location *vis-à-vis* the Russian and British Empires, as well as Afghanistan and Iran. Also, Bukhara was then considered to be the hub of the region – a local equivalent of London or Paris;[22] events that took place here had repercussions throughout Turkestan. The overwhelming impression of fragmentation of authority that one gathers from this examination remained a dominant issue during the Imperial Russian and early-Soviet days. It is, possibly, a useful pointer to the nature of the political entities even today.

The Kyrgyz' epic hero Alaman Bet's relatively effortless transition from the camp of his own people, the Kalmyks, into the service of Er Kokcho, the Uighur prince, and then again to Manas, a prince of the Sary Nogai, is interpreted by the ethnographer Nora Chadwick as an example of the absence of "political consciousness".[23] This exaggerated overstatement indicates a certain fluidity in the Central Asian notion of territoriality. This fluidity is possibly best exemplified if we follow an epic as it unfolds over the region. The Uzbek epic *Alpamysh* for instance, is to be found straddling the entire territory inhabited by the Turkic people – from the Altai, across Central Asia to the Volga and the Urals on the one hand, and to Trans-Caucasia and Asia Minor on the other. As an ancient folk tale, it existed in the mountains of the Altai as early as the seventh and eight centuries. Together with the Oghuz tribes, the tale spread towards the lower Syr Darya in the nineth and tenth centuries, where it was incorporated into the Oghuz epic of *Salor-Kazan*. With the advance of the Kipchak tribes to the west, different versions of the tale were carried into the Kazakh Steppe and to the Bashkirs in the southern Urals, where it underwent a degree of democratisation and modernisation. Ultimately, the nomadic Uzbeks carried the tale to southern Uzbekistan, where the ancient poem took its final form and spread among the Uzbeks, Kara-Kalpaks and Kazakhs.[24] Similarly, most of the important heroes mentioned in *Manas,* a Kyrgyz epic, occur in the Kazakh story of Er Kokshu.[25]

If we accept language as being pivotal to the structure of boundaries, then these epics give no indication of any great difficulty in communication among different groups in the ordinary intercourse of life. However, a linguistic barrier is recognised with the Chinese to the east.[26] Similarly, if we consider a linguistic map of the region, it is evident that in more than one case languages overlap. There are areas in which Uzbek mingles with Tajik, Turkman or Kara-Kalpak, Kyrgyz with Uzbek and so on. Bilingualism among Uzbeks and Tajiks is common in areas of overlap, especially in towns in the Syr Darya basin, from Khojent to Bukhara. Juxtaposition and overlap of Uzbek, Turkman and Kara-Kalpak in the Khivan region and of Uzbek and Turkman in the areas along its eastern frontier has produced border dialects that show strong traces of mutual influence. There is a sharp dialectic divide between the Kazakhs and the Uzbeks – a fact that suggests a social and ethnic divergence between the steppe dwellers and the more sedentary population of the south.[27] Conversely, a case wherein two language groups are inextricably intermingled applies to the Uzbeks and the Tajiks. Assigning stable and contiguous boundaries to each has thus proved notoriously difficult, and strong claims on each other's territory continue even today.

This overlapping of frontiers, however, should not be taken to mean that there was no concept of the notion of territoriality among the Kazakh, Kyrgyz or Turkman nomads of Turkestan. Many anthropologists like Jean Paul Roux have cautioned against the facile assumption that terrain means nothing to a nomad:

> There was a time when one imagined a nomad to be a man detached from all ties of territoriality and moving freely across immense zones of steppes and deserts. Nomadism is neither anarchy nor disorder but organized movement over a space which can be vast but is clearly delimited by custom and treaties or tacit accords between competing or related groups. Of course, these spaces of nomadism were fluid and their limits changed according to the vicissitudes of history.[28]

This was particularly true in the Central Asian situation where a succession of Turko-nomadic invasions and mass migrations meant that borders were broadly determined by contingent expansions of power.

The early State that developed among the nomads of Central Asia was the result of adaptation to a specific ecological situation wherein the nomads and their sedentary neighbours occupied different zones. There is evidence of constant conflict in those early times, both economic and territorial, between Iran (the sedentary world) and Turan (the nomadic world).[29] Lawrence Krader points to the development of the State among the nomadic societies of Central and middle Asia during the first millennium prior to the modern era as being on the margins of the history and territory of the agricultural peoples of China, India and Persia. These States, according to him, were typically "lineage states", which created elaborate, fictitious genealogies tracing the descent of kings back to several centuries. An example of such a fictitious genealogy is the *Secret History of the Mongols*, a document compiled in the thirteenth century, which traces the genealogy of Emperor Chenghiz Khan over fourteen generations. This genealogy, as Krader correctly points out, should not be taken in its literal sense but indicates the transition made by the Mongols from "primitive forest people" to the "pastoral society of the steppes with political economy and the state". At the same time, it is a record of the "social organization of kin, village communities, clan and clan confederation which was maintained by them from pre-historical periods through the Empire of Chenghiz Khan."[30]

Within these loose State formations, which were continually expanding and contracting depending on the political fortunes of the ruling elite of the time, the peoples of Central Asia represented a variety of overlapping identities. The most basic of these was related to place or lineage – to region or clan for the oasis dweller and to tribe and tribal confederation for the inhabitants of the steppes. Elements of collective identity were provided by a concern for nomadic myths of descent. An interesting example is that of the Turkmen, who, despite intensive migration, maintained their "clan identity". Upon meeting a stranger, the knowledge of the position of one's group in the genealogical order was essential. The Kazakhs, on the other hand, who were ignorant of their genealogies, suffered a drastic loss of status.[31] However, a unifying source of identity in the region was Islam.

A certain amount of order was brought into this loose state of affairs by the advent of the Mongols. Even Arminius Vambery, who lamented that the Mongol hordes "put an end to the intellectual life in Central Asia", acknowledges this.[32] Subsequently, Timur and his heirs succeeded in creating a State in which the indigenous Turkic culture, customs and language and the Chengizid political legacy were combined and retained, along with an Islamic identity and institutions and a Sufi folk culture. Kemal Karpat points out that the State created by Timur and his successors, the Ulus Chagatai, formed the nucleus of a proto-nation with a strongly developed sense of an ethno-linguistic identity that coexisted with their Islamic identity.[33] However, the brittleness of this political construct is evident from its short duration.

A brief sketch of the nature of Bukhara's frontiers, just prior to the Russian takeover, will provide an interesting illustration of the constantly shifting nature of boundaries that was so typical of Central Asia.

Bukhara and its Disputed Frontiers

By the end of the eighteenth century, three Uzbeg dynasties had established khanates in the lands between the Syr Darya and the Amu Darya – the Manghits in Bukhara, the Qungrats in Khiva and the Mins in Kokand. In comparison with the last two hundred years, they ensured a degree of internal cohesion and centralisation, but did not produce stable boundaries either with each other or with Persia, Afghanistan and Kashgar in the south and east, or *vis-à-vis* the Russian advance from the west. However, not only did the three khanates have no stable boundaries, the surrounding country did not have them either: Persia disputed Khiva and Herat with Afghanistan; the latter in addition disputed Balk, Hissar, Kulyab, Badakshan and the Pamir *vilayet*s (provinces) with both Bukhara and Chinese Kashgar. The external areas of conflict were the settled lands of Merv and Chardzhou between Khiva and Bukhara; Khojent, Ura Tyube and Karategin between Bukhara and Kokand; and the lower Syr Darya between Kokand and Khiva. The Kazakhs along the northern border of Khiva and the Tekke Turcoman in Trans-Caspia were the main nomadic and semi-settled peoples who did not regard themselves as subject to anyone.[34]

While these were the ground realities, most of the literature of this period provides descriptions of another kind of variable frontier for the region. Though romantically conceptualised by Halford John Mackinder and his German rival Karl Haushofer as the 'Heartland', the region during this period was seen as a pawn between the expanding Russian and British Empires.[35] As such, most descriptions were suffused with a Great Game imagery, and authors such as Demetrius Charles Boulger defined frontiers from an onlooker's perspective. This nineteenth-century imperial historian wrote that Central Asia was

> that portion of Asia which intervenes between the Russian and English frontiers – wherever they are now or wherever they in the future may be. It is consequently a variable tract of country in accordance as those frontiers advance or recede.[36]

However, alternative descriptions are available from the accounts of people who were more favourably situated to do so. These were men who, during the nineteenth century, travelled to the region under various pretexts and left detailed accounts of their adventures. The following pages will attempt to look at Bukhara in the decades just prior to the Russian advance through the eyes of two such travellers.[37] Though obviously coloured by European perceptions and interlaced .with personal prejudices, a clear image of the times emerges from their accounts.[38] This points to the fact that though nominally divided into three khanates, this was a region of segmentary States with disputed frontiers; it was this segmentation which subsequently allowed for a successful Russian advance.[39]

According to Vambery,

Efrasiab, the great Turanian warrior and one of the heroes of ancient Iran, is regarded as the founder of Bokhara. Extravagant fables form the basis of its earliest history. . . .The first thread of real history, properly so-called, only begins at the epoch of the occupation by the Arabs. Upto the time of Djenghis Khan (1225) Bokhara and Samarcand. . .were regarded as belonging to Persia. . . .On the invasion of the Mongols the Persian element was entirely supplanted . . . and the Ozbegs everywhere seized the reins of government . . . . The special history, properly so-called, of Bokhara begins with the House of the Sheibane . . . . However, Central Asia declined after the fall of the Timourides from the height of civilization and true enthusiasm for all that is refined and beautiful into the slough of ignorance and barbarism from which it has never as yet recovered itself. With its civilization, its political importance rapidly decayed; . . and that which was formerly the splendid empire of Samarcand has sunk in modern times to the miserable Emirate of Bokhara.[40]

It was to this "miserable Emirate of Bokhara" that the traveller Alexander Burnes arrived on 27 June 1831, during the reign of the ill-famed Emir Nasrullah. (Vambery arrived later, in 1863, during the reign of Nasrullah's son Mozaffar-ed-Din.) Burnes claimed that it was his desire to visit the conquests of Alexander the Great that led him west beyond Lahore and the British Empire, and only hints at the "information being useful to the British government". Vambery, on the other hand, stated that it was his interest in linguistic sciences and his desire to find out relations between the Hungarian and Turco-Tartaric dialects that led him to Central Asia. There is evidence in both the accounts that point to interests other than the ones that were explicitly stated.[41] Both Burnes and Vambery travelled under assumed names and identities.[42]

The uncertain nature of the extent of the emirate is clearly brought out during the course of both their descriptions of Bukhara. According to Vambery, the frontiers of the emirate were

on the east the Khanate of Kokand, and the mountains of Badakshan; on the south, the Oxus with the districts on the further side of Kerke and Chardjay; on the west and the north the great desert.[43]

To Burnes, it seemed as if

on the north it is bounded by the Sea of Aral, the Sir or the Jaxartes of the ancients and the country of Kokand or Ferghana. On the east it extends to the mountains which branch from the highlands of the Pamir. On the south it has the Oxus, which however, it crosses on the south eastern limit and holds a supremacy over Balkh and the cantons of Andkhou and Maimuna. On the west, it is separated from Orgunje or Khiva by the deserts of Kharasm.[44]

Both agreed that they had assigned the widest possible limits to the emirate and that the exact lines of demarcation could not be defined "for there are provinces within this boundary which owe but doubtful allegiance". Burnes also named cantons which, though tributary to Bukhara, rendered only a nominal allegiance by sending a few horses yearly to the king.[45] Similarly, the Russian traveller N. Y. Khanikov observed that "[t]he Emirate of Bukhara has no fixed boundary sanctioned by time or circumscribed by international treaties".[46]

During the course of the thirty-odd years that had elapsed between the journeys of Burnes and Vambery, there had evidently been some chages in the political divisions of the emirate – and not surprisingly, a number of conflicts also seemed to have occurred during those years.[47] Burnes, for instance, does not include Shahr-i-Sabz, whose stubborn chiefs refused to acknowledge Bukharan overlordship, though he does note that "the Emir has chastised the chief of Shahr-i-Sabz and seized six of his villages, recently".[48] Vambery leaves out the more important province of Balkh.

Shahr-i-Sabz, famous as the birthplace of Timour, was particularly troublesome. Vambery rather unkindly records the death of Emir Nasrullah "in a fit of rage" on discovering that he had been unable to incorporate the province into the emirate even after taking it thirty times; and that one of the first acts of the new Emir, Mozaffar-ed-Din, was to lay siege to it again.[49] The other two khanates were similarly plagued by dissensions. Khiva was enfeebled by the continuous wars that it had to wage to maintain its own tributaries "who were ever ready to renew the contest – the Yomuts, Tchaudors and Kasaks", and Kokand was faced with continuous dissension from the "Kipchaks, Kirghis and Kasaks".[50]

While the principalities faced continual internal upheavals, relations among themselves were far from stable. The khanate of Khiva was situated on the delta of the Amu Darya, to the west of Bukhara. The Khans of Khiva, whom Burnes described as "organized banditti", waged continuous wars with Bukhara, which meant that caravan routes through Khiva were rarely safe.[51] Similarly, Vambery noted that the "Emir was away on a campaign to Kokand" when he arrived at Bukhara.[52] Short-lived alliances between the Khanates of Kokand and Khiva against Bukhara were also not uncommon. Khiva was considered a dependency of Bukhara till the time of Ruheem Khan – though when Burnes arrived in Bukhara it had increased its powers by inflicting injuries on neighbouring countries. It had also recently established a supremacy over the Turkmen hordes south of the Amu Darya.

However, control over the Turkmen could at best be ephemeral. Both Vambery and Burnes noted the extreme individuality of the people and the Turkmen saying, "Biz bibash khalk bolamiz" (we are a people without a head) to be true. They were ruled, according to Vambery, by "a mighty sovereign..."Deb" – custom or usage", though Burnes wrote that they "acknowledged the patriarchal government of their *aksaqals* [village elders]".[53] The essential difference between the oasis population and the nomads in terms of political allegiance becomes evident from Mary Holdsworth's comments to the effect that

> The oasis population had their intensive agriculture, town life, trade, organized crafts and beginnings of home industry; the adjacent nomad and semi-nomad peoples, made up of small units, each with strong inner political cohesion, still had no permanent overriding political loyalty or constant affiliation. Their adherence had to be cajoled, bargained for or secured by force. It continued to be an uncertain element, since they acknowledged no external power for any definitive period of time.[54]

The imperfect assimilation of the Turkmen periphery into Khiva meant a long and continuous struggle, which was carried on by the legendary Turkman Junayid Khan, that ended only with the final creation of the Turkman Soviet Socialist Republic in 1924.[55]

An interesting aspect of this picture of disputed frontiers is clearly brought out by Holdworth when she states that

> The changes in internal boundaries, the breaking off or the adhesion of a *vilayet* from one Khanate to another – though at first sight kaleidoscopic – have coherent significance. It is always the same *vilayets* that change hands and allegiances, the ones that tip the local balances of power and rock precariously established stability. Certain mountain *vilayets* always remained unabsorbable whether by Bukhara, Kokand, Afghanistan or Russia – Tsarist or Soviet. The last strongholds of Enver Pasha, the districts which the partisan Basmachis held until nearly 1930 were the same eastern *vilayets* whose *begs* in the nineteenth century merely presented gifts to the Emir of Bukhara and who never remained under Kokand or Bukhara for more than a dozen years at a time.[56]

This historical examination of the nature of Central Asian boundaries gives a clear indication of the kind of problems involved in the event of a delimitation exercise in the region, some of which have remained unsolved to this day.

The Unsolved Questions

The complexities involved in the process of delimitation are not only apparent today; *Mushtum*, a satirical Turkestani magazine had reported in 1924, the year the delimitation was completed, that "before the partition into nationality republics, we got so completely befuddled that we couldn't figure out which of the nationalities we ourselves might belong to . . . ".[57] This was written at a time when plans for the delimitation of the region along ethno-linguistic lines were being rapidly enacted, and reflected the conflicting emotions of the people of the region. Numerous such reactions to the delimitation plans are being re-examined today in the light of the second phase of transition in the region, that is now comprised of the five Central Asian republics of the Commonwealth of Independent States (CIS).

The delimitation was conducted after the revolution on the basis of the censuses of 1917 and 1920. However, these were not consulted in isolation. There are clear indications that other, pre-existing, records were also consulted, so that it can be safely assumed that certain preconceived notions about the peoples of the region were incorporated within the new structures, as also the fact that often criteria other than demography had a role in the delimitation.[58]

The following tables give an indication of the national composition of the region prior to delimitation, and provide an insight into the nature of population distribution:

Table 1

National Composition of the Population of the Turkestan Republic, 1917–1923

National Groups	Percentage of Total Population
Uzbeks	41.4
Kazakhs	19.4
Kyrgyz	10.7
Tajiks	7.7
Turkmen	4.7

Source: Table compiled from *Tsentralnoe Statisticheskoe Upravlenie Turkrespubliki, Statistichiski Ezhegodnik 1917–1923*, vol. 1, Tashkent, 1924, cited in R. Vaidyanath, *The Formation of the Soviet Central Asian Republics: A Study in Soviet Nationality Policy 1917–1936* (New Delhi: Peoples Publishing House, 1967), 270.

Table 2

National Composition of the Population of Bukhara, 1926

National Groups	Percentage of Total Population
Uzbeks	50.7
Kazakhs	1.6
Kyrgyz	0.5
Tajiks	31.6
Turkmen	10.3
Kara-Kalpaks	0.1

Source: Table compiled from *Materialy po Raionirovaniye Srednei Azii, Treritorii i Naseleniya Bukhari i Khiva,* Tashkent, 1926, cited in Vaidyanath, *Soviet Central Asian Republics,* 272.

Table 3

National Composition of the Population of Khiva, 1926

National Groups	Percentage of Total Population
Uzbeks	79.0
Kazakhs	4.3
Turkmen	14.6
Kara-Kalpaks	0.9

Source: Table compiled from *Materialy po Raionirovaniye Srednei Azii, Treritorii i Naseleniya Bukhari i Khiva,* Tashkent, 1926, cited in Vaidyanath, *Soviet Central Asian Republics,* 274.

Complexities in categorisation arose from the fact that the various peoples in this region lacked group exclusivity and cohesion; this fluidity did not appear merely among the urban population but also among those who lived outside the towns. There were reports from different parts of the region during both census counts that people were innocently misidentifying themselves, and that in some cases it was very difficult to assign clear ethnic distinctions.[59] There were also cases of deliberate misidentification for political reasons, particularly among the Tajiks and Uzbeks. While delimitation on the basis of language was considered a reasonable step, it was not completely successful in the Central Asian region. The Uzbeks and Tajiks, for instance, were multilingual by norm and their only attachments were regional. Moreover, the designations that were to be subsequently given to the people had little historical basis. Most writings on the reconstruction of an Uzbek history, for instance, point out that the press and the world of art were not talking about the

Uzbek identity on a large enough scale to warrant the construction of a separate Uzbek State. While in late 1922 a small core of intellectuals had begun the process of laying the cultural base on which an ethnic identity could be subsequently established, there was no specific political framework around it.[60] What they were projecting was not so much a political vision as a cultural one in line with the numerous other demands that were being made at that time. Ironically, the demands for self-determination of such national groups as the Tajiks were initially ignored, and Tajikistan was formed as an autonomous region within Uzbekistan. That delimitation did not immediately clarify matters became evident when within five years the Tajik ASSR had to be separated and formed into an SSR. The Uzbeks and Tajiks were both concentrated in the Ferghana and Samarkand Oblasts' of the Turkestan Republic. Within this, the Tajiks formed a majority in the city of Samarkand, Pendzhikent, Ura-Tube and Khojent. However, Samarkand city and Samarkand Oblast', excluding three *volosts* (sub-divisions of a district) inhabited by the Tajiks, went to Uzbekistan. The Uzbek SSR was given forty-one volosts of the Djizak, Katta-Kurgan and Khojent *uezds* (districts) of the Syr Darya Oblast'.[61] However, often within oblasts there were some uezds that had a different population composition.

There were also other problems: the 1920 census, for instance, showed that the Samarkand Oblast' which was included within the Uzbek SSR had an Uzbek population of 59.5% and a Tajik population of 29.6%. But in the Khojent Uezd of the Samarkand Oblast' the same census showed a different picture with a larger number of Tajiks (See Table 5).[62] This had been historically true, for the *Ezhegodnik* (statistical yearbook) *Materialy Dlia Statistichiski Turkestanskogo Krai 1872–1879* for the year 1872 shows a similar larger population of Tajiks (See Table 4).[63] On the other hand, the Djizak Uezd of the Samarkand Oblast' always had a larger proportion of Uzbeks. The fact that there were pockets of different groups of people within the same oblast' further complicated the situation, as did the fact that the necessity of contiguity meant that very often a city with one type of population distribution, surrounded by a different ethnic group, had to be carved out and placed within the geographical boundaries of one State in order to maintain that contiguity.

A later writing which critiques the basis of the delimitation shows the large numbers of unrecorded populations in the uezds, and further complicates the picture (See Table 6).[64] An examination of the Uzbek and Tajik populations in the two uezds of Khojent and Djizak makes for interesting reading.

Table 4

Population of Samarkand Oblast', 1872–1879

Population	Khojent	Djizak
Uzbek	21,400	32,885
Tajik	60,070	2,996

Source: Table compiled from *Materialy Dlia Statistichiski Turkestanskogo Krai 1872–1879* (INION Collection; New Delhi: IGNCA), microfiche nos. 11958–11962, p. 127.

Table 5

Population of Samarkand Oblast', 1920

Population	Khojent	Djizak
Uzbek	61,482	89,520
Tajik	113,023	832

Source: Table compiled from the 1920 census, cited in Vaidyanath, *Soviet Central Asian Republics,* 268.

Table 6

Population of Samarkand Oblast', 1926

Population	Khojent	Djizak
Uzbek	15,983	63,683
Tajik	9,841	167

Source: Table compiled from I. I. Zarubin, *Naseleniya Samarkandskoi Oblast'* (INION Collection; New Delhi: IGNCA), microfiche no. 11965, p. 15.

Claims for joining certain Tajik-populated areas to Tajikistan was made by the Tajik Regional Committee of the Communist Party of Bolsheviks of Uzbekistan to the Political Bureau of the Central Committee of the All Russian Communist Party of Bolsheviks. This included certain districts of Samarkand, along with the city of Samarkand and also the Emirate of Bukhara, based on the following population distribution:

Table 7

Distribution of Tajik and Uzbek Populations in Certain Districts of Uzbekistan, 1924.

Name of the Region	The Tajik People	The Uzbek People
I. Khojent Tajik Region		
a) districts of former Kokand District	83,530	17,005
b) from the former Namangan District	64,351	20,153
Total	202,350	64,251

continues

continued

Name of the Region	The Tajik People	The Uzbek People
II. Three Districts of Surkhan Darya Region	78,303	39,093
III. Districts of Samarkand together with the city of Samarkand	70,773	13,192
IV. The Bukharan Emirate together with the city of Bukhara	163,405	45,775
Grand Total	514,368	162,030

Source: Table compiled from Rakhim Masov, *The History of the Axe Type Division*, trans. Anonymous (Dushanbe: Irfon, 1991).

It is interesting to note that the census of 1920 often provided a different ethnic picture from the one given above. According to the 1920 census, the Emirate of Bukhara, for instance, had a different distribution of Tajiks and Uzbeks (see Table 2). Given the complexities of the time, it is undeniable that an accurate estimation of population distribution was difficult to determine. It is possible that, more often than not, estimates were determined by political exigencies.

With the advantage of hindsight, we can note that the relative ease with which the delimitation was accomplished could not hide the long-term difficulties that each of the States of Central Asia was to encounter in the future. Grouping people with local loyalties, such as the Uzbeks for instance, meant circumscribing diverse peoples within boundaries of which they had little understanding. This could not eradicate local division or religious loyalties that reached across boundaries. Labelling Uzbeks as the inhabitants of Ferghana, Zerafshan, parts of Bukhara and Khiva, and of the Syr Daryan and Kashka Darya regions was not a magic formula that could immediately integrate them as Uzbeks.

In *Naseleniya Samarkandskoi Oblast'* written in 1926, I. I. Zarubin, an ethnographer who examined the demographic distribution in the Central Asian region immediately after the delimitation of 1924, points to two major critiques of the delimitation plan.[65] His book on the population of Samarkand was written in the year when the first systematic census of the region was under way. It is interesting that his observations are as significant to the region today as they were then. He stressed the fact that the basis on which delimitation was carried out, i.e., the censuses of 1917 and 1924, were partial, and did not take the entire population of the region into consideration. The necessity of consulting other sources, and his constant reference to the agricultural and settlement data of the Czarist period, hinted at the fact that they may well have assumed an importance in the delimitation plan of the Soviets. He pointed out the interesting fact that the 1917 census was based on agricultural statistics; the rural statistics was voluminous as a result. However, the population of the cities and their surroundings, and settlements along railway lines were not taken into account. This could have been a deliberate attempt at ignoring the large numbers of Tajiks in the region, as they were principally urban settlers.

Historians, geographers and ethnographers had come to this region in the wake of the imperial Russian annexation. Learned societies in Moscow and St. Petersburg established branches in Turkestan; among them were the Moscow Society of Amateurs of Nat...:al Sciences, Anthropology and Enthnography (in 1870), the Society of Oriental Studies (in 1890) and the Imperial Russian Geographical Society (in 1897). The work of these scholars not only laid the foundation for future scientific research in the region, but was also of great help in the delimitation exercise later on. The Turkestan Statistical Commission, founded in 1868, was another valuable source of data. The first census of Central Asia was taken as part of the All Russian Census of 1897, in which dialect provided the basis of ethnic classification. Ethno-linguistic data from this census, along with the partial censuses of 1917 and 1920, formed the basis of delimitation. The confusion with identity among the people was reflected in the censuses, which used numerous overlapping classifications – for instance, Kyrgyz, Kara-Kyrgyz, Kazakh and Kyrgyz-Kazakh. This, in itself, is illuminating, as the *Entsiklopedicheski Slovar* of the Czarist period used similar multiple designations in its definition of the people of Turkestan.[66] The delimitation was thus bound to reflect the ideas and biases of the Czarist period, thus demystifying the myth of a total transition.

Zarubin further pointed to the discrepancy in numbers of the population in the 1920 census and the last listing of the people that was conducted in 1904–1905. For example, in the Samarkand Oblast', the 1920 census registered 221 people for Tubali and Lyanger, whereas the 1904–1905 census had listed 674 people. This difference, however, can be explained by factors like war, famine or revolution and need not necessarily be a statistical error. But he also pointed out numerous other examples where it was difficult to determine whether the census had been done in all the areas, and to the discrepancies of the census data with other sources. Important among these were the surveys for the resettlement plans of 1911–1913, as well as data from unlisted societies which were based on numerous sources, such as data on uezds and city administrations. It seemed to him that in order to make a correct assessment of the area, earlier investigations would have proved to be useful; in Djizak, for instance, the places not cited in the two censuses were investigated during 1911–1912, and were found to be populated by Kyrgyz and Kara-Kalpaks.[67]

His investigation also revealed that there was no evidence regarding the 'tribal' constitution of the population for the unlisted parts of the Samarkand Oblast'; it could only be hypothetically considered to be Uzbek. Indeed the census of 1920 had indicated that all the three unlisted settlements were "possessing" the Uzbek language.[68] This, as is evident from any acquaintance with the Central Asian region, does not necessarily indicate the nationality of the group because the people of the region were often bilingual. A study based on the *kvartals* (blocks) of Bukhara clearly showed that there was a divergence between the language spoken and the idea that people had of their own identity.[69] In fact, a divergence between ethnic and linguistic identity is being increasingly recognised in the region today.

Similarly, there were also cases of omission where, for instance, the 1917 and 1920 censuses failed to record certain groups of people. Zarubin referred to the study of the ethnographer M. C. Andrev, who recorded the presence of Kara-Kalpaks in 1916 near the Nuratinski hills, though the population entered by the subsequent censuses was reported as Kyrgyz. This was because the census failed to record 20,513 people, of whom 1,997 people were Kara-Kalpaks. Similarly, according to P. S. Skwarksy, another ethnographer who worked in that area, the population was largely Kyrgyz in certain parts of Karatashk, though the 1920 census records only 12 Kyrgyz. In Yamskoi Volost there were strong indications of a Tajik population, although sources recorded the population as Uzbek. Skwarksy is quoted as having pointed out that the people there were Tajik, though they did not speak the Tajik language.[70] In Nakrutsk, similarly, the people were categorised as Uzbeks, though the area was also populated by Turkmen, Kyrgyz and Tajiks. Or, as in Bishkend in 1915, a majority of the population was 'Uzbek-Sart', and a small proportion of Tajiks considered themselves to be Uzbeks. In Andijan the Tajiks, rather than the Uzbeks, were in a majority.[71]

Another problem of delimitation was the fact that during the preceding years, identity had been rather loosely determined. Most scholars, beginning with V. V. Barthold, noted that identity was based either on religion or location, and was not 'national'.[72] The most telling example of this was the confusion that resulted from having to point to a single group as the most important in terms of self-definition. This became evident time and again as the centuries-old assimilative process meant that most people spoke the predominant language of the region, yet identified themselves differently. The ethnographer A. D. Grevinkin, for instance, wrote that the Turkmen in the Samarkand Oblast' came from different parts of the region. However, they said that their mother tongue was Uzbek, and on the question of their nationality, pointed out that they were Turkmen-Uzbek.[73] There were numerous such examples of the prevailing sense of multiple identity that remained the predominant characteristic of the region.

Yet complexities notwithstanding, and typical of the revolutionary times, the policy of transition went ahead. It represented, among other things, a break from Czarist designations. The group name 'Sart', for instance, was banned from use, since it was not considered to be an ethnic designation, and 'Uzbek' was substituted for it, on the grounds that there was no separate nation called the Sart, as different from the Uzbeks, and no separate Sart language that was different from the Uzbek language. The word Sart was used to define a group of people who spoke the Turkic language but were seen as the last remnants of the Tajik population. Writing in 1909, I. I. Gier had defined the ethnographic basis of the people of Turkestan and had grouped them as Sarts, Uzbeks, Kyrgyz, Turkmen, Kara-Kalpaks, Tatars, Tajiks, Europeans, Iranians and Indians. Devoting the largest section of his work to the people he called the Sarts, he began by pointing out that their genealogical origin was largely unknown, though they were considered to be of mixed Iranian and Turkish descent.[74] The *Ezhegodnik* (statistical yearbook) of 1872 had, however, pointed out that though they were considered to be of mixed origin, yet they formed a separate *narodno'st* (nationality) and differed noticeably in type and character from the others.[75] While the delimitation plan left no scope for a separate home-land for the Sarts, Zarubin, writing in 1926, continued to identify them in areas of Samarkand as a separate people inhabiting important urban centres.[76] Questions such as who were the people identified as Sarts and why were they not identified as a separate people during the delimitation remain unanswered.

One territorial problem that has defied a solution in Central Asia today is that of claims made by the Tajiks on Uzbek lands. It is interesting to note that the *Entsiklopedicheski Slovar*, a major ethnographical work of Czarist times, referred in its note on Turkestan that the Tajiks, who were the remnants of a Persian population, were about 9.5% of the population living in the hills of Ferghana and the Samarkand Oblast'. It also identified other, smaller groups, and pointed out that they were all assimilated within the Uzbeks.[77] Similarly, Bukhara and Khiva were categorically stated as having been first populated by the Uzbeks and only then by the Sarts, Tajiks, Turkmen and Kyrgyz.

It pointed out that in Bukhara the Uzbeks were known as Sarts.[78] A different picture emerges from the *Ezhegodnik* of 1872, which identified Tajiks as a large group in certain uzeds of the Syr Darya Oblast'. On the section on the population of Turkestan, it identifies Kyrgyz (i.e., Kazakh) to be the largest group, followed by the Sarts, the Tajiks and the Uzbeks.[79] The creation of a separate Tajik and Uzbek nationhood has meant that there is today what Edward Allworth calls a search for "retrospective proof" of nationality in a given territory.[80] Since much of the history of these people was based on the settled population, it left the nomadic elements out.

Not unnaturally, there were apprehensions in the minds of the authors of delimitation about the viability of demarcation along ethno-linguistic lines. The Chairman of the Central Asian Bureau of the Central Committee of the Russian Communist Party had commented that

> It would be extreme self-sufficiency to assume just for a minute that while deciding the national question in Turkestan, we had been free from any mistakes, particularly, that in the process of formation of National Republics, and specifically, in the process of setting territorial boundaries, one could have expected firm decisions not allowing for any further corrections. There was neither sufficient knowledge of statistical economy and national composition of the regions nor sufficient knowledge of certain localities even by indigenous workers. Moreover with the diversity of nationalities, variety of economic relations, etc., of small regional villages, one can say beforehand that it will be impossible to set inviolable boundaries right away. In future, depending on the will and desire of the population, a certain reconsideration and correction of boundaries is possible.[81]

Conclusion

For an accurate appraisal of the historical era in which the region is situated today, a closer examination of the factors that led to the first transition becomes a crucial prologue. This prologue is a clear pointer to the fact that the post–revolution situation represented just one of the many possibilities of the time. It also points to the fact that there was very little that was unambiguous about the frontiers of the three principalities into which the region was nominally divided on the eve of the Russian annexation. Further, reorganisation began with Russian attempts at administering the region, though the Emirate of Bukhara and the Khanate of Khiva maintained their ephemeral existence.

Nor was the creation of the republics in the post–revolution period without its problems, for the months immediately following the dissolution of Czarist rule in Turkestan had ushered in an intense period of short-lived national-territorial dreams. This was also the period when romantics like Zeki Velidi Togan occasionally dreamt of a united Turkestan. The forms that the States assumed from the amorphous mass that was Turkestan was just one of the various historical possibilities of the time.

It is perhaps this situation of fluidity that is being relegated to the background today, in the course of an enthusiastic search for independent existence. To an extent this has meant that "Tsentral'naya Azia" (Central Asia) has become more of a myth than a reality.[82] The reality, however, is that an exercise in the re-creation of separate historical legacies in which the States are involved today has to take note of the fact that, to a very large extent, it would have to be as much of a construct as the States themselves.

Warring Neighbours Coexist and Cooperate: A Review of the India–Pakistan Dialogue

RITA MANCHANDA

I

War and Coexistence

The history of India–Pakistan relations has been seen traditionally as a conflict-driven one. A violent partition in 1947 established two estranged neighbours as unalterably adversarial towards each other. The last fifty-odd years since independence have seen four full-scale inter-State wars, several localised, low-intensity and proxy wars and an endemic exchange of heavy artillery fire across the Line of Control (LoC), where Indian and Pakistani troops are engaged in eyeball to eyeball confrontation. After the 1998 nuclear tests by India and Pakistan, the confrontation between the two antagonistic neighbours threatens to engulf the sub-continent in a nuclear war.

Within a year of India and Pakistan going nuclear, a war-like situation broke out along the LoC in Kargil in the Himalayas. It emphasised not only the limits of an unstable nuclear deterrence but its positive encouragement of the waging of localised wars in an endemic conflict zone. Kargil highlighted the continuing propensity of the ruling elites in the sub-continent to use military force to settle differences. Moreover, by politically de-linking Kargil from Kashmir, the victors of the Kargil propaganda war cast the India–Pakistan confrontation as one of inevitable and irreconcilable hostility.[1] In the new millenium, the India–Pakistan relationship appears as one of the most conflict-prone in the world, and one that could flare up into a nuclear confrontation.

It is therefore surprising to learn that all through the last fifty-odd years of hostility there has existed a multifaceted dialogue that has been quarrelsome as well as cooperative. It significantly demonstrates that there is nothing inevitable or insuperable about the conflict between the two nations and that there is a capacity to resolve differences through dialogue. While the dominant India–Pakistan relational narrative is a history of conflict with interregnums of 'no-war–no-peace', there is also another, more positive, relational narrative of negotiation and cooperation. There has been a history of initiatives towards negotiations, both bilateral and via third parties, that solved political and technical differences between the two. Both governments have been able to reach enduring agreements in a wide field of areas, from disputed boundaries to managing, at an earlier stage, an Indo-Pakistan non-weaponised nuclear deterrence, and are even now working out the ground rules for a manageable weaponsied deterrence.

Even in the midst of conflict the two countries have demonstrated the possibility of pushing through cooperative agreements like the negotiated settlement of the Rann of Kutch boundary dispute, the establishment of a network of diplomatic, postal and civil aviation links and joint mechanisms for promoting trade. A number of Confidence Building Measures (CBMs) have also been agreed upon though they have not succeeded in preventing a Kargil-like situation. But then, CBMs are not peace agreements.

Indeed, the Kargil conflict epitomises the peculiarities of the India–Pakistan 'no-war–no-peace' relationship. For realists on both sides, the Kargil conflict confirmed that the long-standing policy of the political elite in India and Pakistan remains committed to a reliance on military, as opposed to diplomatic, means to resolve differences and further mutually antagonistic national interests.[2] However, the intertwined military and political dynamics of the Kargil conflict show a 'high risk but coexistence' relational model at work. Despite the hostility in terms of the use of air power, war-mongering jingoism and the emotional effects of a heavy toll in casualties, the conflict was determinedly kept localised by both sides. There was no severance of diplomatic, economic or travel links. Although sporting links were temporarily disrupted (a cricket series was called off) this was largely the result of an emotional outburst in a time of superpatriotism drummed up by the media. In the end, the military disengagement in Kargil was a diplomatically negotiated compromise, brokered by the USA. Military die-hards on both sides lamented the loss of a chance of victory in battle, but more sober political analysts regretted the unnecessary double-speak in a continuing diplomatic dialogue that made recourse to a third power necessary.[3] The argument, at least on the Indian side, has been that there is no need for a third party to mediate as India and Pakistan can directly talk to each other.

Except in the periods immediately prior to, and just after, the full-scale Indo-Pakistan wars, there has been no irreconcilable breakdown of communication that makes third-party mediation an imperative to restore dialogue. As we shall see, the role of third-party mediation in managing and containing India–Pakistan differences has been a hotly contested issue. India swears by bilateralism and Pakistan is equally determined to bring in a third party. But as the Kargil experience shows, there is no certainty, in the post–cold war period, that internationalisation of an issue per se will favour Pakistan.

The India–Pakistan War

The relational dynamics of coexistence tend to get obscured in the heightened drama of a conflict. In January 1987, when the military establishments of India and Pakistan were locked in a bout of belligerent brinkmanship set off by Indian military exercises code-named Operation Brasstacks, senior Indian and Pakistani officials in Pakistan were successfully negotiating the normalisation of relations between the two countries. At one level it brutally brought home the fact that the real power centres lie elsewhere, but it also demonstrated the taut balance of confrontation and coexistence at work. Indeed, India's then foreign secretary, R. Venkateswaran, who had been negotiating for normalisation in Islamabad, was summarily sacked on his return. Ironically, it was during the foreign secretary's visit to Pakistan that the decks were cleared for an agreement that stated that there would be no attacks on each other's nuclear installations. The agreement survived the Brasstacks crisis and was initialled in 1988, the first breakthrough in bilaterally managing a nuclear South Asia.

The Brasstacks crisis showed up the weakness of the bilaterally agreed institutional mechanisms to inspire confidence and defuse tension when there are high levels of mistrust.[4] However, the period during the tenure of Pakistan's President Zia-ul-Haq was to see a surprising spurt in official initiatives to normalise relations, including the revival of a no-war pact and a mutual force-reduction exercise, despite the fact that both countries were going in for a maximal defence posture at the time. The talks on the non-use of force were countered by the reality of the ongoing low-intensity war in the Siachin Glacier in the Himalayas and cross-border support for dissidents in Punjab and Sind.

The reassertion of the Kashmir dispute as central to the antagonism between India and Pakisan in the 1990s choked off all efforts at normalisation on the economic front or the settlement of less controversial boundary disputes like Sir Creek in the Rann of Kutch or the Tulbul Navigation Project on the Jhelum River. In the midst of the jingoism inspired by the insurgency in Kashmir, it is easy to forget that for two decades after the Simla Agreement, Kashmir was put on a backburner, and substantial progress was made in restoring disrupted links in other fields. That this progress proved transient reinforces the fundamental importance of dealing more imaginatively with the Kashmir dispute, if India–Pakistan relations are to definitively move out of the adversarial groove.

After the India–Pakistan nuclear tests in May 1998, there had been growing international pressure on the power elites in the two countries to better manage their adversarial relations. Nit-picking official talks on normalisation of relations were consequently resumed, impelled equally by the imperative of the socio-economic costs of non-cooperation and hostility. But it was the February 1998 Lahore Declaration that was trumpeted as a symbolic turning point in the relationship. Both prime ministers had seemingly put their political capital on the line and committed themselves to peace and cooperation, the one representing a Hindu nationalist party, the other the Punjabi power elite. However, the Lahore Declaration came unstuck in less than three months in the face of loud accusations of betrayal of the spirit of peace at Kargil. The chorus of accusations was echoed by the peoples of both India and Pakistan, for the "politics of peace" symbolised in the Lahore Declaration had been legitimised by emerging cross-border avowals of solidarity for the normalisation of relations between India and Pakistan. Despite this setback, it is the democratisation of the peace process that will ensure that the war–peace continuum structurally inherent in the India–Pakistan relational dynamic does not slide into war.[5]

It is evident that civil society processes in the sub-continent, and especially in Pakistan, are nascent. But it is this new element – the emergence of civil society solidarities committed to peace – which holds the promise of substantially transforming the adversarial India–Pakistan relationship for the better. Initiatives like the Pakistan–India Peoples Forum for Peace and Democracy (PIPFPD), for example, go beyond the advocacy of mere normalisation of relations; they also hope for the realisation of peace within a framework of human rights and democracy. They campaign for a cross-border vision of human security that is seen as inversely proportional to the obsessive pursuit of national security as defined by the elites in Pakistan and India.

It is people to people contacts that are proving most effective in chipping away at the adversarial stereotypes in which the two peoples have been cast. Keeping the citizens of India and Pakistan apart by raising walls of prejudice and hate has been an integral part of the nation-state building project of both Pakistan and India. Beyond the statist territorial orientation of the civil–military bureaucracies, there have always been millions of quiet mutinies at the border patrolled by the armed Indian Border Security Forces (BSF) and the Pakistani Rangers – the smuggling of goods in and out of both countries, or the passage of divided families for a wedding or a funeral.[6]

Although the Kargil conflict saw a resurgence, in India in particular, of the demonisation of the 'other' as enemy, it also occasioned assertions by indomitable voices that urged that Pakistan ought not to be reduced to a land of mullahs (Muslim clerics), *mujahideen* (Islamic guerilla fighters) and terrorists in the public perception; and that the majority in both countries did not support hostility but, on the contrary, wanted peace. At a fundamental level, questioning India and Pakistan's adversarial relationship challenges the orthodoxy on which the nation-state edifice is built. It makes the transformative potential of a peoples' dialogue all the more important.

My essay aims at restoring to the conflict-driven history of India–Pakistan relations these dimensions of non-military initiatives to negotiate differences and build understanding and cooperation. It explores the peculiarly Indo-Pakistani 'conflict-with-coexistence' relational structure, and demonstrates that there is nothing inevitable about a conflict-ridden India–Pakistan relationship, for the expanding peoples constituency for peace in India and Pakistan has the potential to transform a seemingly irreconcilable and hostile association by democratising the peace process.

Early Years: The Partition Process

Chronicling the early years of India's relations with Pakistan, Professor Sisir Gupta, the doyen of the Indian international relations establishment, emphasised the spreading network of cooperation between the two newly independent and still interdependent nations. Writing in the early 1950s, Gupta said, "[w]ater continues to flow into Pakistan's canals from Indian headworks, ad hoc agreements have been regularly signed, joint flood control measures discussed, ways of averting border incidents found, border enclaves exchanged and joint tours undertaken by the ministers of the two countries".[7] Joint arrangements were worked out for the exchange of movable refugee property and the recovery of abducted persons, rail traffic links were established, liberal passport and visa systems instituted, trade agreements negotiated and protection of religious shrines pledged.

Transfer of Assets

The hope that, once Pakistan was formed, the two neighbouring States would evolve a healthy and cooperative relationship soon foundered on the dispute over the transfer of liabilities and the distribution of assets of undivided India. Facing empty coffers and the gigantic task of constructing a State, Pakistan was deeply aggrieved over the difficulties in getting its share of the assets. Eventually, in December 1947 an agreement was reached which provided for Pakistan to receive Rs. 750 million as its share. The process of settlement was a bitter one, especially over the sharing of military stores.[8] The tightening sinews of war in Kashmir threatened to choke off the transfer of assets. It took the moral pressure of a fast by Mahatma Gandhi to persuade the Congress government to release the funds and stores. Subtle pressure by the former colonial power, Britain, also contributed to breaking the deadlock. The experience reinforced Pakistan's constant fear that India was working towards its collapse.

Trade

The financial crisis over Pakistan's refusal to devalue its currency sent bilateral trade into a tailspin. In December 1949, the Sterling was devalued; India followed suit and devalued the Rupee, but Pakistan held out. India then refused to accept the value of the Pakistani Rupee, and trade between the two countries virtually broke down. Pakistani growers of raw cotton and jute, which was destined for mills in India, were on the brink of ruination. Already, three months earlier, bilateral trade had come under pressure when Pakistan, desperate for more central revenues decided to unilaterally levy an export duty on jute and import duties on coal. This was despite the understanding that no customs duties would be imposed on inter-State trade. India suspended supplies of coal to Pakistan in retaliation.

India–Pakistan trade never recovered from this setback, although trade agreements were negotiated periodically. In 1957, just before the Kashmir issue was debated in the United Nations Security Council, the two governments reached a comprehensive trade agreement. It provided for a Most Favoured Nation (MFN) catagorisation of each other's goods. But bilateral trade remained marginal to their economies. The war in 1965 brought even this limited trade to a grinding halt.

Protection of Minorities

Mutual accusations of hostile interference in each other's internal affairs continue to be traded by both sides to this day. The fanning of cross-border reactions to communal violence is inherent in the politics of confrontation between the two States. In Pakistan, it is an article of faith in the nation-state orthodoxy that Pakistan, alone, is the protector of Muslims in the sub-continent.

The outbreak of widespread communal violence in the eastern parts of India and Pakistan in 1950 led to the signing of the Jawaharlal Nehru–Liaquat Ali Khan Pact in an effort to provide protection to minorities.[9] This agreement was the first step in evolving a bilateral framework to manage differences, and established the principle that protection of minorities was the responsibility of their respective governments.

The two governments pledged to curb hostile propaganda building upon the earlier post-partition accord in 1948, which urged both governments to discourage propaganda for the amalgamation of Pakistan in India, and the demand for the inclusion of Indian territories like Cooch Behar and Tripura into Pakistan. The 1950 agreement extended this to cover terrorist and other attempts to alter the designation of these areas, with an explicit renunciation of support to terrorism.

It proved to be a brittle agreement. Within months, Liaquat Ali and Nehru, in a flurry of letters in 1951, were trading bitter accusations about officially-sponsored hostile propaganda.[10] The understanding suffered a further setback by the assassination of Liaquat Ali in 1951. Still, at least twice in 1950, the meetings between the prime ministers of India and Pakistan helped to cool down religio-nationalist passions. Reflecting a renewed effort, the August 1953 joint communique stated that the "Prime Ministers attach the greatest import to this friendly approach and to the avoidance of words and actions which promote discord".[11] It helped to bring about a degree of normalcy in the relationship, after a wave of anti-India sentiment in Pakistan following the removal of Sheikh Abdullah from the state government in Kashmir.

No-War Pact

Border incidents continued to trouble relations between the two States. However, it was armed clashes in Kashmir between the regular armies of Pakistan and India which heightened the sense of mutual insecurity of the two States. In the case of Kashmir, India, prompted by Lord Mountbatten, turned to the UN for a settlement of the dispute. Despite this, however, from those early years onwards, there were also attempts at proposals and counter-proposals for a no-war pact to manage the adversarial relationship bilaterally. Its most recent incarnation was the Pakistani Prime Minister Nawaz Sharif's offer to India of a non-aggression pact at the UN General

Assembly in 1997. Its earliest antecedent was Prime Minister Jawaharlal Nehru's 1949 proposal of a no-war declaration.

Writing to the Pakistani prime minister in December 1949, Nehru said, "[o]wing to geography and many other reasons it is inevitable that many issues arise between the two countries which require settlement. A firm declaration that we will in any event settle them by peaceful methods will itself be a great service to our two countries and the world. It will remove the fear of war from the minds of our two peoples."[12] Liaquat Ali welcomed the offer, but proposed a procedure and a timetable to settle disputes – two months negotiate, two months mediate and then refer for arbitration. The arbitration clause stymied progress then, as it does to this day, as India is deeply suspicious of third-party involvement after taking the Kashmir issue to the UN.

Since then, the proposal for a no-war pact has been tossed back and forth, with no consensus in sight. Border skirmishes in the Rann of Kutch in February 1956 once again prompted Nehru to propose a no-war declaration. In April 1959, it was President Ayub Khan of Pakistan who proposed a joint defence arrangement to India against a common enemy from the north – China;[13] it was summarily dismissed by Nehru. But by then Pakistan had become a strategic ally of the West, sucking South Asia into the vortex of the cold war politics of containment of Soviet and Chinese communism. Its fallout in the sub-continent was the military build-up of Pakistan and the attempt to create an artificial parity by equating a bigger and more powerful India with a smaller and weaker Pakistan.

After the 1962 India–China war, there was Western pressure on India and Pakistan to patch up their differences and end the Kashmir dispute. In 1963 India's foreign minister Swaran Singh proposed formalising the ceasefire line in Kashmir as the international boundary between the two countries, but Pakistan's foreign minister Zulfiqar Ali Bhutto summarily rejected it. His view was that without a settlement of the Kashmir dispute there could be no possibility of a no-war pact.[14] The Kashmir dispute was now embroiled in the internal ideological politics of the two nation-states. War broke out in the sub-continent in September 1965, but it did not settle the Kashmir problem. Following a ceasefire, President Ayub declared in the UN General Assembly that India and Pakistan could adopt a no-war pact only after the Kashmir dispute was resolved.[15]

It was only under duress that Pakistan subsequently agreed, in the Soviet-brokered Tashkent Declaration of January 1966, to affirm the obligation "under the Charter not to have recourse to force and [to] settle their disputes through peaceful means".[16] But no sooner had the ink dried on the agreement than a beleaguered Ayub was protesting that he had not agreed to a no-war pact; instead, he had succeeded in getting India to recognise Kashmir as an area of dispute in the Tashkent Declaration. Subsequent moves by Prime Minister Indira Gandhi in 1968 to dredge up the no-war pact proposal met with a contemptuous dismissal by Ayub Khan. "To talk of a no-war pact without settling the Kashmir dispute is only an attempt to hoodwink the world," he said.[17] Indira Gandhi was to say much the same when President Zia-ul-Haq was to propose a no-war pact in 1981.

Rann of Kutch

The settlement of the Rann of Kutch dispute by way of arbitration demonstrated both the value and limitations of a third-party mediated settlement. The 1965 war between India and Pakistan did not dislocate the arbitration proceedings over the final settlement of their disputed boundary in the Rann of Kutch. When trouble first flared up in 1948 along the border between the Indian state of Gujarat and West Pakistan, an exchange of diplomatic notes temporarily put a lid on the dispute. In 1956, however, armed clashes broke out, but the army commanders on both sides agreed to pull back troops and maintain the status quo. At the diplomatic level it was agreed, in the joint communique of October 1956, that "all outstanding boundary disputes. . .should, if not settled by negotiations, be referred to an impartial tribunal for final settlement of the dispute".[18]

But Pakistan attempted to settle the matter through military means in April 1965. Finally, Britain, backed by the US and the Soviet Union, persuaded the two parties to resolve the dispute peacefully. Under the June agreement the dispute was to be referred to the Indo-Pakistan Western Boundaries Case Tribunal, if an agreement could not be reached bilaterally. As war clouds gathered, the August meeting of the two foreign ministers had to be cancelled and the dispute was automatically referred for arbitration. Although the Tribunal's decision in 1969 – which, among other things, demarcated the boundary between the two on Sir Creek – came under severe criticism in India, it was accepted as binding. For India, it reinforced a prejudice against referring disputes for third-party arbitration. The former Indian foreign minister M. C. Chagla summed it up by saying, "[t]he best justice we can get is from our own strength and not from looking at any international Tribunal or Supreme Court, whether it is a question of Kashmir or any other territory".[19]

A boundary dispute left over from the Tribunal's award was the delimitation of Sir Creek that affected both the land and the maritime boundary between the two States.

Indus Waters Treaty

The Indus Waters Treaty is often cited as a model for successful third-party arbitration of a dispute between India and Pakistan. It is also held up as a model resource sharing agreement. As part of the partition process, there had been a 1948 Inter-Dominion Standstill Agreement on the sharing of the waters of the Indus River, which was vital for the irrigation systems of East and West Punjab, but it soon came under pressure. Indeed, the Indus had the potential of becoming as major a source of tension as Kashmir between the two countries. The challenge then was to prevent a manageable technical problem from becoming a politically intractable one.

At this juncture the World Bank stepped in, and after protracted negotiations effected an agreement on a functional plane.[20] However, as the environmentalist Deepak Gyawali observed, the third party in this case was the World Bank–Bretton Woods system, which held out the inducement of substantial aid to the two squabbling States. Describing it as partition and not a water-sharing treaty, he argued that Pakistani passions over Kashmir should be linked to its fears on India's control of the headwaters of the Indus.[21]

Notwithstanding that critique, the agreement has withstood the pressures of two wars: despite the 1965 war, India paid its annual installment of Rs. 80 million towards the building-up of Pakistan's irrigation system. In the midst of the ceasefire period, water was released into the canals of Pakistan despite pressure from farmers in East (Indian) Punjab. Since the creation of a Permanent Indus Commission in 1979, there has been routine cooperation in such areas as sharing of flood forecasting data. The groundswell of disgruntled voices in the downstream reaches with regard to salinity and floods after releases are, however, yet to be fully addressed.

Third-Party Mediation

The involvement of third parties in the management of the India–Pakistan adversarial relationship has been mired in controversy. It was India, the then 'aggrieved' party, which internationalised the Kashmir dispute by taking it to the United Nations in 1948. Not only did the protracted negotiations within the UN process not facilitate a settlement of the problem, but the internationalisation of the dispute also resulted in Kashmir getting caught up in the politics of the cold war. Pakistan's induction in the Western alliance system sealed the fate of Kashmir as a running sore in India–Pakistan relations. The superpowers, keeping their own strategic interests in mind, were keen to 'contain' the dispute.

This containment process, says veteran analyst Bhabani Sen Gupta, was achieved by "trying to create an artificial balance to give Pakistan a sense of security; attempts at limiting the conflict by placing an arms embargo on both sides and finally, mediating the conflict".[22]

The Soviet Union brokered the containment of the 1965 war. The Tashkent Declaration drafted an impressive framework for non-use of force and normalisation of relations, and the Kashmir dispute was shelved for the time being, with each side reiterating its known position. The Declaration led to a public outcry in Pakistan and a hasty disavowal of any acceptance of a no-war pact. According to the former Indian foreign secretary J. N. Dixit, the Indian experience of third-party mediation in the 1948 and 1965 conflicts was that "Pakistan would assume an artificial air of injured innocence and claim compensatory post-conflict compromises".[23]

Bilateralism

The third India–Pakistan war of 1971 again highlighted the use of military means to settle differences, but it also demonstrated the futility of war as a means of resolving the Kashmir problem or fundamentally altering the adversarial relationship between the two. The 1971 war, however, did give rise to a bilaterally negotiated, conceptual framework for a durable peace – the 1972 Simla Agreement. There was to be no repeat of the disaster of third-party mediation as in Tashkent. President Zulfiqar Ali Bhutto in an interview with Indian journalists said, "I am allergic to third-party intervention. It is high time that the nations of the subcontinent solved their own disputes without having to turn to outside umpires for help."[24]

To Bhutto, the man who had vowed a thousand years' war, fell the task of picking up the pieces after the defeat of a second partition. In a volte-face from what had been Pakistan's basic stance – negotiate on Kashmir and then move towards normalisation – Bhutto argued for a step by step approach: before any grand declaration of a no-war pact, there must be a return of territory and prisoners of war (PoWs). Bhutto did not want to reopen the Kashmir issue in Simla. Indira Gandhi had to resist the temptation to overplay India's superior position after the war to push through a package solution on India–Pakistan differences.[25]

India was adamant about the recognition of a new Line of Control in Jammu and Kashmir as against the ceasefire line negotiated by the UN. Linked to it was the requirement that all issues between the two countries be settled peacefully and bilaterally. The deadlock in the negotiations was broken with the inclusion of a clause – "without prejudice to their recognised position". It implicitly confirmed that Pakistan's position on

Kashmir was different from that of India's. At Simla, the two sides agreed that though the Kashmir issue was not settled, the spirit of the Simla Agreement enjoined a bilateral settlement of the issue.

The debris of the 1971 war was cleared, the LoC defined and, after tricky negotiations, the East Pakistani PoWs returned. (A 1993 Delhi agreement brokered the return of non-Bengali PoWs). Diplomatic relations, as well as visa, postal, road, rail, air and shipping links were restored, although India's 1974 nuclear test explosion delayed the process. It took four years for India and Pakistan to exchange ambassadors, and shipping links, disrupted since the 1965 war, were re-established only in 1975. Trade was resumed after ten years with the signing of the 1974 Trade Protocol. But except for an ad hoc agreement on the export of surplus cotton bales, trade remained very restricted, as Pakistan's industry minister opposed the opening up of trade lest it hurt his country's nascent industry.[26]

Salal Dam Agreement

What does stand out during this period is the 1978 agreement on the Salal Dam in Jammu and Kashmir, 64 km from Pakistan. After eight years of negotiations, an agreement was reached whereby India agreed to lower the height of the storage dam and use it only for power generation. The last few snags in the negotiations were removed during the visit of the Indian foreign minister, Atal Bihari Vajpayee to Pakistan, the first such high-level visit in a decade-and-a-half. The agreement was hailed as an example of the two countries being able to work out their problems peacefully. But the initiatives during the Janata Party government in India to promote normalisation between the two countries were all too brief.

Decade of Normalisation: Cooperation Amidst Tension

The decade of the 1980s saw a remarkable resurgence in diplomatic initiatives to rebuild the relationship. Pakistan's President Zia-ul-Haq's 'peace offensive' promoted the emergence of a structured framework of interaction between the two countries. Cross-border road and rail transport, civil aviation, post and telecommunication links were revived and cooperation in trade and finance encouraged. At the diplomatic level, after a fifteen years of not talking to each other, high-level ministerial exchanges were re-established, including the practice of ad hoc meetings between the two leaders of India and Pakistan. Official contacts were stepped up between the home affairs, defence and water resources ministries. A Joint Commission was set up to spur cooperation in economic, cultural and agricultural sectors. An understanding was reached on consular access to nationals in each other's jails. The two Army Chiefs began talking to each other about Confidence Building Measures to defuse tensions along the border. The home secretaries discussed the mapping-out of ground rules for the border and joint patrolling to check illicit trafficking and terrorism.

There were also symbolic gestures, like permitting the visiting Indian foreign minister, P. V. Narasimha Rao, to address the Pakistan Institute of International Affairs in 1983. It was the first time in a decade-and-a-half that an Indian politician had spoken at a public forum. President Zia attended the Indian Republic Day celebrations in Pakistan in 1985. For the first time since the hardening of their adversarial relationship, there was a conscious effort at lowering the barriers inhibiting people to people contacts. The visa regime was liberalised, especially for Sikh pilgrims. Sporting and cultural contacts were revived, and India agreed to the establishment of a Pakistani consulate in Bombay.

But parallel to this efflorescence in cooperative initiatives was a sub-track of tension and confrontation. The 1980s saw India and Pakistan caught up in an escalating arms race, this time both conventional and nuclear. Pakistan's induction as a front-line State in the US-sponsored war on Afghanistan sucked South Asia back into the vortex of cold war politics. While there was no outbreak of a full-scale war, a low-intensity war broke out in Siachin. Furthermore, India and Pakistan almost drifted into a full-scale war as a result of a show of brinkmanship during the massive Operation Brasstacks military exercises in India. The cooperative dialogue was further buffeted by reports of cross-border support for insurgency in Indian Punjab, and to a lesser extent, in Pakistani Sind. The flare-up of communal violence in India provided Pakistan with a renewed propaganda opportunity to project itself internationally as the champion of the 'aggrieved' Indian Muslims.

Seen in this light, was President Zia's peace offensive an empty public relations exercise to neutralise Western anxiety over the destabilising implications of the revival of arms supplies to Pakistan? It was no secret that Pakistan's renewed interest in a non-aggression pact came at the tail-end of the official announcement of a $3.2 billion US aid package.

To expect that President Zia would deliver a structure for a durable peace is to be deliberately naive about his authoritarian rule. The military establishments and the Islamic fundamentalists, both of which he fostered, underwrote the regime of President Zia, the 'usurper' of power from Bhutto. The military could hardly be expected to shed its adversarial view of India and undermine its claim on defence spending and privileges. Zia candidly acknowledged that Kashmir was so wrapped up in the internal politics of Pakistan that he could not isolate it, even if he wanted to. Moreover, as Samina Ahmed analyses, regime legitimacy may have eluded successive military rulers, but there has always been a domestic consensus on security policies posited on an uneasy relationship with India. So long as regime legitimacy remains internally disputed, the threat from India will be used to enhance internal goals.[27]

Whether it was democratic or authoritarian, civilian or military rule in Pakistan, foreign policy and in particular its India policy has been largely controlled by the military. That the anti-India mindset is essentially centred in the dominant Punjab–Pathan elite axis, and gradually diminishes towards Sind or Quetta, would make a difference only with the democratisation of the policy process. However, Zia the general, more than any civilian president, was only too aware of the costs of a war with India and thus the need to contain the adversarial relationship.

Joint Defence

What was once the strategic unity of the undivided sub-continent's defence had been disrupted by the adversarial India–Pakistan relationship. On occasion though, there have been tentative, though abortive, initiatives to evolve a mutual security-perception vis-à-vis third-party threats. President Ayub Khan had proposed a joint defence against China before embarking on the strategy of 'the enemy of my enemy is my friend'. Subsequently, Prime Minister Indira Gandhi was to sound out Pakistan on a mutual security assurance to ward off instability following the Soviet intervention in Afghanistan. At the time, Pakistan was being wooed by the West to become a front-line State in their support for Afghanistan. India had also just concluded a $1.2 billion defence supply agreement with the Soviet Union. In an effort to allay Pakistan's security fears, Foreign Minister Swaran Singh offered security assurances to enable Pakistan to shift its forces from its eastern border to the western border with Afghanistan. However, in an interview with Rajendra Sareen, President Zia scoffed at the proposal: "What is the guarantee from the Indian side? We have fought three wars. . .how should I be reassured. . . .[We have asked you to] just lift even a twentieth of your forces as a token. . . [but] we have seen no reaction."[28]

In a continuing effort to manage India–Pakistan tension against the backdrop of an emerging arms race, Zia revived the no-war pact proposal. Indira Gandhi responded with a counter-proposal for a friendship treaty. The talks got bogged down over issues such as the erosion of the principle of bilateralism for dispute settlement and the use of air bases by foreign military aircraft. In any case, the talks were not taken seriously by either side. As Indira Gandhi said, "the proposal makes no sense; you can't talk peace and prepare for war".[29]

Confidence Building Measures – Conventional and Nuclear

What proved more successful were the discussions between the military commanders on proposals to keep border conflicts and tensions under control. The two army chiefs, in an exchange of letters, suggested a framework of regular contacts between the Director-Generals of Military Operations (DGMOs) and an exchange of information on troop movements.[30]

The spurt in a programme of Confidence Building Measures was spurred on by a perception of parity in military strength, where the asymmetry in Pakistan's conventional defence was compensated for by its covert nuclear weapons programme. In the mid-eighties, there were incremental leaks about Pakistan's clandestine nuclear weapons programme. In 1984, a cluster of reports appeared in the American press on an imminent Indian attack on Pakistan's nuclear facility at Kahuta, much in the same vein as the Israeli attack on the Osirak reactor in Iraq. In December 1985, Prime Minister Rajiv Gandhi and President Zia discussed the possiblity of a non-attack on each other's nuclear facilities.

Zia, under pressure to deflect US non-proliferation laws inhibiting aid, engaged in a show of preventive nuclear diplomacy. Proposals were mooted for a Nuclear Free Zone in South Asia, a joint declaration renouncing the acquisition of nuclear weapons, simultaneous accession of India and Pakistan to the Non-Proliferation Treaty (NPT) and a mutual inspection of each other's nuclear facilities. India rejected all these proposals, as it would have meant forfeiting its policy of keeping open its nuclear option. What survived of Zia's nuclear diplomacy was the 1988 agreement on the safety of nuclear installations and the first Confidence Building Measures in managing a stable, non-weaponised nuclear deterrence. It was brought into effect in 1991 and the two sides have since been annually exchanging lists on nuclear sites.

However, the crisis which blew up over Operation Brasstacks in 1986–87 raised uneasy questions about the value of the CBMs in place. The lack of trust between the two adversaries effectively undermined the value of the nascent framework of communications between the field commanders and the political leaders. Both India and Pakistan did not use the hotline between the DGMOs, despite growing tensions over Indian military exercises and the massing of troops on either side of the border.

A study of crisis management during Operation Brasstacks shows that information shared was not deemed reliable by both sides, and that India only minimally complied with Pakistani requests for information about the scale of the exercise.[31]

Eventually, the Indian and Pakistani prime ministers did use the hotline to defuse tension. The role of the American and Soviet ambassadors was also significant in prompting India and Pakistan to begin official-level talks once again to work out force withdrawals. President Zia gave a political impetus to the de-escalation of tension through his 'cricket diplomacy', when he visited India to watch a cricket match in Jaipur and used it as an occasion for an informal bilateral summit. India and Pakistan were thus able to contain the crisis, but this experience exposed the propensity of the two countries to drift towards war even in a situation of normalcy, and the absence of any bilateral mechanism to reduce escalating tensions over border disputes.

By September 1987, Indian and Pakistani troops were again at war over the undemarcated boundary along the Siachin Glacier. Two rounds of talks between the defence secretaries of India and Pakistan in 1986 had failed to evolve a peaceful framework to settle their competing claims. In Pakistan, opposition leader Benazir Bhutto made propaganda capital of the Chief of Army Staff (CoAS) President Zia's loss of 1500 kilometres of territory to India. Talks were resumed against a military stalemate in Siachin. After six rounds of talks, an understanding on disengagement and re-deployment of troops, without prejudice to the respective claims of either side, was reached by 1992. But the all-but-signed agreement on Siachin has become yet another casualty at the altar of irreconcilable historical differences: the insistence that there must first be progress on settling the core issue – Kashmir. The jettisoning of the 'step by step' approach, which called for building on areas where an agreement could be reached, has meant that an attempt at solving the Tulbul Navigation Project and Sir Creek boundary disputes has had to be shelved.[32]

Joint Commissions – A Mechanism for Exchanges

Despite the armed clashes and the heated exchange of words across the border, the dialogues for normalisation pushed ahead. Mechanisms were put in place to promote exchanges, though pragmatists like J. N. Dixit argued with good reason that the emphasis was on the process of dialogue, with President Zia balking when it came to actual decisions or implementation.[33] Eventually, the long-awaited agreement to set up an Indo-Pakistan Joint Commission was formalised during the visit to Pakistan in June 1983 by Indian foreign minister, P. V. Narasimha Rao. Four sub-commissions were identified to promote economic cooperation and trade and exchanges in agriculture, education, science and technology, information, culture, travel, tourism and consular matters.

These commitments were meant to be on a long-term basis, but the actual implementation was often short-lived. In the area of bilateral trade, for example, the trade embargo imposed during the 1965 war was lifted in 1974. Although the trade protocol of 1976 opened up imports of coal, cast iron, tea, pharmaceuticals and power generation equipment, it failed to make much impact. In July 1978, Pakistan unilaterally prohibited its private sector from trading with India. The ostensible reason was that Pakistan's worsening trade balance prompted a protectionist approach. By 1985, Pakistan's exports to India were worth only Rs. 190 million, while its imports from India were worth Rs. 350 million. Fears were raised about Indian goods swamping Pakistani markets.

Trade talks between the commerce ministers in 1986 removed restrictions on channelling imports through the Trading Corporation of Pakistan. But the expectation that the Indo-Pakistan Joint (Sub-Commission on Trade) Commission would be able to remove the hurdles in the way of bilateral trade were not fulfilled, although by 1988 the list of items Pakistan allowed for import was up from 42 to 249. Even the momentary impetus given to the India–Pakistan relations in the wake of the Benazir Bhutto–Rajiv Gandhi meeting in 1989 failed to make a dent in Pakistan's refusal to extend Most Favoured Nation (MFN) status to India.

The Joint Commission was to have met annually. The third and last meeting of the Joint Commission in 1989 took place in the wake of the bonhomie generated by Prime Minister Rajiv Gandhi's visit to Pakistan, the first visit by an Indian prime minister in thirty years. A cultural exchange programme was approved, but the restrictions that continue to this day in the exchange of books, periodicals and newspapers testify to the lack of progress made in this field. Efforts to revive the Joint Commission in the 1990s were stymied by the Kashmir dispute taking centre stage.

There had been considerable optimism that a popular Rajiv Gandhi in India and a democratically elected Benazir Bhutto in Pakistan would put past confrontations behind them and restructure a new relationship. Moreover, with the Geneva agreements on Afghanistan signed the US, too, wanted the situation in South Asia to stabilise, especially in view of the nuclear capabilities of the two adversaries. Rajiv Gandhi took the initiative to keep up the pace of interaction established during Zia's peace offensive. Three bilateral agreements were signed: the first was on a non-attack of each other's nuclear facilities, the second on cultural cooperation and the third on the avoidance of double taxation. In trade, Pakistan expanded the list of permissible items for import from India to 571.

There were a flurry of exchanges of high-level delegations in the spheres of tourism, railways and transport. Talks on resolving differences over the Tulbul Navigation Project, Sir Creek and Siachin also continued. It was in the late eighties that the present programme of CBMs was instituted, an example of which was a Memorandum of Understanding to prevent violation of each other's airspace by military aircraft, and the rationalising of ground rules for patrolling the border. In conditions reminiscent of the East–West cold war conflicts, here too, the CBMs were crisis driven, based on a sense of military parity and conditions of relative detente.[34]

However, even in the midst of the Benazir Bhutto–Rajiv Gandhi summit in July, there were warning signals that the resurgence of the Kashmir dispute would derail the dialogue process.

The Kashmir Dispute takes Centre Stage: Saving a Working Dialogue

An internally fuelled insurgency in the state of Jammu and Kashmir catalysed the politics of a hostile confrontation between India and Pakistan in the 1990s. The sabre-rattling in both countries got louder, and pressure mounted for the breaking-off of all dialogue other than that between the DGMOs. Pakistan's arming and training of Kashmiri militants raised the spectre of a drift towards war between India and Pakistan, two non-weaponsied nuclear powers. India–Pakistan relations were reduced to jingoistic rhetoric, the physical attack on each other's diplomats, armed clashes on the LoC and a 'proxy war' in Kashmir. India and Pakistan baiting became the obsessive sport of their respective diplomats in inter-national fora. It seemed that realists like Pakistan's Abdul Sattar and India's J. N. Dixit had reason to argue that India and Pakistan could not normalise relations.[35]

Ironically, the end of the cold war had raised optimism about a lowering of tension in the area. Russia was disengaging from South Asia and the US was working out a non-competitive strategic relationship with both India and Pakistan. But the sub-continent continued to become more, and not less, conflict-prone.

Throughout the rapid backslide in relations, however, the dialogue survived. Prime Minister P. V. Narasimha Rao explained in Parliament in 1992, while taking note of the evidence on Pakistan's State-sponsored terrorism in Kashmir and Punjab, that the bilateral dialogue with Pakistan would have to continue. Prime Ministers Rao and Sharif met six times to try and salvage a working relationship.

The US was also to prod India and Pakistan to de-escalate tension. It is still a matter of speculation whether it was the US National Security Advisor Robert Gates' mission to India and Pakistan that averted a war and a threatened nuclear exchange. But within weeks of his visit, the two foreign secretaries began their first round of talks on CBMs. In August 1992, the two ratified the instruments relating to an agreement on advanced notification of military exercises, manoeuvres and troop movements. An agreement was reached on the prevention of air space violations. A joint declaration was made on the prohibition of the use of chemical weapons.

But the tentative moves to keep afloat a working dialogue broke down in the wake of a wave of violence that swept the sub-continent following the destruction of the Babri Mosque in India. India then blamed Pakistan for abetting the perpetrators of the serial bomb blasts in Mumbai. The Indian home minister publicly rejected a Pakistani offer that the two home secretaries meet to discuss the issue of the whereabouts of the Memon brothers, allegedly implicated in the bomb blasts. It took a year-and-a-half before the two foreign secretaries met again.

Prime Minister Rao provided a fresh impetus for talks by directing in 1994 that Kashmir should be put on the agenda. But the crisis over the siege of the Hazaratbal mosque in Srinagar cast a long shadow on the seventh round of talks.[36] About a fortnight later, Pakistan submitted two proposals for CBMs, including one which set out the modalities for a plebiscite in Kashmir. India rejected them both. Pakistan in turn rejected the six working papers sent by India, which contained proposals for a resolution of the disputes over Sir Creek, Siachin, the Tulbul Navigation Project, as well as the revival of the Joint Commission.[37]

It was during this freeze in the official dialogue, with both sides locked in mutually antagonistic positions, that the growing efforts at people to people contacts became crucial. The business lobby was particularly persuasive about the costs of non-cooperation in commercial terms. A study commissioned by Prime Minister Benazir Bhutto on the pros and cons of opening up trade with India established that the economic advantages far outweighed the disadvantages. The study, "Pakistan–India Trade: Transition to the GATT Regime", estimated unofficial trade between India and Pakistan to be anything from $100 million to $500 million. If Indian goods routed via third countries were added, the figure would reach $1 billion. This implied a substantial loss of revenue to the cash-strapped exchequers of India and Pakistan.

Moreover, the process of establishing, within the South Asian Association for Regional Cooperation (SAARC), a South Asia Preferential Trade Agreement (SAPTA) put pressure on Pakistan not to slow down trade. The SAPTA process entailed regular interaction between the commerce ministries of India and Pakistan, and also a timetable for lowering regional trade barriers. The setting up of structures like the Standing Committee on Customs Cooperation institutionalised regular and structured interaction. But the issue of Pakistan extending MFN status to India had got so politically wrapped up with Kashmir that any progress on the trade front was seen in Pakistan as selling Kashmir short.

Prime Minister Nawaz Sharif, a businessman himself, had, in the new trade policy of July 1997, identified 14 new groups of items that could be traded with India. Commerce Minister Ishan Dar justified the move by saying, "We have to be economically sensible. If we can get a product for $5 [from India] why should we pay $7 or $10 for it?"[38] But Dar had to retract his statement in the face of a barrage of criticism from hardliners on Kashmir, who couched their opposition in a concern over a level economic playing field, given India's higher tariff walls. But the real sticking point was clearly Kashmir. As Foreign Minister Gohar Ayub Khan said, "trade in the region can only flourish in a stable and conducive environment free of conflict and tension along with visible forward movement towards the resolution of the Jammu and Kashmir dispute".[39]

The Gujral Doctrine

The coalition Janata government in India was committed to a policy of good neighbourliness. It was determined to break away from the politics of reciprocity characteristic of earlier Congress governments. I. K. Gujral, both as foreign minister and subsequently prime minister, was committed to walking that extra mile. As a result of Gujral's determination and the pragmatism of Nawaz Sharif, an official-level dialogue was revived. Sharif even mooted the idea of Pakistan selling surplus power to India. But events once again got stuck in the familiar quagmire of India pitching for a step by step normalisation, with Kashmir to be put on a backburner, and Pakistan adamant on normalisation only after tackling the Kashmir issue. In the second round of talks between the two foreign secretaries in June 1997, it was agreed that all outstanding issues, including Kashmir, were to be discussed. A mechanism was to be set up to include working groups to discuss all issues in an integrated manner. But even that understanding seemed to come apart when the two foreign secretaries met again in

September and traded charges over what had, or had not, been agreed to on Kashmir.

The September talks were held when the air was still reverberating with the sound of heavy artillery fire on the border. Rising tensions over the heavy exchange of fire in August had been defused when the two prime ministers talked on the hotline. In the India–Pakistan context, it is not at all surprising that the official talks on peace have a fiery underside – in this case, the hotting-up of the missile race. Incidents of terrorist violence in India and Pakistan prompted the conventional knee-jerk reactions. The Pakistani Inter-Services Intelligence Agency (ISI) and the Indian Research and Analysis Wing (RAW) were, as usual, implicated. Gujral openly blamed Pakistan for the terrorist bomb blasts in Julandhar and Coimbatore, and Sharif blamed the RAW for the bomb blasts in Lahore.[40]

In the statist India–Pakistan relational structure, rigidified as it is along an antagonistic axis, could the historic changes of a completely different party coming to power in India and the transition from military to civilian government in Pakistan make much of a difference to their outlook vis-à-vis each other? With a Bharatiya Janata Party (BJP)-led coalition in India and Nawaz Sharif at the head of the Pakistan Muslim League (PML) government in Pakistan, there was both the possibility of a political breakthrough towards normalisation, and the dread of the ultra-nationalist anchorage of the two pushing them both into military adventurism. The dye was cast when the BJP government crossed the firebreak and tested nuclear weapons in May 1998. Pakistan, inevitably, followed suit, locking the two neighbours in a competitive nuclear and missile arms race. It catapulted India and Pakistan onto the international security agenda as a 'nuclear flashpoint' region. Pressure mounted to work out a framework of CBMs to manage an unstable nuclear relationship, to reduce tensions and promote normalisation.

Lahore Declaration: A Detour to Kargil

The Lahore visit of India's Prime Minister Atal Behari Vajpayee was as sudden as it was dramatic in the political initiatives to which both leaders were seemingly committed to give a new direction to the relationship. The euphoria that followed the visit gave rise to a wild optimism that relations between the two countries would at last improve. But the giddy embrace of the two was not underpinned by substantive preparatory work or subsequent follow-ups. The February 1999 Lahore Declaration promised a commitment to resolve differences through a dialogue process and immediate steps to reduce the risk of an 'accidental' use of nuclear weapons. The Memorandum of Understanding, signed by the two foreign secretaries in Lahore, spoke of bilateral consultations on security concepts and nuclear doctrines, and an initiative on the structure of CBMs. Also, the two affirmed their respective unilateral moratorium on further nuclear tests. An agreement on the prevention of incidents at sea was also to be concluded. But a follow-up on these measures did not materialise. To say that it was the reduction of the Vajpayee government to the status of a caretaker government which came in the way of transforming the symbolic gains of Lahore into something more substantial is simplistic. It misses the political dynamics at work in Pakistan and India as well as the ad hoc nature of the Lahore event.

The Kargil conflict was a major setback to the hopes that something could be made of the Lahore process. The intrusion by Pakistan was projected as a betrayal of the spirit of Lahore and the trust of not only Vajpayee but also every Indian who believed that peace was possible between India and Pakistan. Without getting caught up in the political dynamics of the whys and wherefores of Kargil, its escalation and the political agendas of beleaguered leaders, what is significant is that despite the jingoistic belligerence on both sides, parleys, direct and indirect, continued throughout. Ultimately, it was a negotiated compromise (facilitated by the US) which effected the military disengagement.[41]

Throughout the Kargil war, despite the fact that the dominant mood was of belligerent jingoism, there were nonetheless audible and persisting dissenting voices condemning the use of force and calling for a ceasefire and peace. It needs to be kept in mind that the Lahore process was legitimised by the emerging peoples' peace constituency in India and Pakistan. Their voices, on both sides of the border, were not silent during Kargil as they demanded accountability for the breakdown in the process. Eventually, it is the democratisation of the peace process that holds the promise of transforming the adversarial India–Pakistan relationship by creating new networks of social solidarities capable of reordering the priorities of both nations.

II

Non-Official Dialogues and the Peoples' Track

Soon after independence in 1947, as State-to-State relations turned adversarial, keeping the two peoples apart became integral to the politics of demonising the other. In the last fifty years, a generation has grown up in

India and Pakistan that does not know each other. History has been rewritten, a common past distorted and adversarial stereotypes reinforced.[42]

At the peoples' level there had been little or no communication once the residual process of the transfer of power had been dealt with. Bilateral trade, which could have made for wide-ranging contacts, whittled into insignificance. Reciprocal visa restrictions made contact between divided families difficult. War legitimised the protracted closure of road, rail, air, shipping and postal links. Exchanges of newspapers, books and periodicals were not allowed. And even more effective in keeping the two peoples apart were the walls of prejudice and hate. Communication was reduced to exchanges of artillery fire and hostile propaganda across the border. Their respective diplomatic missions were viewed as the outposts of spies, and people interacting with them were denounced as fraternising with the enemy. Intelligence agencies rather than diplomats began to define the official dialogue. On both sides of the border, there was a remarkable fit between the State ideology based on adversarial relations and popular acceptance of hate politics, and its corollary, a national security obsession.

It is this fit that is under threat as more peoples' contacts are being established. As Nirmal Mukarji, the co-chairperson of the Pakistan–India Peoples Forum for Peace and Democracy, said at the 1996 Calcutta convention of the PIPFPD, "[t]he more people come across and see for themselves, the more they talk to each other, the more they are exposed to each other's writings, the more the process of demonising the other will come apart".[43] Clearly there is a change in the attitudes of intellectuals, social activists and businessmen about the cost of non-cooperation and confrontation. Even sectoral groups, like the business community, environmentalists, women and human rights organisations are becoming aware that to cooperatively tackle their sectoral agenda, they have to engage with the bigger agenda of peoples' peace and peoples' security in India and Pakistan.

Stray Initiatives to Mend Fences

In sharp contrast to the wasteland of non-official contacts of the early decades, President Zia-ul-Haq's peace offensive saw the beginnings of people to people contacts. Although Zia's politics of Islamisation sought to hitch Pakistan to its Persian–Arab cultural moorings, the 1980s saw a spurt in non-official interaction between the peoples of the sub-continent. Visa restrictions were made relatively more liberal; in this, Zia may have been playing the 'Sikh card', but in the process thousands of ordinary Indian citizens – Sikhs, Hindu pilgrims and many more Indian Muslims – visited Pakistan. Many more journalists were allowed to visit accompanying official delegations.

Sporting contacts in cricket and hockey were revived and a tentative beginning was made in cultural exchanges. In 1989, Indian theatre groups performed for the first time in Pakistan, following a cross-border theatre workshop involving cultural groups from India and Pakistan. The Centre for Science and Environment took fifty Indian environmentalists to Lahore for an Indo-Pakistan meet on the environment, resulting in the publication of a book titled *Beyond Shifting Sands*.

Concern about the escalating India–Pakistan arms race in the 1980s prompted the Centre for South Asian Studies of the University of Punjab to organise in 1985 a seminar in Lahore with South Asian military experts to review rising defence expenditure. The seminar was extremely critical of Prime Minister Rajiv Gandhi and President Zia for sacrificing peoples' development at the altar of a nuclear and conventional arms race. Another initiative was the University of Illinois' South Asian Visiting Scholars project sponsored by the Ford Foundation. Since 1984 it has brought together hundreds of scholars from India and Pakistan. Efforts to promote friendship inspired the former foreign secretary, Kewal Singh, to set up the India–Pakistan Friendship Society in 1987. Its counterpart in Pakistan, however, has still to be founded.

The Business Community

The 1980s were also to see the nascent growth of cross-border linkages between business associations and the possibility of the business community emerging as a powerful lobby in asserting the economic benefits of cooperation. It was backed by the parallel growth of the SAARC structure and its non-official offshoot, the SAARC Chambers of Commerce. The SAARC process has delivered the South Asian Preferential Trade Agreement which promises to transform the trade relations of the SAARC Seven. It has put enormous pressure on Pakistan to keep up with the other South Asian countries. Opening up trade between India and Pakistan would do more than open up markets—it would set up a spreading network of non-official contacts and build a vested interest in the continuance of economic cooperation for which peace is a necessary condition.

As early as 1969, N. T. Parekh, the visionary Managing Director of ICICI Bank, formed an informal group of Bombay-based businessmen and financiers to lobby for a South Asian Common Market. Seminars were held, followed by consultations with the government. Advocacy articles were published in newspapers, and a book entitled *India and Regional Development* appeared. The 1971 war cut short this initiative. It was not till 1987 that Parekh was able to revive his campaign with a seminar attended by Indian and Pakistani scholars and businessmen.

Commercial contacts between Indian and Pakistani businessmen were minimal until the end of the 1980s. But since the 1970s, influential periodicals like *The Pakistan Economist* had been advocating cheaper imports from India rather than buying commodities like iron ore more expensively from a third country. While most Pakistani newspapers backed the protectionist argument that import of Indian goods would adversely affect Pakistani industry, there were newspapers like *The Khyber Mail* that supported the opening up of trade.

In 1981, the Federation of Pakistani Chambers of Commerce and the Lahore Chamber of Commerce took the initiative to hold talks with their counterparts in India. A year later a delegation of Indian businessmen visited Pakistan and agreed to set up an Indo-Pakistan Joint Business Commission, which held its first meeting in 1983. An enduring result of the visit of the Indian delegation was the setting up of an Indo-Pakistan desk in the Punjab, Haryana and Delhi Chambers of Commerce and Industry (PHDCCI). It continues to be a catalyst for the growth of commercial relations in both countries.

Within the business community there were sectors like the Indian Cotton Traders Association that were particularly active. Visits to Karachi were made by a delegation of the Indian Cotton Mills Federation in 1988, followed by a delegation of the East Cotton Association in 1989. Inquiries were made about the possibility of buying cotton from Pakistan. A seven-member Indian tea delegation also went to Karachi to revive the tea trade; after 1948, Pakistan had reoriented its tea imports towards Kenya and Sri Lanka. Four years later there was a trial shipment of 50,000 tons of Indian tea to Karachi. In 1997 another delegation of tea exporters was to try its luck, after waiting over six months for visa clearance. But bilateral trade, restricted to only 571 items at the time, remained insignificant. Beyond trade in the listed items there were ad hoc agreements to import cotton, iron ore, cement, sugar, wheat, potatoes and onions.

The SAARC Chamber of Commerce promoted a series of seminars and the exchange of business delegations to lobby for an increase in trade, special business visas and the opening up of the overland route for Indian and Pakistani goods to come by road. The Confederation of Indian Industries (CII) set up a task force to promote trade, and a CII delegation visited Pakistan in 1996. These exchanges not only helped the business communities to become aware of each other's markets but also helped to remove certain State-sponsored prejudices.

Pakistani officials maintained that the public would not countenance trade with India as long as tension-generating issues remained unresolved. But Indian businessmen were to find, in their exchanges with representative from the Federation of Pakistani Chambers of Commerce and private entrepreneurs, a keenness to trade with India.[44] Indeed, it was businessmen-turned-politicians like Senator Ilyas Bilour from the North-West Frontier Province who, as members of Nawaz Sharif's government, were instrumental in strengthening commercial relations with India, battling, along the way, to overcome the anti-Indian prejudice of the bureaucratic mindset.

In 1990, when India won a competitive bid to supply onions and potatoes at short notice, Pakistani government officials insisted that the issue should not be publicised. J. N. Dixit, who was then the Indian High Commissioner in Pakistan, found that everyone in the markets of Pakistan knew that the onions and potatoes were from India, and that the tradesmen were just relieved that the shortage had been met.[45] However, during a later trip to Pakistan, I found that a section of the press had communalised the shipment of onions and potatoes in newspaper headlines as "Hindu onions" and "Hindu potatoes". The story doing the rounds in Pakistani official circles was that the consecrated tubers had to be put on special offer with a bagful of not-so-sweet Indian or 'Hindu' sugar.[46]

But businessmen on both sides of the border were to find that trade could not be excluded from politics. In 1997 when Pakistan opened up its tyre market, a number of Indian tyre manufacturers rushed to Pakistan as part of the PHDCCI delegation. The market for Indian tyres was estimated at Rs. 2,500 million. Moreover, Pakistan had just announced the opening up of 14 new groups of items for trade with India in its new trade policy. With considerable enthusiasm, in July 1997, the visiting thirty-member Indian business delegation from PHDCCI agreed with their counterparts in Lahore to set up an India–Pakistan Chamber of Commerce. The announcement was greeted with a chorus of criticism in the Pakistani press. "Trade and economic relations cannot improve unless political issues are resolved", the Pakistani finance minister warned.[47] The Lahore Declaration was to give a fillip to commercial interaction in the form of discussions on the purchase of power and sugar. The political controversy over the sugar deal, however, epitomises the peculiarity of the Indo-Pakistan relationship, as the sugar was exported by a company associated with Nawaz Sharif's industrial empire. Although the Kargil conflict did not dislocate business flows, the elections in India inevitably politicised trade.

Sections of the business community, only too aware of the contradictory pulls of economics and politics in India–Pakistan relations, have shown considerable interest in the non-official dialogues to promote peace. But more often than not, they have been supportive only from the outside. Businessmen have been reluctant to directly participate in dialogues that focus on political and security issues. An exception was the 1991 dialogue organised by the Calcutta-based businessman, O. P. Shah. The two-part India–Pakistan dialogue was sponsored by prominent Indian and Pakistani businessmen. Held in Islamabad and New Delhi, the Shah initiative brought together fifty professionals to discuss cultural and economic issues between the two countries. An interesting aspect of these discussions was the participation of representatives of fundamentalist organisations as well. More recently, however, sections of the business community, especially in West Bengal in India and the North-West Frontier Province in Pakistan, have been proactive in their support of the mass meetings of the Pakistan-India Peoples Forum for Peace and Democracy.

Track Two Diplomacy and the Peoples' Track

The 1990s have seen a remarkable burgeoning of non-official contacts and people-to-people dialogues, which are chipping away at the old antagonistic orthodoxies, and for the first time expanding the space for independent debate on even such contentious issues as the Kashmir dispute. This is despite the recurring war hysteria and the endemic risk of the two countries drifting into a war even while efforts are on at normalising relations. The fact that the diplomatic dialogue is often deadlocked, with only the artillery speaking, makes it all the more imperative for civil society to keep open as many channels of communication as possible. The heightening of inter-State tension, however, makes political dialogue at the peoples' level difficult and even risky. Visa difficulties, for instance, had hampered the efforts of some Non-Governmental Organisations (NGOs) to organise a peoples' level joint celebration in India and Pakistan on the fiftieth anniversary of independence. It needs to be kept in mind that high levels of tension have reinforced bureaucratic privileges, and the ruling elite have a vested interest in maintaining the ideological underpinnings of the structure of conflict. On the other hand, the Pakistan–India Peoples Forum for Peace and Democracy has been more fortunate in being able to get mass visa clearances for delegates to their conferences. Evidently, even within the politico-military–bureaucratic establishments of both countries, there are those who are keen to break the deadlock in the official dialogue and allow the non-official and peoples' initiatives to take place, so that an atmosphere conducive to more flexible policy options at the State-to-State level is created.

Within the cluster of non-official and people-to-people dialogues are seminars and workshops for the establishment of bilateral and regional linkages between academic and sectoral institutions – women's groups, environmentalists, lawyers, labour unions, cultural groups, old boys/girls networks, school and college exchange programmes and mass-based joint peoples' organisations.

At one end are the non-official, classic Track Two initiatives concerned with conflict resolution and defusing tensions. They involve selected groups of retired civil servants, eminent academics and journalists who informally interact with policy makers. It constitutes a parallel track to the official dialogue, providing a discreet forum for testing alternative policy options that could then become the basis for State-to-State diplomatic initiatives. They help to prepare public opinion for changes in State policy.[48]

At the other end are the socially broad-based people-to-people dialogues that try to foster new constituencies for change by reaching out to networks of trade unions, grass-roots activists, women's organisations and environmental and cultural groups. The agenda is a political and transformative one that questions the costs of the politics of confrontation and intolerance in terms of the militarisation of civil society and the undermining of democracy. To them, the process of the dialogue itself is of value as an assertion of civil society.

Neemrana and Track Two Initiatives

Inspired by the impact of the 'Track Two' diplomacy on conflict resolution between the US and the Soviet Union and on the Middle East peace process, American institutions organised a series of seminars and workshops to promote conflict resolution in the sub-continent. Against the sharp deterioration in the official relationship, the need to open up non-official channels to pave the way for defusing tensions was acutely felt. In the American perception, the dangerous drift towards war, furthermore a nuclear war, made it all the more urgent to encourage influential citizens in India and Pakistan to design and popularise a nuclear restraint regime. However, it was soon evident that the nuclear issue could not be separated from the India–Pakistan adversarial relationship as long as Kashmir was its epicentre.[49]

The most prominent effort was the Neemrana Dialogue launched in 1991 at Neemrana, a picturesque fort in Rajasthan. The initiative brought together former diplomats, military personnel, academics and journalists from both countries into a structure of regular seminars moderated by Paul Kreisberg, a former American diplomat. About twelve rounds of discussion were held around the themes of conventional arms race, nuclear proliferation, Kashmir and economic relations, and a joint policy paper on Kashmir was presented to the two governments. The process itself was an important exercise in that former policy-makers were exposed to each other, some of them for the first time. But with no formal mechanism for reporting back to the two governments, the interface between the Track One (governmental) and Track Two processes was dependent on personal and informal contacts.

Hampering the Track Two process is that there is no 'revolving door' concept in the sub-continent, as there is in the US, with academics, journalists and officials shifting in and out of government. Foreign and security policies are the jealously guarded preserves of a closed bureaucracy, with access to information a privilege and not a right. While the governments have supported the holding of the Neemrana dialogue by facilitating visas, the ability of Track Two channels to make an impact on policy makers is limited. Moreover, US sponsorship of these Track Two initiatives raises questions over the neutrality of the agenda. Funding, too, remains a highly controversial issue in these initiatives.

The United States Information Service (USIS) has also sponsored a series of workshops on conflict resolution, conducted by Dr. Harold Saunders, who had been involved in the US-facilitated Israeli-Palestinian peace talks at Camp David. In 1993 and 1994, the US Institute of Peace organised two workshops on the Kashmir issue conducted by Dr. Saunders. Decision makers and activists from Pakistan and India were brought face to face with Kashmiris from both sides of the LoC to discuss conflict resolution on Kashmir. In addition, the USIS sponsored a series of travelling seminars in India and Pakistan. Moderated by an American, this Track Two initiative in conflict resolution brought together eminent academics and journalists. The process provided for freewheeling discussions on how to build bridges. These town hall meetings provided for a wider exposure of groups used to closed-door meetings. Also active is the Ford Foundation-supported South Asia Dialogue series patterned on the Pugwash conference of scientists for nuclear disarmament. Structured around annual meetings between policy-making and academic elites, the sessions focus on confidence building and conflict resolution, human rights and economic reforms.

More recently, European organisations like Friedrich Naumann Stiftung have become active in promoting Track Two processes like the

Initiative for Peace and Conflict Resolution. The plenary meet was held in 1995 in Strasbourg. The core group of the Initiative is committed to drafting a South Asian Peace Charter and organising parallel summits.

Bilateral and regional initiatives have been reinforcing each other in the emergence of non-official channels of communication like the Coalition for Action of South Asian Cooperation. The regional consultations organised by the Kathmandu-based South Asia Forum for Human Rights (SAFHR) have become catalysts for generating networks of cross-border constituencies to develop a cooperative framework for addressing the issues of refugees, minorities and black laws, which provide legal sanction for the suspension of constitutional rights and liberties.[50] The Delhi-based South Asia Human Rights Documentation Centre, the Bombay-based Centre for Peace Initiatives and the Karachi-based Pakistan Peace Coalition are also active.

The bilateral, inter-elite dialogues sponsored by the Rajiv Gandhi Institute for Contemporary Studies (RGICS) promote a shared perspective from which to examine contentious issues. The RGICS India–Pakistan dialogue has focussed on human security and economic cooperation, arguing that the two countries should go ahead and improve relations without waiting for a final resolution of contentious issues like Kashmir or the nuclear and missile race.

The more official relationships have deteriorated, the more third party-sponsored Track Two initiatives have mushroomed. But the lack of mutual trust between Indians and Pakistanis has constrained these inter-elite dialogues. A study of the Track Two dialogues by Navneeta C. Behra, Paul M. Evans and Gowhar Rizvi in *Beyond Boundaries: A Report on the State of the Non-Official Dialogue on Peace, Security and Cooperation in South Asia* found that both sides seemed to feel that their counterparts had less ability to deviate from the official position.[51] Moreover, the study felt that the Track Two channels largely involved the elites, who in any case had a vested interest in sustaining the structure of power underpinned by the political myths of negative identity and confrontation. In spite of this, the very process of interaction revealed the existence of pluralistic positions on even such contentious issues as Kashmir and the armed forces. These dialogues have been important in bringing into the open a more variegated debate on national security, exploring more flexible policy options like freezing the status quo along the LoC. In a book recently published in Pakistan, Professor Nasir Ahmed Shawl, while rejecting the LoC freeze proposal, states that "if any other division proposal is advanced keeping in view the interests of Kashmiris, it would be considered".[52]

The Track Two dialogues, both home-grown and sponsored, have provided channels for the exploration of alternative policy options and to build up pressure on the two governments to review their rigid positions. Its impact on policy makers has been limited, given the high levels of tension and mutual mistrust. Still, they have helped to reshape public opinion, to make it possible for political leaders to don the cloak of statesmanship and talk the language of reconciliation with honour.

People-to-People Initiatives

The peoples' track, or initiatives like the Pakistan–India Peoples Forum for Peace and Democracy, are inspired by a vision of building cross-border democracy. By drawing in representatives of mass-based organisations, women's groups, environmentalists, trade unions, professionals, human rights activists, artists and professionals, the PIPFPD seeks to foster new constituencies (beyond the inter-elite security dialogue) capable of reordering national and regional priorities.

Halfway between the Track Two inter-elite dialogue and the PIPFPD is the activity of the Peoples of Asia Forum. The core group consists of eleven Indian and eleven Pakistani academics and activists who subscribe to the basic principle that India's, and Pakistan's, territorial integrity be respected and that Hindu–Muslim and India–Pakistan relations be dealt with as separate issues. The group's activity includes an objective study of the Kashmir dispute to create a better-informed public and a study of the factual distortions in the writing of history. Its more public activities have included the co-sponsorship of an initiative for India and Pakistan to jointly celebrate the fiftieth anniversary of independence both in India and in Pakistan. That effort, however, proved abortive.

The Pakistan–India Peoples' Forum for Peace and Democracy is the most ambitious of the region's initiatives for people to empower themselves. The catalyst for this movement was the Human Rights Conference in Vienna. When jingoistic hysteria was at its peak in the two countries in 1993, and India and Pakistan were battling it out in Vienna over Kashmir, a small group of Indian and Pakistani human rights activists were seized of the idea of initiating a mass-based joint peoples' forum. Their experience of the Vienna process had demonstrated that Indian and Pakistani NGOs had no problems working together and pursuing common concerns, while the official delegations were embarrassingly hurling jingoistic rhetoric at each other. It was to be a home-grown people-to-people dialogue that would cut through the chicanery of State-sponsored prejudice and hate.

The journey from Vienna to Lahore was taken with small, halting steps. The Pakistan–India Peoples Forum for Peace and Democracy was launched in Lahore in September 1994. A small group of Indians and Pakistanis, comprising former civil servants and politicians, academics and activists agreed that the people-to-people dialogue should be a political one that reached out to new constituencies beyond the inter-elite track. For the founders of the PIPFPD, peace was inextricably linked with fostering a movement for cross-border democracy. Confrontation had fostered militarisation of the polity and the subversion of democratic rights. The politics of cross-border enmity held hostage minority communities who were majority communities on the other side. It generated bigotry and religious intolerance within and an undying hostility across the border.

The Kashmir dispute was acknowledged as the major hurdle in India–Pakistan relations for which a democratic solution had to be found. The principles of the declaration centred around the four issues of Kashmir, demilitarisation and denuclearisation, religious tolerance and governance. They form the backbone of the PIPFPD.

Their proposal, that a hundred Pakistanis and a hundred Indians could come together in New Delhi, was met with open incredulity. The official dialogue at that point in time had virtually broken down, and Prime Minister Benazir Bhutto had ordered the closure of the Indian consulate in Karachi. In such an atmosphere, visas would surely not be issued. But surprisingly, good sense prevailed and non-reporting visas were issued. Despite a negative campaign in the Pakistani media warning against a "sell out" to India, nearly one hundred Pakistanis came to India. The first ever mass-meeting of citizens of India and Pakistan was held in February 1995. There was a definite consciousness among the people present that they were making history. For most, it was their first opportunity to talk to one another and discover that the areas of agreement were more than the areas of disagreement, even on such contentious issues as Kashmir.[53]

It took courage for these two hundred people in New Delhi to ignore such pronouncements of the State orthodoxies as "Kashmir is an integral part of India", or, "Kashmir [is] Pakistan's jugular vein" and listen to each other instead. They were able to agree that Kashmir was not merely a territorial dispute between India and Pakistan and that a democratic solution required the involvement of the people of Jammu and Kashmir on both sides of the border.

The successive joint conventions in Lahore, Calcutta and Peshawar have demonstrated that the initiative can be sustained. Its spread to Calcutta and Peshawar showed that the PIPFPD's roots were spreading beyond

New Delhi and Lahore. In the Calcutta convention in December 1996, the objective was not only to double the number of delegates but to have the Pakistanis come to India over land. Of the 165 Pakistani citizens who came, 145 came by road and rail, a symbolic gesture to persuade the two governments to review the border policy on closed roads. The running theme of the PIPFPD is that people-to-people contacts will pull down the walls of prejudice and hate. In Calcutta, the PIPFPD made a strong plea to both governments to remove restrictions and facilitate contacts. As I. A. Rahman, the co-chairperson of the PIPFPD said, "the elite can visit by aeroplane but for the others road and rail links are blocked. The elite can telephone each other, but the poor cannot send to each other even a postcard."[54]

The Calcutta convention marked the transition of the PIPFPD from an activity in seminar rooms to a movement that took to the streets. Arm in arm, 500 Pakistanis and Indians marched down the streets of Calcutta asserting with one voice, "no to war, we want peace," and the city responded. The West Bengal chief minister had set the tone saying, "if 200 Pakistanis have the courage to come to India then the least West Bengal can do is to make them welcome".[55]

The Peshawar convention in November 1998 brought home the divergence in perspective the further one moved away from the heartland of the nationalist orthodoxies of India and Pakistan. For the 300 Indians who had journeyed by road to Peshawar, the experience highlighted the complex, multi-layered inter-connectivity in the histories of the two peoples. Their hosts were people who had been followers of Badshah Khan, or the 'Frontier Gandhi' as he is known in India, whose non-violent, secular politics were a reminder that in the years before martial law a secular tradition had flourished in the region. A journey to Peshawar brought home the shared heritage of the Gandhara Buddhist sculptures and its ruins at Taxila. At a time when both countries are busy erasing a common history, a journey through this historic countryside was a binding experience and an important political statement.

The grim fallout of the May nuclear tests by India and Pakistan spread over the Peshawar convention, instilling a sense of urgency in the PIPFPD to facilitate a process for breaking the antagonistic deadlock and signing a peace treaty. The PIPFPD's appeal for a "dignified exit" from the nuclear and missile race carried an added resonance when it came from the Indian co-chairperson, Admiral L. Ramdas. Here was a former chief of the naval staff, a man who for 45 years had been in uniform, standing up before Pakistanis and Indians in Peshawar to openly urge both governments to renounce nuclear weapons.[56]

The joint conventions of the PIPFPD are, admittedly, 'talk shops', 'travel and tours' and 'jamborees'. Nevertheless, their value is in no way lessened by being all these, for they nonetheless provide the opportunity for an ever-widening network of ordinary Indians and Pakistanis to come together and celebrate the diversity and pluralism which their governments deny. Keeping people apart is what feeds fear and prejudice. People-to-people dialogues bridge that divide and spawn uncountable offshoots, like the theme focus on Pakistan at the prestigious Calcutta Book Fair, held a couple of months after the Peshawar convention.

The PIPFPD's strength has been in the fostering of unplanned networks. In Lahore in 1995, representatives of the fishermens' unions met and agreed to work for the welfare of the fishermen and their children who were languishing in each other's jails because they had strayed across the maritime boundary. The result of their joint lobbying was that by the time of the Calcutta meet, the two governments had agreed to release the fishermen, their children and the boats. In Peshawar, a channel of communication was established between the Aurat Foundation, a Peshawar-based NGO, and the PIPFPD to rescue three minor children who had been locked up in a Pakistani jail for over three years. It eventually resulted in a campaign to free child prisoners, who are the most abject victims of the policy of denial of consular access to each other's prisoners. Four months later, in February, the three children were released.

The chapters of the PIPFPD have spread to at least nine cities in India and to almost every province in Pakistan. Funding is derived from contributions by members, the business community and Indians and Pakistanis abroad who subscribe to the concerns of the PIPFPD. The real dynamism of the PIPFPD lies in its potential to build new networks of national and cross-border constituencies capable of re-defining the governments' agendas in favour of the peoples' agenda. The Vajpayee– Sharif Lahore Declaration was preceded by another Lahore Declaration of the citizens of India and Pakistan. The peace politics of the two prime ministers were prompted by the growing community of civil society groups on both sides of the border who are committed to peace. It is the growing strength of these groups that hold out the promise of transforming the adversarial India–Pakistan relationship.

Conclusion

There is nothing essentialist in the conflict as demonstrated above by the alternative relational narrative of India and Pakistan. The dominant logic of the necessary co-existence of two neighbours make peace not only desirable but necessary. India and Pakistan have demonstrated the capacity to negotiate differences as well as the propensity to use military force. The nuclear dimension in their confrontation makes it all the more imperative to eschew the use of force. Moreover, increasing democratic pressure demands that the adversarial relationship has to be so managed as to enable the two governments to deliver on the economic and social commitments to the people. New security challenges need to be met, like those of environmental degradation, management of water resources, cross-border trafficking in drugs, arms and people, refugees and migrants. If India's weight in the international system is not to be assessed as other than 'India minus Pakistan', it will be incumbent on India to shed the albatross of confrontation for the realisation of its aspirations to become a Great Power. Above all, a new security paradigm, shaped by a non-statist human security perspective, is being articulated in the emerging people-to-people networks. These networks have the potential to not only manage, but transform, the India–Pakistan adversarial relationship.

SEVEN

Plural Dialogues

RANABIR SAMADDAR

Semantic Twist?

India and Pakistan conducted their respective ritual acts of initiation into the club of nuclear powers in May 1998. In reaction, there were the expected cries of pride, breast beating, despair and alarm. Experts assembled round many tables to think, advise and debate – should these two countries, now powers, talk bilaterally of arms control, disarmament, confidence restoration and normalisation? Many doubted if they would. Both right- and left-wing alarmists thought that, for good or bad, South Asia had given up on dialogue. When the Indian prime minister visited Lahore, however, the alarmist hype gave way to expressions of relief. But the ink on the Lahore Declaration had barely dried when cross-border shoot-outs started in the snowy heights of Kargil in the Himalayas. The very organs that had been effusive over the 'bus diplomacy'[1] to Lahore now raised doubts over its efficacy. The zig-zag of events from arms build-up, to talks, to clash of arms had, indeed, confused even the most hardened realists.

It is within this context that this essay outlines a possible approach to a dialogic situation between India and Pakistan. It does not, however, develop the argument in its entirety, but rather makes brief remarks that are more in the nature of a parenthesis. For this reason, I shall preface my submission with a thesis, which I shall then attempt to prove.

Dialogue, according to the Oxford Dictionary, is conversation; a piece of written work in conversational form; a kind of composition (sometimes in a novel); a conversational text or tract. Dialogue, thus, does not automatically suggest an improvement in relations. Though ancient wisdom tells us that to talk is to relate, to reflect, to befriend and to moderate – the antithesis, in fact, to hostility – we must qualify this in the light of our modern experiences of war, armament and disarmament. There is a violence in words: not only in the form of verbal duelling but also in the form of words that create, foster and exacerbate violence. Dialogue, thus, could crystallise and solidify violence. Therefore, I wish to dispel any notion that the relationship between India and Pakistan is rocky because there has been no dialogue: indeed, these countries talk so that they can fight; they speak of confidence-building measures because they are confident of the power of words to sustain violence. Their dialogue is the background against which they proceed to war and create artefacts of war; they then stage the next round of dialogue to pause and assess the preceding violence. Dialogue in this scenario is a part of violence. There is, therefore, a politics of dialogue – as a theorist has said, a "politics of friendship".[2] Dialogue is, then, a matter of strategy. My submissions that follow try to address this issue of strategising dialogue.

Distortions in a Given History

The history of disarmament talks in the nuclear age and among nuclear powers shows that disarmament talks are basically arms limitation talks.[3] A nuclear power cannot be disarmed; neither is there a precedence for it. The arms limitation talks that centre around conventional arms are also tied to nuclear arms. A nuclear power now cannot be disarmed in the way conventional powers were disarmed in the past, unless a power suddenly collapses; and even then, that power is not disarmed. If we are not to think in the convoluted manner in which the age of nuclear rivalry appears as a period of "long peace",[4] we have to accept the fact that nuclear rivalries produced arms limitation talks and treaties that modulate merely the pace by which nuclear armament was to proceed. The end of the cold war, which brought nuclear rivalry to a close, did not arrive as a result of the disarmament process; the end to the superpower nuclear armaments race came about as the result of a sudden collapse of a power, which, even then, did not spell total nuclear disarmament. For nuclear disarmament to be completely effective, the collapse has to be sudden, dramatic and total.

In other words, nuclear disarmament is always incremental, be it strategic or tactical. Interestingly, the notion of disarmament, subsumed as it is under the narrative of arms control, has a paradoxical nature. A doomsday spirit seems to move it. While it assumes that disarmament averts war and the final catastrophe, it simultaneously builds itself up and sustains itself by naturalising its 'incremental' nature; in other words, it reconciles itself to incremental (dis)armament. It is thus both a finite and infinite concept.[5] This paradoxical nature of disarmament is a specific historical product. Born into, and characteristic of, an age of panic, superpowerism, helplessness of smaller and weaker countries and the inexorable progress of armament, disarmament was looked upon as an imperative to avert doom. And yet, also characteristic of that age, was the fact that the disarmament experts, backed by 'nuclear politicans'· and national security lobbies, made the disarmament process an arms-limitation exercise, aimed at an incremental arms build-up, modifying the nature of arms and balancing disarmament with the growth of arms. Disarmament is thus an infinite process with a finite profile – an irreducible historical exercise. Any standard history of that era will tell us of the successive arms control measures: the Hotline Agreement (1963), the Strategic Arms Limitation Talks (SALT) I (1972), the Threshold Test Ban Treaty (1974), the never ratified SALT II (1979), the Intermediate Range Nuclear Treaty (1987), the Chemical Weapons Destruction Agreement (1990), the Strategic Arms Reduction Talks (START) (1991), the START I Protocol (1992) and START II (1993). But this history will not elucidate that this progress in arms limitation talks resulted in greater arms sales, further development of missile technology and a growing sophistication in electronic warfare. It is important to draw attention to the historicity of this discourse of disarmament, which seems to be more a mode of declaration and an announcement of promise rather than a restrictive exercise.

There is another aspect to this historicity. Apart from the inherent paradox in the concept of disarmament, there is an interesting feature to note – its secrecy. I do not mean that the narrative is secret, but rather that it is a narrative of concealment – of disarmament as much as of armament; what it hides, in fact, in terms of narration. For example, being a general discourse on arms limitation, it does not tell us that during the period of the cold war, there were other, bilateral, dialogues between the US and the USSR, West Europe and the USSR and between the two Germanys. Although these talks were also in the theatre of dialogue, the overall grand theme had dwarfed their importance. The history of dialogue thus tells us only, or mostly, of SALTs, STARTs, the Test Ban treaties and sometimes of the Helsinki Process.

Given this history of concealments, how are we to judge what position yesterday's *Ostpolitik* has in today's history of disarmament? How are we to be sure, as the cold war history would have us believe, that the stabilisation of the Polish–German border, or the velvet divorce of the two nations of erstwhile Czechoslovakia was the result of the fall of the Berlin Wall in 1989 and not a product of a polyphonic dialogue?[6] Or, how are we to rule out the possibility that the Treaties of Locarno and Rapallo, through the reworking of their own duality in today's context, may have a narrative distinct from the dominant history of the dialogue of disarmament?[7] The hegemonic discourse of dialogue has succeeded in burying events like the campaigns for peace in 1951, the Pugwash Conference of scientists for nuclear disarmament, the Campaign for Nuclear Disarmament (CND) in the 1960s and the massive demonstrations for peace in Europe and America in the 1970s and 1980s. As small steps on the road to peace they are not insignificant, but as elements of a narrative of dialogue they remain buried in the secret annals of disarmament, dialogue and normalisation. Indeed these efforts have been so submerged that it is difficult to recover them from the given narrative of disarmament, whose historicity succeeds in placing other dialogues in a 'prehistoric' framework.

For the countries that are countries by virtue of being powers, there is no freedom, then, from the imperative of developing the artefacts of nuclear politics, rivalry and weaponry; nor is there freedom from the subsequent disarmament talks that can only be arms-control talks. Freedom from this causality will amount to 'opting out' of global compulsions and behaving 'locally'; to be obliged to then claim a history of other relations and other dialogues.[8] In short, we have here a case of finite history that admits of many histories of disarmament and dialogue.

The relationship between Pakistan and India after the nuclear tests of May 1998, that include such events as the Lahore Talks, will now become part of the master discourse of dialogue that I have outlined. In this scenario, it is hardly necessary to judge whether relations will improve one way or another; any predictions with regard to this are equally banal. Of course, relations between the two countries may improve; certainly they may talk, decide to talk, produce papers to categorise these as non-papers and non-papers to eventually come out with papers; they may meet to decide the modalities of meeting anew. They can also strut and posture, and say that though they have nuclear warheads, rockets, missiles, bombs and computer simulations demonstrating the blasts of real bombs and delivery systems of real missiles, they would instead parley, and not unleash what these simulations so graphically illustrate. If they do not have a doctrine, they will sit down to formulate one, so that they can then claim that the doctrine is ultimately to prevent the implementation of any other doctrine of use. Finally, they can say that they interacted so that they could prepare meanwhile for 'the day after'.[9] This is the indeterminacy indicated by that misleading phrase 'nuclear option'. To say that with one nuclear test a country exercises that option would be inaccurate. The question of option surfaces not only in the form of choice: to weaponise or not; to weaponise, but to what extent; and whether to rely on a system of weaponised or non-weaponised deterrence. Further, the option is how to test these weapons, and to what degree; to sell the technology and/or the weapons or not; and finally, of course, whether or not to use the weapons. But the question of option does not end even here. For example, in the case of India, should these issues be linked with Kashmir, as some politicians in the sub-continent think? Should these issues be limited to a conventional arms build-up? Be conclusive with an overall settlement? And so on, ad infinitum.[10]

Such a scenario is based on the historical precedents of arms-tension-talks-Confidence Building Measures (CBMs)-reduction-balance-confidence-arms-tension-talks cycles. Thus, improvements and deteriorations in situations are inevitable and predictable. This is an incremental scenario; there is little possibility of a sudden collapse of one combatant, and therefore the withdrawal of one adversary, from the scene. The only historical example we have of such a caving-in was not a military collapse, nor even a technological collapse, but a political one. This collapse, though, was unanticipated and dramatic, not incremental. A similar template of attrition and incremental advance is applicable to, and will continue in, South Asia also. Indeed, from the viewpoint of utility, this scenario is a must for the nuclear politicians, the new power elite, the national security estate, and for the scholars who live off the discipline of strategic studies. But the interesting aspect is that the process of dialogue on arms control, arms reduction, disarmament, Kashmir – in fact, everything that is indicated by the word 'normalisation' – will also take on the pattern of a hegemonic narrative. Thus, the history of India–Pakistan relations will appear as one of an endless round of discussions by secretaries, ministers and prime ministers, and we may be pardoned for not remembering the number of their meetings.[11] If the Simla Agreement in July 1972 established bilateralism as a principle of conflict management, we do not know which major conflict in particular was resolved through it. Pakistan may have secured the release of its prisoners of war, and India may have succeeded in persuading Pakistan to accept the existing Line of Control (LoC) as sacrosanct and in relying on bilateral discussions for a solution to the Kashmir problem. It can be argued that by establishing the principle of bilateralism, India won in the long run; but it could equally be argued that Pakistan won substantively, despite being the weaker party, by gainfully using the timing of the negotiations and the existing international opinion to its advantage.[12] The Simla Agreement may thus offer us lessons in negotiating styles and their effectiveness; for example, the 'high context' approach (declared intentions of maximum nature but readiness to settle for incommensurate results) as opposed to the 'low context' approach (minimum declaration of intentions accompanied by a very real desire to achieve targets reasonably determined), both of which are important lessons in diplomatic history.[13] But apart from this, the received history of dialogue has little to offer in terms of the more mundane need for peace in the region. In fact, the existence of other dialogues (which I will write of later) tends to get buried by this received narrative. Just as other histories of disarmament and coexistence lie buried in the master history of arms-control talks, so also other dialogues for coexistence and their documentation lie hidden in this received narrative.

A Question of Language

The language and mode of dialogue is thus no less important than the content and theme. As an example, I can cite the instance of the official dialogue in October 1998 between India and Pakistan that had, expectedly, failed. The instance supports my argument that the problem is not that these two countries do not talk among themselves, but that the structure of their dialogue, the dialogists' mode, is at fault. How, for instance, are the 'soft' issues and the 'hard' issues to be managed – first one then the other, or the reverse, or concurrently? Then again, how can these countries reconsider the structure of their dialogue, when a very senior leader in power in India set a hostile pre-dialogue tone by branding Pakistan a "terrorist" State, and the Pakistani ministers in Islamabad responded in equal measure? It is no surprise, then, that leave alone the hard issues of terrorism or arms control, even soft issues like Sir Creek and the Tulbul Navigation Project/Wular Barrage defied solution in this round of talks.[14] Pakistan was unwilling to talk with any kind of commitment if the agenda did not include, definitively, the 'core issue' of Kashmir. Equally noticeably, India's attitude was neither open nor flexible. In essence, the Tulbul Navigation Project/Wular Barrage question was a simple trade-off: India would adhere strictly to the 1960 Indus Waters Treaty, and not impound any waters (as planned under the Kishenganga Hydroelectric Project), and Pakistan would in turn accept India's assurances that the barrage would not reduce the inflow of water to the Jhelum river flowing into Pakistani territory. Neither offered this trade-off. The talks collapsed, setting the tone for a dialogue of the deaf – a sure recipe for failure.

This failure became obvious with the continuing inability of both countries to reach an agreement on the Siachen Glacier. Siachen has come to symbolise the world's most strategically absurd high-altitude war, fought over a non-demarcated border beyond a point known as NJ-9842. Battle is being waged at elevations exceeding 6,000 metres, and costs India three men and Rs. 5 crores (Rs. 50,000,000) a day, with thousands of soldiers being exposed to frostbite, hypoxia and severe mental stress. Siachen, contrary to starry-eyed journalists and defence reporters, is proof not of anyone's bravery, but of the expendability and low value of Indian and Pakistani lives. India's assertions that Pakistan had always planned to occupy the area were countered by Pakistani claims that the LoC actually ran further east, to the Karakoram Pass, and that they had always been in occupation of this area. Given that the extension of the LoC was unilateral, as was India's decision to airlift soldiers and thus militarise the dispute, the bilateralism of the Simla Agreement was of no value, notwithstanding the five rounds of talks between 1986 and 1989. When at one point it looked as if an agreement seemed possible after the fifth round of talks in 1989, it was inexplicably repudiated. It is probable that with Hindutva passions on the up over the Babri Masjid demolition issue in India on the one hand, and the surge in sentiments over Kashmir in Pakistan on the other, neither India nor Pakistan wanted to take the 'risk' of appearing to 'capitulate' to the other.

As a result, none of the participating government secretaries, military experts and advisers could propose any firm measure to reduce tensions between the two countries. Nor could the political leadership of the two countries resolve to take sensible steps towards the withdrawal of the unilateral extension of the LoC; establishment of a demilitarised zone; joint delimitation of a line from NJ-9842 northwards to the border with China; formulation of ground rules to govern future operations; and finally, redeployment of forces to mutually agreed positions. Instead, only a cease-fire, prior to talks on other 'modalities', was proposed. In effect, this meant that the Indian government was not willing to compromise on the advantage of having its troops at elevations 2,000 feet above the Pakistani entrenchments on the Saltoro Ridge, no matter what the cost and how little the strategic advantage of such a position. This reaction is a classic example of a free-for-all dialogue in which any subject under discussion gets instantly connected to 'national security'. To these two negotiating parties nothing seems to constitute 'unacceptable damage', and therefore there can be no question of arriving at a solution to avoid it. The Siachen impasse shows that this assumption is self-defeating; that the language based on this assumption is potent enough to create a gridlock, and thus, as conflict-resolution language, is totally ineffective.[15] It is an over-powering dialogue, aimed at thwarting other dialogues. Its objective is to convince the citizens of the two countries that grave security concerns cannot allow for any other mode or occasion for talks, or any other party to participate in the talks. Such is the hegemonic discourse of dialogue that succeeds in 'naturalising' the imperative for one strategy as the driving force for others, for all time, in every way.

The aim of dialogue here seems to be to establish "relational control", which, according to one expert, aims to establish an influence over the structure of interaction between the interlocutors, in order to have the capacity to set the "rules of the game" in conflict and cooperation. Such a strategy aims at being able to exercise a degree of control over the actions of a neighbour in order to control the consequences flowing from such actions. Its purpose is also to enable a country to have a degree of leverage over the cultural orientation of "near abroad".[16] In a dialogue guided by such a concept, the aim is to prevent the multiplication of talks, to see that they do not stray beyond the charted brief and to set the agenda in such a way that dialogue becomes a tool of power, hegemony and total control. Dialogue then becomes a watchdog, rather than an exchange, of ideas. By embracing unilateralism, dialogue then becomes a unidirectional quest for power, a mode of gaining direct behavioural control, not only of the neighbouring State, but of non-State actors such as oppositional groups and insurgent forces within the country, where their existence impinges on the structure of a relationship.

India's first prime minister, Jawaharlal Nehru, was always sagacious in these matters. On 14 August 1962 he told the Indian Parliament that, "There is a world of difference between negotiations and talks; a world of difference. One should always talk, whatever happens, whatever the position and whatever the chances. If I have the chance to talk, I will talk to [the Chinese]. It is quite absurd not to talk. . .talking must be encouraged whenever possible. Negotiation is a very formal thing; it requires a very suitable background, it should not be taken up unless a suitable background comes . . . . Talking is an entirely different thing."[17] If his successors, and their counterparts in Pakistan, have not displayed the same wisdom, they have nonetheless practised the dictum. There is nothing to lose in talking, so they talk, but they do not negotiate; that is serious business. Thus one cannot expect anything "substantial . . . out of a discussion of [the] Kashmir issue on [an] official level. The only possibility is noting down various lines of approach without commitment."[18] That style and philosophy of dialogue continues even after fifty-five years of partition. The dialogue of 15–18 October 1998 was the most recent instance, where all that the two parties could agree on was to talk again in February 1999. When talks at the level of the foreign ministry officials fail, as they invariably do, it is always up to the two prime ministers to resolve the deadlock through political initiatives. Hierarchies in levels of dialogue are also a part of the structure of the dialogue under discussion. The officials must meet so that the leaders can meet, but these officials can accomplish little, since they know that rules, procedures, outlines and drafts are all meaningless (or perhaps meaningful), as their role is simply to stymie their counterparts. In an endless merry-go-round, the leaders meet so that their officials can meet subsequently. The length to which this charade is played is absurd: in January 1998 at Dhaka in Bangladesh, for example, the then Indian prime minister I. K. Gujral had proposed that all the eight subjects for which working groups were to be formed should be discussed simultaneously to avoid the slightest emphasis on Kashmir. Pakistan picked up on the trick and reciprocated amply by stressing that without a discussion on Kashmir no other discussion would take place. This manoeuvre clearly demonstrated the irreconcilable dialoguing strategies of the two countries: on the one hand, talk, discuss and try to settle any other issue except Kashmir on the one hand, and if there is no talk, discussion and settlement on Kashmir, there is going to be no talk on anything else on the other. The nuclear weapons question is now a part of this master plan: to pass off unilateralism in the name of consultation, and to naturalise the strategy of relational control. To talk is to dialogue, to relate and ultimately to control by domination. This leads us now to the other meaning of dialogue, which has not yet been discussed, namely, "a form of composition, a conversational text (in a novel or play)". Dialogue in a play is memorised and delivered; it is an accessory to the part of an actor. This definition amply illustrates the unilateralism embodied in the word dialogue. The point to note is that the second meaning hides itself behind the first, which succeeds in naturalising the word.

But there remain other complexities beyond this hegemonic narrative of dialogue. A companion essay by Rita Manchanda in this volume analyses the multiple trajectories of the India–Pakistan dialogues. The essay shows how India and Pakistan have been involved in not just one stream of dialogue but many – sometimes successive, sometimes alternate, sometimes concurrent; how the themes for these dialogues have remained the same and how they have changed; as well as their dynamics, architecture, forms, impact and agencies. The essay not only draws our attention to the divergent trajectories of the themes, but more importantly, to the divergent trajectories of their agencies. Thus we have a revealing profile before us of who argues for dialogue with whom and when; at what stage do governments tire out; when do the civil-liberty activists, cultural activists and various non-governmental organisations move in; when do the professionals start dialoguing; at what point do the respective journalists take upon themselves the task of getting to know each other; when does the public at large join in; and when do businessmen at last start showing an interest in peace. By tabulating the relative fortunes of these themes in terms of the attention paid to them and their duration, the essay highlights the myriad aspects of this subject.

Finally, there is the interest of the world community in normalisation and peace in this region. Their efforts towards this end are focussed on the sponsoring of unofficial dialogues, non-official backing of official dialogues and official patronage of unofficial dialogues, as well as dialogues at international forums, shuttle dialogues, secret dialogues and dialogues promoted by others. These efforts are necessary, since normalcy in this nuclear age is rarely achieved by internal efforts alone, and peace even less. Normalcy is 'restored', peace is 'restored' or 'waged' – as these words signify, this can only be done from the outside. The well-known studies of external linkages to internal conflicts, and internal repercussions of external conflicts remain enmeshed in the mindset of the pre-globalisation days (examples of which are the conflict in the Chittagong Hill Tract in northeast India, the Kashmir dispute, the Tamil separatist issue in Sri Lanka and the Baluch demand for secession from Pakistan, among others.) They ignore the fact that 'externalities' and 'internalities' are only relative terms. With the rise of the 'region' as the crucial intermediary layer between the 'world' and the 'country', we can look back and say that, only in the enveloping milieu of post–colonial State formation did we think of them as internal or external; today, however, they are issues of the region.[19] Apart from this, we can see that such a 'restoration' of normalcy or peace is linked, as conflict studies show, to a restoration of constitution, of a State, of politics, 'normal' politics and even, in extreme cases, of 'civil society', so that dialogues can commence under this all-encompassing canopy. An amusing scenario? Certainly not, though a ludicrous one. In short, a situation that invites the perennial enforcement of all desirable things from the outside, and that too, never dramatically: hesitant and cautious beginnings are inevitably followed by long drawn-out endings. Peacekeepers in the contentious regions of the world, for example, may become fatigued by their work, but, by the very fact of their involvement, have to continue to promote peace-seeking dialogues. The situation is akin to riding a tiger, with no hope of disengament and no conceivable end in sight. The issues discussed above thus illustrate the wide, incremental nature of dialogue.

Plurality of Dialogue

Since this perspective of the structurally incremental nature of dialogue is crucial to an understanding of the future prospects of relations between India and Pakistan, I wish to draw attention to the obvious conclusion: that dialogue is essentially a plural process, and hence, to be of any effect whatsoever, must be converted into a multilogue. The structure of a multilogue draws its strength from the phenomena of the pluralities of dialogists and dialogic modes and themes. It is free, disengaged from the hegemony of a narrative of dialogue that concentrates on arms parity, deterrence, reduction of weapons of mass murder, meetings of the security lobbies, security conferences of ministers, generals, think-tanks and various foundations for strategic studies. That the Organisation of Security and Cooperation in Europe (OSCE), which is the apex forum of dialogues on security and cooperation in that region, could not prevent the catastrophe in Bosnia or the Balkan crisis as a whole is a testimony to the failure of hegemonic dialogue. The OSCE is centralising; the structural constraints of the Helsinki Process do not allow it to be concerned with the general prerogatives of peace and human rights except in a marginal way. Again, its structure has little proactive role *vis-à-vis* the peace requirements of the continent, for its concern is with a security that has almost nothing to do with peace. Therefore, such consultations as are held under its auspices always suffer from what one observer has termed "security delusion".[20]

In South Asia, the structure of consultations over security is even more stultifying: there is no room for pluralism in the bilateralism and multilateralism of the South Asian Association for Regional Cooperation (SAARC) process. Important constituents such as peace and human rights are given scant attention within this organsiation. Peace in region, therefore, can only be fragile, being a by-product of these consultations, and not an end in itself. A fragile peace, we are told, is due to the fundamental "asymmetries of power", and thus peace is bound to be "elusive".[21] An equally possible reason, however, could be that democratisation of the consultative process is tedious and shorn of the glamour and high profile of nuclear diplomacy, and therefore seemingly unattractive in some quarters. But by dealing with pluralist streams of dialogue, peace politics can aim at involving the constituencies of human rights and democracy; peace built on such a foundation is bound to be more durable. Such a dialogue holds no promise of radical breakthroughs, but remains convinced of the need to link security with peace. It is frankly non-statist in its fundamentals. It is avowedly dialogic both within a country and in its external relations, and remains convinced of the need for dialogue between the internal and the external. Thus we come to the other significant element in plural dialogues, namely, transparency.

In essence, multilogue implies acknowledgement of plurality and transparency. In this context, it may be fruitful to refer to the specific experiences of dialogues hosted by Pakistan–India Peoples Forum for Peace and Democracy (PIPFPD). The PIPFPD deals with the questions that it considers central to an interlinked-issue format, namely (a) demilitarisation, denuclearisation and peace, (b) promotion of tolerance and protection of minorities, (c) governance and democracy and finally, (d) the Kashmir imbroglio. The PIPFPD has thus opted for a 'clubbing together' of the central issues. This linkage can be sustained only on the basis of transparency, consensus, and recognition of the fact that the will of the people is essential for the solution of hard issues that include, above all others, nuclear weapons and Kashmir. The political truth quite simply is, then, that the constituents of democracy and peace are interrelated, though not identical. The clubbing method goes further: it draws on the resources and goodwill of the vast sub-continental diaspora – not the wealthy Non-Resident Indians (NRIs) and Non-Resident Pakistanis (NRPs) but the working class. This distinction is important, for in their faraway lands the latter display little or none of the jingoism evident within the region, while remaining very much an organic part of the sub-continental population. They retain their pre-partition social links, thrive on reflexivity and remain in a mentality of exile; in short, they are the perfect material for bridge-building between the two nations. How has the PIPFPD been able to use this critical mass to its best advantage? One reason for its success is that the PIPFPD is more of an umbrella organisation, where people working towards peace gather of their own volition. The PIPFPD is thus not a homogeneous group, but is composed of several associations whose concerns and agendas vary. It is not so much a coherent organisation as a movement; this ensures its transparency and its polyphonic character. It is possible that in an assembly of hard-nosed realists the PIPFPD sounds almost like an anarchist charter; but what it offers here is an alternative: a choice between a primarily statist approach, and a citizens' approach. Since neither are stand-alones, it is possible to find ways to link the two; how the basic mapping of this interaction is perceived is, however, fundamental.

This issue can be taken even further, as for instance, the concern over demilitarisation, which includes the issue of nuclear risk-reduction measures in this region. While India, Pakistan and China have decided on a variety of confidence-building measures over the past decade, their implementation has remained tardy. Nuclear risk-reduction efforts call for a serious consideration of new, security-related measures directed at the likely causes of miscalculation and nuclear accidents on the sub-continent. Since the origin of the nuclear programme in the region is complex, the non-deployment of missiles, along with associated nuclear risk-reduction measures, offer the best prospects for nuclear safety. But the missile programme is based on sustained hostility between India and Pakistan; therefore, one obvious solution will be to increase transparency in the various measures. It is vitally important to ensure frequent communications between regional commanders along the Line of Control, reduction of cross-border infiltration and prevention of artillery firing with consequent loss of life, all of which can be based on a phased demilitarisation of the border. These can be coupled with alternative 'open skies' arrangements for the sub-continent, which means that monitoring the build-up of conventional forces may be as important as keeping watch on the deployment of ballistic missiles. There can be other steps, like a reduction of the defence budget by, say, twenty-five per cent over three years, a treaty over fission material, a Memorandum of Understanding (MoU) over non-proliferation of nuclear weapons, an agreement for the presence of mutual observers at military exercises and a public scrutiny of the business of defence. These steps are only possible if they are based on a commitment to transparency in dealings. The nuclear question is then part of the larger politics of dialogue in the sub-continent.[22]

Besides demilitarisation, the issues of tolerance, protection of minorities and governance are crucial in their import for trans-border tranquillity. There is enough in the inadequacies of past enactments, institutional experiences and records of agreements, like the ones between Liaquat Ali Khan and Jawaharlal Nehru (in 1948 and 1950), to critique. But there are also positive experiences which can, and should, be shared: India's record of gradual decentralisation; the restoration of civil liberties through vigourous civil resistance after any autocratic swings in polity; the strength of small producers and the small-scale sector in the economy; the alternative tradition of tolerance; and the scientific, technical and intellectual resources of the country. On its part, Pakistan's entrenched power elites are meeting opposition from peoples' organisations such as the Pakistani chapters of the PIPFPD, the Human Rights Commission of Pakistan and the Pakistan Coalition for Peace. These can have a bearing on dialogue: they can make it cooperative, positive and proactive, not adversarial, negative and preventive. This is particularly applicable to the issue of Kashmir, where discussions, consultations and dialogue, in effect, demilitarisation, remains the precondition for any hope of settlement. The PIPFPD offers a platform on which civil liberty activists collaborate with retired admirals and generals; trade unionists with representatives of chambers of commerce; lawyers, jurists and intellectuals with ex-bureaucrats; journalists with professors; pacifists with militants; and hardened political activists with do-good liberals.

A Culture of Dialogue, A Dialogue of Cultures

Readers of this essay will notice that, while commencing with the culture of dialogue, I have almost unwillingly concluded with a suggestion for a dialogue of cultures. Absolute categorisations, obsessions and 'hate speeches' are all born out of misunderstanding and mutual hostility. Can such a situation produce reconciliation, let alone peace, among two warring countries? Is such a thing possible after the massacres of 1947, four wars, regular acts of frenzy and destruction and the constant rationalisations of these violent acts? A forum of citizens for trans-border dialogue, as I see it, cannot hope for any immediate success. The reports of governmental dialogues invalidate all the official claims to reconciliation, security and peace. The only alternative lies, therefore, in the "goodness of the collective soul", what one calls a "little kindness", which is invincible: a gesture selflessly given, with no expectations in return. One's own responsibility towards one's own kind is "a spirituality whose future is unknown".[23] Under these circumstance, then, any sceptical questioning of the success of such a tenuous process has no meaning and no relevance.

I end by referring to that extraordinary study by a group of five researchers on the Operation Brasstacks military exercise conducted by India. They have mapped out a complete history of such an exercise: how a crisis originates, the incoherence in its responses, lessons in crisis management, policy conclusions and other relevant matters.[24] I am attracted, however, to another aspect present throughout the study – communication between the two countries, or the lack thereof, which resulted in the commencement of an encounter in the form of a dialogue of arms, only to revert, once again, to the dialogue of speech. Particularly applicable are the appendices the authors provide, especially "A Chronology of Cooperation 1947–1995" and "Brasstacks and Its Antecedents". By reading them together, by transposing one onto another, it is clear that the chronology, which appears as a sequence, is actually an overlapping narration, that is to say, one event not only follows the previous one in chronological order, but also causes and influences the other, reinvents itself in the form of the other. To my mind, the two series captioned above are simultaneous acts, though this idea seems impossible at first. Perhaps one could call this the chiaroscuro effect, for half-revelations are precisely the effects of a chronology, of a master narrative.

Dialoguing, then, is an act. It has its architecture, its poetics and its politics. We must read into its language, rhetoric, power and history. If one can remain aware of these aspects of dialogue, one can act appropriately: have a dialogue for peace and peaceableness for dialogue.

EIGHT

State in the Revision of Space and History Today

RANABIR SAMADDAR

The Compulsion of Representation: Short Wars or Long Peace?

In 1985, impressed by the elements of stability in the post–war international system, John Lewis Gaddis, an eminent historian of the cold war, called this the period of the "long peace". In an interesting essay, he argued that although the peacemakers fell out among themselves immediately after the Second World War, and built up an almost unprecedented stock of weapons of destruction to keep each other in check, there was at least no war among them. Without a formal treaty, the world had been at relative peace since 1945. Even though small, localised wars, hunger, pestilence, deprivation and domination remained and continued to characterise the world, there were no hostilities like the two world wars. Although nothing survived of the wartime affability and cooperation between the Great Powers, they had withheld the use of their guns against each other. The post–war settlement survived "twice as long as the far more carefully designed World War I settlement, has approximately equalled in longevity the great ninteenth-century international systems of Metternich and Bismarck, and unlike those earlier systems, after four decades of existence, shows no perceptible signs of disintegration. It is, or ought to be, enough to make one think."[1]

Gaddis, in fact, did not leave it to the readers to "think". With a flourish he concluded the essay with these words,

> The Cold war, with all of its rivalries, anxieties and unquestionable dangers, has produced the longest period of stability in relations among great powers that the world has known in this century; it now compares favourably as well with some of the longest periods of great power stability in all of modern history. We may argue among ourselves as to whether or

not we can legitimately call this "peace": it is not, I daresay, what most of us have in mind when we use that term. But I am not at all certain that the contemporaries of Metternich and Bismarck would have regarded their eras as "peaceful" either, even though historians looking back on those eras today clearly do.

What is to say therefore, how the historians a century from now – if there are any left by then – will look back on us? Is it not at least plausible that they will see our era, not as "the Cold War" at all, but like those ages of Metternich and Bismarck, as a rare and fondly remembered "Long Peace"? Wishful thinking? Speculation through a rose-tinted wordprocessor? Perhaps. But would it not behove us to give at least as much attention to the question of how this might happen – to the elements in the contemporary international system that might make it happen – as we do to the fear that it may not?[2]

This is clearly a Hobbesian argument: the prospect of total war would maintain peace, since people would realise that such a war would destroy everybody. Evidently written in the age of a Thatcherite belief in 'deterrence as peace', detente and Strategic Arms Limitation Talks (SALT) talks (which held that a mutual acknowledgement of the respective strengths and influence of the two superpowers held the key to peace and a working relationship), *cold war* in an argument like this transformed into *long peace*. Yet there will be no dearth of historians in another ten years who will tell us contrarily that peace began with the end of the cold war. At the end of the Second World War Winston Churchill said that peace had returned to Europe with the end of what he called the "second Thirty Years War" – roughly the period between, and including, both the World Wars. It seems that definitions such as war and peace can be juggled not only within a single time-frame but also within the framework of a single incident. All that we need to do is to use these two terms interchangeably, depending on which point in the past we define for ourselves as a starting position.

But what happens to those for whom there is no 'world' in their history, whose conflicts are 'local' and relegated by geopolitics to the 'rim' of world affairs? Those who were ravaged by wars in Biafra in Africa, the Gulf and Vietnam? Those who are constantly engaged in fending off "insurgency crossfires"?[3] It seems that world history has not taken cognisance of these peoples and regions, for their wars did not feature in a world conflagration, the latest weapons were not used, international interventionist armies were not despatched, axes, alliances, dual and triple ententes were not formed, and the 'virtual transparency' in international diplomacy ruled out intrigues and made humanity return to the barbaric wars of the old ages.[4]

Are we then to conclude that "long peace" is made up of short wars, a reformulation of the old Clausewitzian argument that peace is the condition of war?[5] It is true that the end of the cold war has created a paradigm shift in international relations, but if we cannot hold on any more to a balance-mechanism-dominated world system as the explanatory device for today's wars and peace settlements, what are we to fall back on?

This essay is on the problem of war and peace in the context of globalisation. For those who are not privileged to be participants in world wars, and are consequently left out of world history for the most part, the problem of war and peace requires to be defined differently; the received definitions, unfortunately, do not have much to offer to this group.

The short wars of the last fifty years have had world-wide consequences, particularly so after the restoration of liberal democracy in 1989. Yet the historiography of these conflicts in the period of the cold war does not attach much importance to these short wars, not because they did not cause huge losses in lives and resources, but because they were thought to have had little effect on the pattern of superpower domination and rivalry, arms build-up, disarmament negotiations and alliance configurations. Therefore, these conflicts are represented only as footnotes in the main body of post–war history, which is preoccupied with the 'larger' issues of the balance of power and the systemic compulsions of holding the peace, howsoever precariously. 'Little' wars thus remain bound to be represented in another image; not surprisingly, they are considered mere reflections in the mirror of the 'bigger' wars engaged in by the Great Powers.

Take, for example, the Vietnam War. The loss of life and resources, the use of chemical weapons and the new methods of aerial warfare are by now well documented and evoke little discussion (except for the need for atonement in some quarters, or the desire to exorcise the ghost of defeat once and for all), for the Vietnam War is acknowledged today as one of a scenario of 'killing fields'. It is also now acknowledged that it was one of the greatest national liberation wars of the twentieth century, comparable only with the liberation of China, and that it brought the age of decolonisation to a close. But in terms of world history, i.e., in terms of the world pattern of competition and collaboration, in the rise and fall of powers, the Vietnam War is not given much importance. Perhaps justifiably so, for it is a myth that wars and victories by themselves empower a country. How a war is executed, how it is sustained, how weaponry is deployed and used, how peace is made, how the strength behind all these is perceived, and above all how war and peace change relations with other countries, these issues become crucial for the Great Power status that is ascribed to a country after a war. Seen in that light, the Vietnam War changed little. It did not create a new system, nor did it undo one; it did not reduce an individual country's status nor did it enhance it; in fact, it did not even affect the attacking country's position in terms of power. Thus the war remained 'local' despite the intense reactions it provoked world wide. The history of the wars of ex-colonial nations remains enmeshed in the history of the peace of the developed world; it is the latter which allows for the definition of the former. For example, the greatest defeat in a war in the post–1945 era did not at all affect the losing power in its world standing; ironically, the power on the victorious side in the Vietnam War crashed out within fifteen years of that famous victory. The superpower compulsions of representing history thus make a mockery of events such as these. Inasmuch as they are not of consequence to the 'world' they do not make 'world history'.

How does one escape the compulsions of representation? Before arriving at a tentative answer we can make a contrasting reference to the Gulf War. The Gulf War was a short war: it was not one of attrition, but showed how modern weaponry could be swiftly mobilised, deployed and used to telling effect. It quickly ended the battle cries of one of the antagonists, who had promised a "mother of all battles", and a "thousand years' war". Yet world history judges the Gulf War as one of greater significance than the Vietnam War because it enhanced the world status of one party. War and peace in the Gulf thus assumed significance much beyond what it would otherwise have had in that area. The implicit message of red republicanism in the Arab lands, the spectre of a Napoleonic adventurer upsetting a carefully constructed system of peace treaties in the region, the symbolic rise of a new concert of powers locked in a holy alliance against any adventurer, the emergence of a 'new South' engaged in a partnership with the 'new North', made the dimension of power in the Gulf War, and its subsequent peace, immensely significant – much more so than the oft-cited factor of oil. Thus, both war and peace are judged by the power of their impact and are accordingly represented in the hierarchy of world history – itself the only privileged discursive field to have a measure of power.

Spheres of Influence: 'Provincial' versus Global History

Power is measured in terms of influence; international relations theory
has no hesitation in admitting this. But it skirts the issue when it tries to
naturalise this by eschewing a genealogical exercise, as if 'spheres of
influence' are as natural as biospheres. The logic, in effect, is that if in the
post–war era there had been no wars, it was because the spheres of
influence worked well; if there had been wars, then these were because
of collisions over spheres of influence. In other words, the fact that there
were no wars showed that all countries were either in one camp or the
other, and that this showed how spheres of influence were a reality of
life. This strange conclusion is based on a refusal to trace a situation back
to its roots.

This representation is obviously unfair, since it includes nations not
privileged to be actors in world history and politics, who have been drawn
into the vortex of world history by those whose acts influence others. A
limited history of the emergence of spheres of influence in the Atlantic
world, and partly in the Pacific world, is universalised, and a provincial
history takes on a global form. The history of some nations which have
their own, specific, dynamics of war and peace, quite separate from the
discourses of the Atlantic world and the great Eurasian landmass, is
colonised by a history which in reality is equally local and equally specific:
specific to the clash of spheres of influence between the Atlantic allies and
a power from the Eurasian landmass. This historiography of the post–war
world is as much a problem as is, ironically, the ability of nations not
privileged to be world actors to make their own wars and their own peace.
The peculiarity of the situation is that the discourse and diplomacy of war
and peace, constrained as they are by power relations, then fetter the
capacity of the weaker nations to act on their own. If it is argued that "for
every thousand pages published on the causes of war there is less than one
page on the causes of peace",[6] the problem bounces back at us: is it
possible for the received discipline of history – (particularly in its form as
power-oriented world history) – to unearth the history of peace? In a
chronology such as this, minor peace efforts are bound to remain encapsulated in the histories of the Great Powers, and conversely, therefore, little
wars remain buried under the discourse of their grand peace.

The disproportion from which the study of the history of peace suffers
is, therefore, a deeply rooted problem. Power and influence – the elements
that make world history and create hierarchies in the grand format –
remain incompatible with a dispassionate study; it is, at present, largely a
record of the dominant parties of this world. Discursive experience has

shown that no matter how minute an examination of a nation's history, it cannot be free from being fated to be a "part of the world".[7] In this respect the revisionist history of the cold war has not been of much help either; it has concentrated almost solely on the internal reasons for America's cold war policy, and merely traced the interconnections between its domestic and foreign policies. This may have enriched our knowledge of the beginnings of the cold war, but the epistemological basis of cold war historiography has remained uncritiqued in such revisionist historical writings.[8]

Twentieth-century perceptions often over-valorised the cold war to the extent that all other conflicts during that period were minimalised. Yet it remains obligatory to show how wars in the post–war era have had their own characteristics to such an acute degree that they cannot be subsumed under the success story of the long peace. The demise of the cold war has refocussed attention on the differential effects of war and peace on the well-being of the world.

In Europe, the Metternichian age was shattered by the wars of 1848; indeed, the historian Eric Hobsbawm calls it the age of revolution, and not the age of peace. The restoration of pre-revolutionary power and politics in the Bismarckian world, which was again not an age of peace, ended with the war that began in 1914. The post–war world since 1945 continuously experienced wars amidst the long peace: if we are to go by the estimates of the University of Michigan's *Correlates of War* project, of the two hundred odd wars, at least 96 are notable as violent civil, inter-State and extrasystemic conflicts.[9] The wars in the Gulf, Rwanda, Afghanistan, Algeria and Bosnia in particular have brought the cold war/long peace to a close in a bizarre way. Going by the arguments of mainstream history, of the cold war/long peace discourse, its end in 1989 should have brought back wars; but this history would have us believe that the cold war ended only because of the capitulation of a warring party. The fact remains that the so-called dominant powers have only a limited ability to control; they can at best restrain the antagonists, and peace prevails not always because of them but despite them. In short, the problematic in the study of peace is to discover the link between the word (denominator of war and peace) and the world (the site of history) that will allow peace to remain free of a master discourse of grand war and grand peace.

But let us resume our discussion of specific wars. The turmoil in Eastern Europe towards the end of the Second World War and its immediate aftermath was certainly linked to the issue of spheres of influence, but was not a product of it.[10] In the case of countries like Greece, Poland and Czechoslovakia, the old imperial power, Britain, which knew the region most intimately was found to be too weak to intervene, which it would surely have done had it the required strength.[11] The collapse of Britain and France, but Britain in particular, signalled the end of the old imperial tradition and the beginnings of decolonisation. This theatre of change stretched from the borders of the Oder-Niesse to the deltas of the Irrawaddy, Mekong and Yangtze, and took almost the same period of time (late nineteen forties till the end of the sixties) as of the long peace to complete. The very process of State formation in the newly created areas in world politics was shaped in a substantive way by the Great Powers' strategy of partition to strengthen their spheres of influence. Thus Germany was partitioned; so was Korea, Vietnam, India, Yemen, Palestine and Cyprus. Radha Kumar's recent researches on Bosnia have shown that partition has been, for several years now, a managerial strategy for stabilising a situation that is seemingly totally out of control; a process which inevitably spawns a new round of instability.[12] The extent to which the States mentioned above have been influenced by this mode of origin has not been historically measured and appreciated, not even in the case of Germany.[13]

Although the Second World War had a justifiable, centralising narrative, there were several histories of the end of the war that went beyond it. Indeed, whereas in some cases the victorious parties in the war went by the supposedly discarded percepts of Woodrow Wilson by re-establishing a representative international organisation, following a global policy of national self-determination and proclaiming a liberal world order, in other respects they were found to have proceeded not much beyond the nineteenth-century concepts of the balance of power, a committee of world policemen and a series of alliances.[14] This is amply clear from the fact that Europe behaved in an unprecedented manner when it welcomed the Marshall Plan for the reconstruction of the continent after the Second World War. In fact, Europe was so compromised by threats of revolution and the awareness of its own inability to maintain its earlier power and influence that it requested America to stay on in the period after the end of the war, reviving, in the process, the nineteenth-century notion of a balance of power even at the cost of partitioning the continent. The history of the cold war thus encapsulated many histories, some rooted in the past, some characteristic of the new age.[15]

In the same way, the post–Second World War conflicts also have their specific, historical contexts. First, the partitions that brought in their wake wars, some of which are still continuing: although the war over Kashmir was fought four times between India and Pakistan, the dispute remains unsolved. Wars in the Congo, Palestine, Lebanon, the Horn of Africa and Bosnia are other instances. Second, low-key wars as a form of diplomacy in many regions where State formation could not solve the nationality question, as in Nagaland in northeastern India and in Kashmir. Third, the rise of republicanism: the unending rounds of war in Afghanistan, for example, are evidence of the effects of that 'forced march of history'. Fourth, border issues in various parts of the globe have not only occasioned Great Gamesmanship, but some major wars as well, as, for example, between China and Vietnam. Fifth, the build-up and sale of arms, in which the "baroque arsenal" itself becomes a temptation to be used.[16] Sixth, covert wars fought by outside powers with mercenaries and trained émigrés as in Nicaragua, El Salvador, Cuba, Angola, Laos, Myanmar and elsewhere. Seventh, the classic peasant revolutionary wars, such as those fought in China, the Malay Peninsula and Indonesia, though such wars are now on the decline. And finally, the wars of self-determination in places like Sri Lanka, Myanmar, Kashmir and the Kurdish region between southern Turkey and northern Iraq and Iran. It is important to remember, however, that most of these cases cannot be limited to their catagorisations: ethnicity, border issues, partition, arms sales and a variety of other factors often combine to produce wars.

Ironically, wars become scattered with the weakening of political policing in this age of globalisation. The policemen who are left on duty are often tired of their role and overwhelmed by war fatigue. Thus, a curious combination of a yearning for isolationism and the lingering desire for a world role marks the Great Powers at this time. Only a new political arrangement can take off some of their burden, but this can only be when the post–Second World War process has exhausted itself. The long peace was the first half of that process; the scattered wars and their aftermath mark the second one. In this era, therefore, we shall see more security doctrines, more efforts to erect a system that could limit or control scattered wars while avoiding deployment commitments – security doctrines that will be, in effect, markedly different from that of the cold war/long peace years.

Restoration: A Workable Solution or an Unstable Structure?

Throughout the ages, a restoration was supposed to bring peace to the lands ravaged by war. In some instances, this peace created the conditions for new wars; in others, it strengthened its own foundations. The question to be asked today, therefore, is: where do we stand after the restoration of 1989?

Johan Galtung attempts an answer by arguing that there is a "peace structure", a "war structure" and a "non-war structure". A peace structure implies a system of positive exchanges and cooperation between nations, which satisfies five conditions, namely, symmetry, homology, interdependence (symbiosis), institution building and dispersion (entropy). If a structure exhibits only one or two features, however, it will not be enough to sustain peace. For instance, there may be symbiosis as well as entropy between a big power and a dependent country, but since there is no symmetry, acute conflicts may arise. On the other hand, there may be symmetry and entropy, yet due to a lack of the other elements stated above, there may be rigidity, and consequently, conflict and war. The war structure also has these elements, with "only one major difference – instead of positive exchange and cooperation, there is negative exchange and destruction". In such a scenario, highly interdependent parties could be involved in mutual destruction; institution building could increase, rather than decrease, the chances of war. In the non-war structure, *"the system is unstable, and may move towards the peace structure or towards the war structure"* (emphasis Galtung's).[17]

While there may be no disagreements about the conditions which support a structure of peace or a structure of war, or, for that matter, a structure of neutrality (neither war nor peace), what is interesting is the premise that peace and war structures are similar, i.e., potentially interchangeable. Galtung himself admits that there is no structural difference between the two. In other words, we cannot offer any irreducible structural explanation on the origins of war or peace. Conditions in Europe in the period 1919–1939 produced a war; these conditions were equally present between 1945 and 1975, yet there was no war. One explanation may be that a strong peace-consciousness developed soon after 1945 (which was more effective than a similar consciousness in 1935–1939), that resisted many a possibility of war, especially because that consciousness was evident in different countries across all levels of society and political classes. But Galtung does not include consciousness as a structural element; consciousness is only an extra-structural factor in distinguishing between positive and negative conditions. Indeed, it would be tempting to take these extra-structural factors into account when studying a 'non-war–non-peace' situation, since the presence or absence of certain extra-structural factors is bound to effect or retard a slide into a war situation. Inevitably, therefore, we come back to the history of war and the difficult task of unearthing within it the history of the consciousness for peace. A comparison with events of the past in discussing the possibilities of peace in the post–1989 restoration period may thus be gainful.

The Napoleonic wars in Europe in the first half of the nineteenth century were concluded by the restoration of an order that was so suffocating that it needed a series of revolts for fresh winds to blow through the continent. On the other hand, the rigid Bismarkian order unwittingly allowed the labour movement and democratic charters to develop in the last quarter of the nineteenth century. The early twentieth century saw some dramatic political upheavals in which new States were formed or destroyed. The restoration of some old-style regimes in Eastern Europe after the war in 1945 was patently untenable, and they quickly collapsed. In Asia too, the old order was sought to be restored in China after 1945; however, American intervention in support of restoration could not prevent its overthrow and the revolutionary war succeeded, with the new order quickly attaining stability and gaining the people's confidence. In Myanmar the converse held true, as an old order was forcibly imposed upon its people; peace has not returned to that country since then. In the entire Far East Asian and Pacific-rim region, the Atlantic world led by the United States buttressed its position after 1945 by constructing a defence perimeter around China. The US troops did not withdraw from the Korean peninsula, the Philippines and Okinawa in Japan, while British forces remained in the Malay Peninsula as did the French in Indo-China. Corrupt regimes were held up the world over and wars therefore raged in those regions for a long time.

Today we have a similar scattered picture before us. The old system cannot be restored in Bosnia, so peace and order are being imposed upon the region with the help of NATO troops. It is a moot point, however, whether the experiment of setting up a State in an effort to restore peace and order will be successful – whether peace restoration will ever be complete without State restoration. As in Somalia, Palestine, El Salvador, Algeria, Yemen, Lebanon, Rwanda, the Congo, Afghanistan, Cambodia and elsewhere, restoration of peace and order can no longer be instituted by merely restoring the old order. Such a situation is ruled out by the 'state' of the State itself, which is often ravaged by attrition, militarisation, fratricide, corruption, elite gangsterism or outright destruction by an occupant army. In countries like these, the introduction of a constitution and the erection of a State structure has become an essential part of the task of restoration. In 1848, it was the declarations of constitutions that signalled a challenge to the restored order. But when peace was restored in 1919 on the basis of a liberal world order the forces of aggression, militarism and revanchism overturned the settlement within ten years of its formulation. Less than twenty years later, the liberal order could be restored in the heart of the Atlantic world only at the cost of partition in 1945. The colonised world was invited to participate in that order through such an unnatural form of decolonisation that they are still reeling from its impact more than fifty years later.

It can thus be clearly seen that the core of the task of peace restoration, of the issue of war and peace, lies in the mysterious origins of the formation of a State. The various state-systems prevailing in the world have been exhaustively discussed; strategies, alliances, diplomacies and policies have been amply analysed, just as much as whether a state-system had to be strengthened or reformed, maintained or changed. But what if the basic edifice – the State itself – becomes unsustainable? When a State incessantly occasions war and is then consumed by it? When peace is actualised even at the State level by private initiatives, that is, by truly public initiatives? When the history of the State becomes inadequate in chronicling the history of peace initiatives and dialogues? When restoring peace becomes inseparable from changing the structure of the State in order to restore it? It is at this juncture that we understand that the module of the State as handed down by a globalised history – world history – has become unworkable. It is now possible to see through the mysteries of war and peace – mysteries that succeed in making a period of the breakdown of the State appear as a period of long peace.[18]

The Play-Off: Globalisation and Fragmentation in Today's World

The triumphalist literature emerging in the aftermath of the cold war has developed around two main themes. The first theme claims that with the failure and collapse of the socialist system, there is now no ideological rival to liberal capitalism (by implication, to the liberal system), no other aspirant backed by any kind of popular legitimacy. The second theme sees in the decline and departure of parallel (socialist) politics the emergence of a genuine world system whose last obstacles are being removed. States, particularly of the Third World, cannot fantasise any more about national paths or national alternatives. Global economic institutions and the international division of labour have finally made capitalism the basis on which States are to be managed. Political programmes and economic practices are to recognise that State management, liberal values and economic openness within a world capitalist system have to go comfortably hand in hand.

The triumphalist literature of the late eighties and nineties that captured the spirit of globalism does not, however, fully reckon with the fact of the breakdown of the State in many parts of the globe. The crisis of the State, as evinced in Bosnia, Afghanistan, Rwanda, Cambodia and other places, still appears within this literature as more of a managerial problem. Peacekeeping, peace enforcing, stabilising and 'constitutionalising from outside' are considered a part of an international managerial strategy for salvaging the State. The problem is defined as stabilising the State against the forces of 'ethnicity', which threaten and sometimes succeed in internationalising an essentially local phenomenon. Therefore, the international strategy is to quarantine the sickness, to closely monitor the situation and apply multilateral, multi-pronged therapy, with various degrees of force, to cure the State of a problem that is not intrinsic but which is seen essentially as an internationalisation of the local. The scenario is, in effect, one of the globalisation of fragmentation.[19]

There is, however, a sense of unease among the votaries of this brave new world, which is amply reflected in this genre of literature. Some authors have held that though the State is not under interrogation, the agenda of reconciling the State with the post–restoration world is hard and arduous. Others have opined that even in these stable times the State is under severe threat from such enormous problems as the massive migrations of populations, ethnic extremities, hunger and pestilence in large parts of the world, unpredictable rogue behaviour (by States such as Serbia, Ethiopia and Afghanistan), laxity of international laws, hordes of unemployed labourers, unruly currencies and above all, the remains of a political class uneducated in the liberal doctrines of governance. While some authors have felt that globalisation is threatened by a clash of irreconcilable civilisations, others have pointed out that the global system, particularly the economic system, is essentially unstable; therefore, the world itself is unprepared for the cohesive forces of globalisation. The fears, suspicions and uncertainties so revealingly expressed at such a triumphal moment in time are reminiscent of the world as it was in the nineteenth century.[20]

The nineteenth-century European States were not prepared for the post–restoration world; alliances, ententes, congresses and treaties were all indicative of nations in flux. The Metternichian age, which had appeared to Gaddis as the period of peace, had appeared to others as the "age of revolution".[21] By the time these States had been educated in the rules of a system, too many imperatives and imponderables broke them up. The unanticipated factor of expanding globalisation played havoc with the carefully constructed edifice of state-systems, so much so that the truly monumental agenda in the Versailles deliberations after the First World War was in achieving national self-determination, home rule and border settlements – a familiar picture to the observers of the late-twentieth-century political scene.

With the end of the cold war, attention has once again shifted to the problems of the Third World, which stand in the way of the successful completion of the Westphalian project for the creation of a global order and the maintenance of peace.[22] Drawn into the vortex of global events and developments like decolonisation, partition, citizenship laws, emergence of minority issues, ecological destruction, hardening of borders, immigration realities and a geographical widening of capital and labour markets, the career of a State in the Third World today symbolises the intractability of the problems of race, ethnicity, citizenship and alienness. States are either crashing out of existence or becoming shadows of the past. In an eerie re-creation of the past, when States had to be formed *de novo* after 1918 and 1945, the same imperative has raised its head in today's moment of triumph. Today the subject of State formation has emerged out of the sedate chambers of social anthropology to become an issue of world politics.[23]

An example of this modern crossover is immigration in international politics. There was a time when for its own formation a State required a subject population. However, it was the territory which more or less marked out this subject population.[24] This is not so today. States now require a definition of who their citizens are and by implication or by explicit formulation, who is an alien. The category of immigration functions as a political marker for these two definitions. The sociological implication of this signification is immense. An ethnic 'core', a differential modus operandi of statehood (that separates a State from others, separates its core from the periphery in its internal structure, and defines its citizens as different from other groups) and the representation of hostility as essential for the State to function – all these point to the fact that from a biological theory of subject population we have arrived at a sociological theory for the same, with the consequence that a State can explicitly claim today the fact or the need for positioning itself in a 'particular' culture. Immigration in this way is not only an issue of labour economics, but of the politics of this time, when State and nation are almost undifferentiated, when the subject and the citizen are almost synonymous terms and the ideology of the State has, in effect, made a return to antiquity. Paradoxically, in this era of State enterprises we seem to have moved back in time, when the cultural basis of a solidarity was taken for granted. These trends have had an immense impact on conflict patterns in the world today, as well as on the capacity of the international order to tackle these conflicts.

Once again, a comparison with the past is instructive. Europe took nearly two centuries for its States to find their cultural bases. Europe's principal aliens, the Jews, after having been substantialy decimated, finally emigrated and formed their own Jewish State after the Second World War, even as Christianity was repeatedly being invoked to stabilise the newly restructured state-systems.[25] With the recent immigration of Turkish, Arab and Bosnian workers into the west European countries, we find that Europe is having to reaffirm its historic cultural basis. Islam, Slavism and religious orthodoxy are the new invasions against which States in Europe have raised their guard – a situation which confirms the "presence of the past".[26] Thus we have the reworking of the problematic of State formation in a situation where the past history of the State refuses to vanish, like a ghost that hovers over a site, despite it having witnessed repeated constructions after periodic demolitions. The questions of State formation, statelessness and the prevention of conflicts have thus become indubitably political: nationalisation of a society for the purpose of imparting stability to the State is not complete if aliens are not marked out.

The irony is clear, especially when we recall the circumstances of South Asia. The post–colonial nation was to be the ultimate form of a political institution. For a realisation of this form, constitutional processes and the development of nationhood required the production of non-state people from time to time. Thus the entire process of decolonisation, including partitions, wars and deliberate acts of enforcing territoriality, produced non-State persons in the country and also in the states within it. But this violent process of production gave rise to anxiety over its ultimate form: would not the massive flows of population give rise to other structures that rupture the fusion of the State and the nation? Indeed, we find that an influx of peoples makes the process of nationalisation ever delayed and incomplete. Since every community produced by the process of State making is essentially fictitious, there always remains the possibility of newer communities being created on the basis of ethnicity by the nation.

South Asia was decolonised through the strategy of partition, but partition has not been unique to the sub-continent as a key element in State formation. As we have seen, Rwanda, Ethiopia, Korea, Cyprus, Bosnia, Iraq, Afghanistan, Germany and many other countries were either partitioned or virtually partitioned or were on the verge of partition during post–war settlements, new State-formation processes and the creation of new state-systems. These issues remain inadequately studied as to their significance in terms of "globalisation and fragmentation".[27] A crucial aspect in such studies is the generation, through these processes, of the continuing waves of migrants and refugees, and their impact on State formation and subsequent State development. The emergence of modern India was through one of the biggest population transfers in human history. Between 1946 and 1951, nearly nine million Hindus and Sikhs came to India and about six million Muslims crossed over into Pakistan. Of the said nine million, five million came from what became West Pakistan and four million came from East Pakistan. Immigration into India, particularly eastern and northeastern India, has continued under the shadow of that historic migration with, of course, new patterns but with very substantive continuities also.[28] Its impact on the State and politics at national, regional and local levels in terms of institutionalised and non-institutionalised domains has been critical, but again, inadequately studied. Though we now have some studies on its impact in the northeast, we are yet to generalise them as elements of State formation in South Asia. The impact of non-State people like the Chakmas on the politics of the Indian states of Arunachal Pradesh and Mizoram, the Bangladeshi aliens in Assam, the Sri Lankan Tamils in Tamil Nadu, the Biharis in Bangladesh, the Bhutanese in Nepal, the Afghans in Pakistan and Tajikistan or the Bangladeshis in Karachi, Lahore and other parts of Sind and Punjab is a potential and actual issue of violent conflict in the region. The effects of the movements of various groups of people from and into Myanmar has been similarly acute, not only for the Myanmarese State, but also for the whole of South and Southest Asia.[29]

War, the struggle for national identity, and ethnicity have created in this region, as elsewhere, a 'virtual' partition situation. Yet in a sense these conflicts are not new to history. Ethnographic and anthropological studies have documented that population movements were a crucial factor in State formation in past ages, associated as they were with kin-linkages. What is new to the situation is the backdrop of citizenship against which alienness is defined, immigration is characterised, policies on 'near abroad' are formulated, the nation periodically defined and announced, and the hierarchy integral to the subject population is catagorised. In this situation the old differences between *jus soli* (right of soil) and *jus sanguinis* (right of blood) do not mean much, for both are equally operational in marking off the non-State persons and where in fencing in the (territorial) State.

Non-State persons are non-citizens, often non-nationals; they are equally unwanted where they were born and where they now live. Citizenship is an essential attribute of the State, not only for defining the subject population, but also for defining the other point of a transactional relationship whose one end is the State. That is why today the 'citizen' is often taken as the 'national', for *State* and *nation* as different entities hardly exist,[30] though at one time the State had tried to adopt non-national forms. Religion, language, tribe, territory – all these define 'minority', and as such they define a particular category of citizenship, which is related to the general problem of the national acceptance of the reality of immigration. In this respect, the experiences of Europe and South Asia are not very different.[31] If we take into account the experiences of Germany and Italy as moderate examples, and Yugoslavia or the Caucasian States as extreme examples, the whole issue is clearly not restricted to the Third World – the "revenge of the nations", in fact, visits States right across the globe.[32] Hatred, violence, an exclusionist legal system of beneficiaries, a system of identifying the potential disruptors or groups of disruptors of statehood – each of these now seems to be the prerequisite for the formation of a State. Seen in this light, the categorisation of non-State persons shows that State formation is not a one-off affair but an exercise in perpetuity, inasmuch as State legitimation remains a permanent plebiscite.[33]

Admittedly, migration is as old as human history; but as suggested earlier, international migration several decades or even one or two centuries ago creates implications for the revisionist strategy of a State, and thus begins to exercise an acute impact on its intra-State and international agendas. Thus Indians in Fiji or Uganda, the Chinese in Southeast Asia, some groups of Tamils in Sri Lanka, Armenians in Azerbaijan, the Turks in Germany, Palestinians in Jordan, Lebanon and elsewhere in West Asia are classic non-State groups who pose a problem because they are perceived as a threat to the sovereignty of that State; for by the very fact of their minority status they remind the majority of their own ethnicity. Involuntary migrations, consequent upon natural disasters, civil wars, political persecutions, repression of minorities and total economic break-downs, involve millions of people who become the subjects of a new 'slavery'. The international system requires migrant labour, sex slaves and émigrés but is yet to devise a system for managing them. Widening information networks, greater mobility of capital, the oil-powered economic boom, a redivision of global labour, the proliferation of small arms and of other methods of low-key insurgency, the growth in world population, the historical "revenge of the nations" – all have a correlation with voluntary and involuntary immigration. The overall well-being of a State has thus become of pressing concern in the list of global anxieties.

Globalisation, in its first true incarnation in the form of colonialism, was the initial impetus to migration. About 30 million people had arrived between 1861 and 1920 in the United States, a country of immigrants already responsible for the displacement and extermination of the indigenous population. Europe saw huge intracontinental migrations to the Baltic regions, the Black Sea and the central lands of the continent. The period between the potato famines in Ireland; the pogroms targetted at the Jews in Poland and Hungary; the forced migration of an estimated 15 million slaves in sub-Saharan Africa and the migration of indentured labour from India, Sri Lanka and China, more widespread than American slavery and encompassing some forty countries and involving 37 million people, began in the seventeenth century and ended as late as 1941. Its duration was equal to that of colonialism, but its political effects are only now being felt.[34] New migration patterns then emerged with the changes in labour markets and the general process of decolonisation, which led to immigration into the West of people from countries in Asia, southeastern Europe, the Mediterranean and North Africa. Western xenophobia saw to it that immigration studies prospered. It is notable that such studies escaped the cold war framework in which the refugee question had remained.[35]

Here indeed is the point. Immigration studies and refugee studies represent a paradox in international relations theory. International relations theory was bound by the reality and rhetoric of the cold war to such an extent that the world which lay beyond the cold war and the 'Great Game' of the post–1945 era was ignored; so much so that 'international' concerns actually became very 'provincial'. Post the cold war though, international relations theory tried to apprehend a phenomenon that may have had something to do with the cold war realities but which, in its complexities, was beyond it, being extra-cold war in its origins. Thus international relations theory now remains in limbo. Immigration studies have became a subject of political history, world history and the history of diplomacy, but hardly of international relations. Tentative responses to the complex realities of today's world, ranging from the neo-Nazi movements in Europe and elsewhere to international institutions like the UN organisations or the peacekeeping forces, as well as its anxious reaction to trends that have long been in human history but are new in their significance in terms of politics – both of the State and of the globe – reveal the uncertain state of international relations as a form of knowledge today.[36]

Today, the discipline of international relations is like an emperor without clothes. How has this come about, and what are the reasons for the uncertainty mentioned above? This state of affairs is probably because international relations theory cannot satisfactorily answer three questions: do contemporary borders exist primarily to control movements of people? Are border controls effective in stopping the entry of aliens? Are these controls instruments of human rights abuses and injustices? These issues remain insignificant to a discipline long obsessed with Great Powers, Great Gamesmanship, great outcomes and great destinies. This neglect has an ironical consequence in terms of political theory also. Among the defining features of liberal politics has been the graduation of the State from the bondage of kinship, the constitution of the subject in the form of an individual citizen, the evolution of the State as one end of a transactional relationship and the uncertain merger of two forms of power – the centralised, juridical power of the sovereign and its 'capillary' form. Yet the current conflict patterns show this graduation as highly suspect. The constitution of a (fictive) ethnicity as the basis/core of the State, the configuration of minorities as immigrant communities, the invasions on territoriality which has all along been the prime attribute of a modern State, show that the State may not be that modern after all; that while the State takes up the agenda of modernising itself through nationalisation, decentralisation, citizenship laws and above all, accepting, and negotiating with, globalisation, the State is in fact through such a process reinventing kinship.[37] A revisionist State thus ends up by seeking forms of the past; its moment of triumph is in many ways a moment of admission of defeat. International relations at the end of the twentieth century, therefore, as featured by the globalisation of fragmentation, looks extremely similar to the international relations of the nineteenth century. One could say, perhaps, that it never really left that age.

Conclusion

Up to this point, we have argued that globalisation and fragmentation today are companions of each other. The issues of statelessness, dispersed conflicts and the imperatives of coercing a State to enforce peace in the post-cold war world are a product of that complex situation. Such a state of international affairs is also demonstrative of the fact that international relations theory is hopelessly inadequate in dealing with this phenomenon. Thus, while today's mood of triumph is disturbed by widespread statelessness, its importance reflects on the agenda of State building to such an extent that we may say that we are in the age of State formation once again. In Afghanistan, as much as in Myanmar, Cambodia, Bosnia and Somalia, peace making is actually 'peace enforcing', for peace here can no longer be achieved through dialogue. The State in most of these cases has been weakened to such an extent that the State edifice has to be erected from outside, so that peace can be enforced within. Conflict theory dealt with asymmetries; conflict-prevention theory now finds these asymmetries too real – so real that the politics of negotiation is often unable to cope with the situation. Peace, and with it stability and a sense of belonging, has become "elusive".[38]

Yet such a condition of the world has not suddenly come upon us: if the First World War showed how fragmented the world had been for the past hundred years, the end of the Second World War brought no decisive change to that situation. The contradictory trends of globalisation and fragmentation played their part in preventing any resolution of a beleaguered world. In the beginning it seemed that individual States were being reconciled to a systematised world. Keynesian theory, now acknowledged as limited in its efficacy as therapy for an individual State, was supposed to be more applicable in a global context. The international economic order was growing, and it was felt that where Keynsianism might fail, monetarism would bring rogue States to order. European imperial control was to give way to a new charter of control, domiciled in America, which would fine-tune state-systems the world over. However, the universalism of the Atlantic Charter was, ironically, defeated by the very instruments it had promoted – monetarism, Americanisation, neo-imperial controls and the fusion of globalisation and Americanisation. Within Atlanticism lay the seeds of its failure; its very universalism has contributed to its downfall. The contradiction is elemental. The realities of globalisation, and the characteristics of the cold war era, namely, trans-national corporations, territorial segmentation of production, financial integration, choices between orders and ideologies, the preponderance of the nation-state and the fusion of globalisation and Americanisation were seemingly absolute. Yet, immigration, labour flows, ethnicity, the creation of new nations and new regions, global recessions, monetarism and outright plunder have ruled out any lasting impact of the cold war and the way this 'war' has ended. The "removal of the geopolitical constraints of the cold war" has erased the certainties of the preceding decades.[39] It ushers in a period of regression to pre-existing times.[40]

Notes

NOTES to Chapter 1

This is a revised version of a paper presented at the seminar on "Asian Geopolitics: Borders and Transborder Flows", organised by Maulana Abul Kalam Azad Institute of Asian Studies, Calcutta, on 23 and 24 March 1998, at New Delhi. I am grateful to Professor Kanti P. Bajpai, School of International Studies, Jawaharlal Nehru University, New Delhi, for his insightful and constructive comments.

1. Ladis K. D. Kristof, "Geopolitics as a Field of Study," The Ford Foundation Lectures in International Relations Studies, The Ford Foundation Programme in International Relations Studies, Department of Political Science, Maharaja Sayajirao University, Baroda, 1992, 2.

2. G. Ó Tuathail and J. Agnew, "Geopolitics and Discourse: Practical Geopolitical Reasoning in American Foreign Policy," *Political Geography* 11, no. 2 (1992): 195.

3. P. J. Taylor, "Geopolitical World Orders," in *Political Geography of the Twentieth Century: A Global Analysis,* ed. P. J. Taylor (London: Belhaven Press, 1993), 31–61; G. Smith, "Ends, Geopolitics and Transitions," in *The Challenge for Geography: A Changing World, A Changing Discipline,* ed. R. J. Johnston (Oxford: Blackwell, 1993), 76–99; S. B. Cohen, "Geopolitics in the New World Era: A New Perspective on an Old Discipline," *Reordering the World: Geopolitical Perspectives on the Twenty-First Century,* eds. G. J. Demko and W. B. Wood (Boulder: Westview Press, 1994), 15–48.

4. J. Agnew and S. Corbridge, *Mastering Space: Hegemony, Territory and International Political Economy* (London: Routledge, 1995); P. Knox and J. Agnew, *The Geography of the World Economy: An Introduction to Economic Geography* (London: Edward Arnold, 1994).

5. J. Agnew, *Geopolitics: Re-Visioning World Politics* (London: Routledge, 1998).

6. G. Ó Tuathail, *Critical Geopolitics: The Politics of Writing Global Space* (London: Routledge, 1996), 15.

7. Agnew and Corbridge, *Mastering Space,* 52.

8. J. Houbert, "Russia in the Geopolitics of Settler Colonization and Decolonization," *Round Table,* no. 344 (1997): 549–561.

9. M. Bassin, "Russia between Europe and Asia: The Ideological Construction of Geographical Space," *Slavic Review,* no. 50 (1991): 1–17.

10. Agnew and Corbridge, *Mastering Space,* 52.

11. Agnew, *Geopolitics,* 89.

12. Ó Tuathail, *Critical Geopolitics,* 225.

13. K. M. Pannikkar, *Asia and Western Dominance: A Survey of the Vasco Da Gama Epoch of Asian History 1498–1945* (London: George Allen and Unwin, 1959), 314.

14. M. H. Fisher, *The Politics of British Annexation of India 1757–1857* (New Delhi: Oxford University Press, 1993), 1–10.

15. B. S. Cohn, "Representing Authority in Victorian India," in *The Invention of Tradition,* eds. E. Hobsbawm and T. Ranger (Cambridge: Cambridge University Press, 1996), 182.

16. T. Metcalf, *Ideologies of the Raj* (Cambridge: Cambridge University Press, 1996), 110–111.

17. Agnew and Corbridge, *Mastering Space,* 56–65; L. W. Hepple, "Metaphor, Geopolitical Discourse and the Military in South America," in *Writing Worlds: Discourse, Text and Metaphor in the Representation of Landscape,* eds. T. Barnes and J. Duncan (London: Routledge, 1992), 136–154.

18. C. Darwin, *Journal of Researches into the Geology and Natural History of the Various Countries Visited by the H. M. S. Beagle* (London: Henry Colburn, 1839), 520.

19. Agnew, *Geopolitics,* 95–96.

20. Ó Tuathail, *Critical Geopolitics,* 21

21. J. Klein, "Reflections on Geopolitics: From Pangermanism to the Doctrines of Living Space and moving Frontiers," in *On Geopolitics: Classical and Nuclear,* eds. C. Zoppo and C. Zorgbibe (Dordrecht: Martinus Nijhoff, 1985), 45–76.

22. G. Sloan, *Geopolitics in the United States Strategic Policy: 1890–1987* (Brighton: Wheatsheaf Books, 1988), 87–95; M. I. Glassner, *Political Geography* (New York: John Wiley, 1995), 326–327; M. Bassin "Friedrich Ratzel," *Geographers: Bibliographical Studies,* no. 11 (1987): 123–132; K. Kost, "The Conception of Politics in Political Geography and Geopolitics in Germany until 1945," *Political Geography* 8, no. 4 (1989): 369–386; Ó Tuathail, *Critical Geopolitics,* 45–50; S. Holdar, "Political Geographers of the Past; IX: The Ideal State and the Power of Geography: The Life-Work of Rudolf Kjellen," *Political Geography* 11, no. 3 (1992): 307–323; G. Parker, *Western Geopolitical Thought in the Twentieth Century* (London: Croom Helm, 1985).

23. Agnew, *Geopolitics,* 102.

24. G. Parker, *Geopolitics: Past, Present and Future* (London: Pinter, 1998), 28–29.

25. Agnew, *Geopolitics,* 102.

26. Parker, *Past, Present and Future,* 26–45.

27. Y. Fukushama, "Political Geographers of the Past; X: Japanese Geopolitics and Its Background: What is the Real Legacy of the Past?" *Political Geography* 16, no. 5 (1997): 407–421.

28. Wm. R. Louis, "The Era of the Mandate System and the Non-European World," in *The Expansion of International Society,* eds. H. Bull and A. Watson (Oxford: Clarendon Press, 1984), 213.

29. Fukushama, "Japanese Geopolitics," 411.

30. Parker, *Past, Present and Future,* 96–117.

31. Ó Tuathail, *Critical Geopolitics,* 41.

32. Sloan, *Geopolitics in the United States,* 91.

33. Ó Tuathail, *Critical Geopolitics,* 31.

34. P. J. Taylor, "From Heartland to Hegemony: Changing the World in Political Geography," *Geoforum* 25, no. 4 (1994): 404.

35. Sloan, *Geopolitics in the United States,* 16–18.

36. Glassner, *Political Geography*, 327.

37. Agnew and Corbridge, *Mastering Space,* 68.

38. J. O'Loughlin and H. Heske, "From 'Geopolitik' to 'Geopolitique': Converting a Discipline for War to a Discipline for Peace," in *The Political Geography of Conflict and Peace,* eds. N. Kliot and S. Waterman (London: Belhaven Press, 1991), 43.

39. J. Nijman, "The Limits of Superpower: The United States and the Soviet Union Since World War II," *Annals of the Association of American Geographers* 82, no. 4 (1992): 681–695; J. Nijman, *Geopolitics of Conflict and Power: Superpowers in the International System* (London: Belhaven Press, 1993); S. Dalby, "Geopolitical Discourse: The Soviet Union as Other," *Alternatives,* no. 13 (1988): 415–442; S. Dalby, *Creating the Second Cold War: The Discourse of Politics* (London: Pinter, 1990); C. S. Gray, *The Geopolitics of the Nuclear Era: Heartlands, Rimlands and the Technological Revolution* (New York: Crane, Russak, 1977); C. S. Gray, *The Geopolitics of Superpower* (Lexington: University of Kentucky Press, 1988).

40. P. J. Taylor, *Political Geography: World Economy, Nation-State and Locality,* 3d ed. (Essex: Longman Scientific and Technical, 1993), 53–64.

41. Taylor, "From Heartland to Hegemony," 405.

42. G. Ó Tuathail, "Second Cold War," in *Dictionary of Geopolitics,* ed. J. O'Loughlin (Westport: Greenwood Press, 1994), 214–217.

43. M. Walker, *The Cold War and the Making of the Modern World* (London: Fourth Estate, 1993), 143.

44. M. Kaldor, "The World Economy and Militarization," in *Towards a Just World Peace: Perspectives from Social Movements,* eds. S. Mendelovittz and R. B. J. Walker (London: Butterworths, 1987), 49–78.

45. G. Ó Tuathail, introduction to *The Geopolitics Reader,* eds. G. Ó Tuathail, S. Dalby and P. Routledge (London: Routledge, 1998), 51.

46. A. P. Rana, "The Non-Hegemonical Imperative: The Non-Aligned Regulation of India's National Security Problematic and the Universalisation of International Society," *Indian Journal of Social Science* 4, no. 1 (1991): 20.

47. Parker, *Past, Present and Future,* 129.

48. G. Krishna, "India and the International Order: Retreat from Idealism," in *The Expansion of International Society,* eds. H. Bull and A. Watson (Oxford: Clarendon Press, 1984), 276.

49. *Ibid.,* 277–278.

50. M. S. Rajan, *Nonalignment and Nonaligned Movement: Retrospect and Prospect* (New Delhi: Vikas, 1990), 193.

51. Jawaharlal Nehru, *Discovery of India* (Calcutta: Signet Press, 1946), 539.

52. A. K. Damodaran, "Before Non-Alignment," in *Interpreting World Politics: Essays for A. P. Rana,* eds. Kanti P. Bajpai and H. C. Shukul (New Delhi: Sage, 1995), 196.

53. *Ibid.,* 203.

54. A. P. Rana, "Back to Basics: Non-Alignment after the Cold War," *World Affairs: The Journal of International Issues* 1, no. 2 (1997): 56–57.

55. In the Indian Ocean, for example, a fishing and coconut-growing community, the Ilois, were forcibly removed from Diego Garcia in the 1960s on security grounds and to pave the way for a huge US air and naval base.

56. S. Akiner, "Environmental Degradation in Central Asia," *Central Asia and the Caucasus Review* 3, no. 7 (1994): 129–138.

57. S. Dalby and G. Ó Tuathail, "The Critical Geopolitics Constellation: Problematizing Fusions of Geographical Knowledge and Power," *Political Geography* 15, no. 6–7 (1996): 451–456.

58. G. Ó Tuathail, "(Dis)placing Geopolitics: Writing on the Maps of Global Politics," *Environment and Planning; D: Society and Space,* no. 12 (1994): 527.

59. K. J. Dodds and J. D. Sidaway, "Locating Critical Geopolitics," *Environment and Planning; D: Society and Space,* no. 12 (1994): 515–524.

60. I. B. Neumann, "The Geopolitics of Delineating 'Russia' and 'Europe': The Creation of the 'Other' in European and Russian Tradition," in *Geopolitics in Post–Wall Europe: Security, Territory and Identity,* eds. O. Tunander, P. Baev and V. I. Einagel (London: Sage, 1997), 148.

61. G. Ó Tuathail, "Critical Geopolitics and the Development Theory: Intensifying the Dialogue," *Transactions of the Institute of British Geographers,* no. 19 (1994): 228–238.

62. G. Ó Tuathail and S. Dalby, "Critical Geopolitics: Unfolding Spaces for Thought in Geography and Global Politics," *Environment and Planning; D: Society and Space* 12, no. 5 (1994): 514.

63. Ó Tuathail and Agnew, "Geopolitics and Discourse," 195.

64. Taylor, "From Heartland to Hegemony," 403–411.

65. R. A. Falk, *On Human Governance: Toward a New Global Politics* (Cambridge: Polity Press, 1995), 177.

66. Agnew and Corbridge, *Mastering Space,* 205–206.

67. *Ibid.,* 206–207.

68. A. Bameazizi and M. Weiner, eds., *The New Geopolitics of Central Asia and its Borderlands* (London: I. B. Tauris, 1994); A. Z. Rubinstein, "Russia in Search of a New Role: Changing Geopolitical Compulsions in Central Asia," *World Affairs: The Journal of International Issues* 1, no. 2 (1997): 62–79; D. L. Smith, "Central Asia: A New Great Game?" *Asian Affairs* 23, no. 3 (1996): 147–175; S. Huntington, "The Clash of Civilizations?" *Foreign Affairs* 72, no. 3 (1993): 22–49.

69. K. Dawisha and B. Parrot, *Conflict, Cleavage and Change in Central Asia and the Caucasus* (Cambridge: Cambridge University Press, 1997); M. M. Puri, "Central Asian Geopolitics: The Indian View," *Central Asian Survey* 16, no. 2 (1997): 237–268.

70. D. I. Hitchcock, "Internal Problems in East Asia," *Washington Quarterly* 21, no. 2 (1998): 121–134.

71. D. Hale, "Is Asia's High Growth Era Over?" *National Interest* 47 (Spring 1997): 44.

72. B. De, "Moving Beyond Boundaries: Contradictions Between People and Territory," in *States, Citizens and Outsiders: The Uprooted Peoples of South Asia*, eds. T. K. Bose and Rita Manchanda (Kathmandu: South Asia Forum for Human Rights, 1997).

73. S. Dalby, introduction to *The Geopolitics Reader*, eds. G. Ó Tuathail, S. Dalby and P. Routledge (London: Routledge, 1998), 179.

74. S. Dalby, "Ecopolitical Discourse: 'Environmental Security' and 'Political Geography,'" *Progress in Human Geography* 16, no. 4 (1992): 503–522.

75. Ó Tuathail, *Critical Geopolitics*, 253.

76. W. M. Adams, "Sustainable Development," in *Geographies of Global Change: Remapping the World in the Late Twentieth Century*, eds. R. J. Johnston, P. J. Taylor and M. J. Watts (Oxford: Blackwell, 1995), 354–374.

77. S. Visvanathan, "Mrs. Brundtland's Disenchanted Cosmos," in *The Geopolitics Reader*, eds. G. Ó Tuathail, S. Dalby and P. Routledge (London: Routledge, 1998), 237–244.

78. D. Lal, "Eco-Fundamentalism," *International Affairs* 71, no. 3 (1995): 22–49.

79. V. Shiva, "The Greening of the Global Reach," in *Global Visions: Beyond the New World Order*, eds. J. Brecher, J. B. Childs and J. Cutler (Boston: New End Press, 1993), 59.

80. Rana, "Back to Basics," 57.

81. R. Roy-Choudhury, "The Indian Ocean Rim-Association for Regional Cooperation: An Overview," *World Affairs: The Journal of International Issues* 1, no. 3 (1997): 45–52.

82. R. A. Falk, "Regionalism and World Order after the Cold War," draft paper presented for WIDER/IPSA Workshop and Panel, Berlin, Germany, 20–23 August 1994, 13.

83. P. Routledge, introduction to *The Geopolitics Reader*, eds. G. Ó Tuathail, S. Dalby and P. Routledge (London: Routledge, 1998), 245.

84. *Ibid.*, 245.

85. P. Routledge, "Critical Geopolitics and Terrains of Resistance," *Political Geography* 15, no. 6-7 (1996): 509–531.

86. R. Mulgan, "Should Indigenous Peoples Have Special Rights?" in *One World Many Voices: Global Perspectives on Political Issues*, ed. G. Hastedt (Eaglewood Cliffs: Prentice Hall, 1995), 258–267.

87. F. Wilmer, *The Indigenous Voice in World Politics: Since Time Immemorial* (Newbury Park: Sage, 1993), 218.

88. B. K. Roy Burman, "'Indigenous' and 'Tribal' Peoples and the U.N. and International Agencies," RGICS paper no. 27, Rajiv Gandhi Institute for Contemporary Studies, New Delhi, 1995, 17–18.

89. C. von Fürer-Haimendorf, *Tribes of India: The Struggle for Survival* (New Delhi: Oxford University Press, 1982), 322.

90. Roy Burman, "*'Indigenous' and 'Tribal' Peoples*," 29.

91. *Ibid.*, 30.

92. P. Lauderdale, "Frank Justice Rather Than Frankenstein Injustice: Homogenous Development as Deviance in the Diverse World," in *The Underdevelopment of Development: Essays in Honour of Andre Gunder Frank,* eds. S. C. Chew and R. A. Danemark (Thousand Oaks: Sage, 1996), 327–331; Falk, *On Human Governance,* 172–206.

93. V. Shiva, *Ecology and the Politics of Survival: Conflicts Over Natural Resources in India* (New Delhi: Sage, 1995), 274–302.

94. Wilmer, *Indigenous Voice,* 36–37.

95. M. G. Weinbaum, "The Three Asias: Security, Economic and Cultural Linkages Across Central, West and South Asia," *Swords and Ploughshares,* no. 10 (1996–97): 1.

96. G. Ó Tuathail, A. Herod and S. M. Roberts, "Negotiating Unruly Problematics," in *Unruly World: Globalization, Governance and Geography,* eds. G. Ó Tuathail, A. Herod and S. M. Roberts (London: Routledge, 1998), 1–24.

97. Ó Tuathail, *Critical Geopolitics,* 248.

98. Rubinstein, "Russia in Search of a New Role"; A. Melville, "Post–Communist Russia: Problems of Transition," *World Affairs: The Journal of International Issues* 2, no. 2 (1998): 68–85.

99. T. T. Thien, "New Alignments, New Realities: East Asia in the Post–Cold War Setting," *World Affairs: The Journal of International Issues* 1, no. 1 (1997): 82–83.

100. *Ibid.,* 90.

101. M. Ahmar, "The Emergence of Three Asias," *World Affairs: The Journal of International Issues* 2, no. 2 (1998): 131.

102. Ó Tuathail, *Critical Geopolitics,* 256.

NOTES to Chapter 2

I am indebted to Professor Madhavan Palat and Professor Ranabir Samaddar for their comments and suggestions.

1. Malcolm Anderson, *Frontiers: Territory and State Formation in the Modern World* (New York: Blackwell, 1997).
2. Ranabir Samaddar, *Memory, Identity, Power: Politics in the Jungle Mahals 1890–1950* (Madras: Orient Longman, 1997).
3. A. E. Moodie, *Geography Behind Politics* (London: Hutchinson, 1947), 73–74.
4. J. R. V. Prescott, *Political Frontiers and Boundaries* (London: Routledge, Chapman and Hall, 1987), 1. Peter Sahlins also stresses that boundaries and borders evoke a precise linear division, while frontiers are more zonal. See Peter Sahlins, *Boundaries: The Making of France and Spain in the Pyrenees* (Berkeley and Los Angeles: University of California Press, 1989).
5. Michael Berube, *Marginal Forces/Cultural Centres: Tolson, Pinchon and the Politics of Canon* (Ithaca: Cornell University Press, 1992), 4–5.
6. Frederick Jackson Turner, "The Significance of the Frontier in American History," in *Selected Essays of Frederick Jackson Turner,* ed. R. A. Billington (New Jersey: Holt, Rinehart and Winston, 1961).
7. Richard Hofstadter and Seymour Martin Lipset, eds., *Turner and the Sociology of Frontiers* (New York: Basic Books, 1968), 3.
8. Turner, "Significance of the Frontier."
9. Donald W. Treadgold, *The Great Siberian Migration: Government and Peasants in Resettlement from Emancipation to the First World War* (Princeton: Princeton University Press, 1957); see also Donald W. Treadgold, "Russian Expansion in the Light of Turner's Study of the American Frontier," *Agricultural History* (October 1962): 147–155.
10. Alistair Hennessy, *The Frontier in Latin American History* (London: Edward Arnold, 1978), 12. Professor Tapan Roychowdhury has tried to apply the Turner thesis in his reportage on the southern frontier of Bengal in India, specifically the district of Barisal.
11. The debate probably began in 1942 with G. V. Portus, "Americans and Australians," *Australian Quarterly* (June 1942): 30-41. P. F. Sharp, "Three Frontiers: Some Comparative Studies of Canadian, American and Australian Settlements," *Pacific Historical Review* (1955): 369–377; W. V. Wyman and C. B. Kroeber, *The Frontier in Perspective* (Madison: University of Wisconsin Press, 1957).). See also the collection of essays in the forum "The Formation of Ethnic Identities in Frontier Societies," *Journal of World History,* 4, no. 2 (1993); Treadgold, "Russian Expansion," 147–155.
12. David A. Chappell, "Ethnogenesis and Frontiers," *Journal of World History* 4, no. 2 (1993).
13. In the 1990s, the Ford Foundation announced a five-year project grant under the rubric of "Crossing the Border." New Mexico State University received the grant for 1998.

14. Friedrich Ratzel, *Politische Geographie* (Munich: Oldenburg, 1897).

15. P. de Lapradelle, *La Frontiere: Etude de Droit Internationale* (Paris: Les Editions Internationales, 1928). The desire of States to have clear and uncontested borders formed the basis of most classic works on borders even in English. See S. Whittemore Boggs, *International Boundaries: A Study of Boundary Functions and Problems* (New York: Special Libraries Association, 1940).

16. J. Ancel, *Geopolitics* (Paris: Les Frontieres, 1938).

17. Norman J. G. Pounds, *Political Geography* (New York: McGraw-Hill, 1972).

18. Michiel Baud and Willem Van Schendel, "Toward a Comparative History of Borderlands," *Journal of World History* 8, no. 2 (1997): 214.

19. The State elites used maps to support their claims by creating discrepancies. According to Karunakar Gupta, many such maps were exchanged between India and China during the Sino-Indian crisis of 1959–1962. Karunakar Gupta, *Spotlight on the Sino-Indian Frontier* (Calcutta: New Book, 1982), 18. On this subject see also Kuldip Nayar, *Between the Lines* (Bombay: Allied, 1969), 133–227. Some countries such as Ecuador double their land possessions in maps. Others in Latin America forbid anyone other than the military to make maps.

20. James R. Akerman, "Cartography and the Emergence of Territorial States in Western Europe," *Proceedings of the Tenth Annual Meeting of the Western Society for French History,* ed. J. F. Sweets (Lawrence: University of Kansas Press, 1984), 84–93.

21. Stephen B. Jones, *Boundary Making: A Handbook for Statesmen, Treaty Editors and Boundary Commissioners* (Washington, D.C.: Carnegie Endowment for International Peace, 1945).

22. See J. Elliott, *The Frontier 1837–1947: The Story of the Northwest Frontier of India* (London: Cassell, 1968). Also Anthony Oye, *The Settlement of Boundary Disputes in International Law* (Manchester: Manchester University Press, 1967); D. E. T. Luard, *The International Regulation of Frontier Disputes* (London: Thames and Hudson, 1970).

23. D. R. Sack, *Human Territoriality: Its Theory and History* (Cambridge: Cambridge University Press, 1980); D. R. Sack, *Conceptions of Space in Social Thought* (Minneapolis: University of Minnesota Press, 1980).

24. Such ideas were articulated by Lord Acton who said, "Power tends to expand indefinitely and in so doing [to] transcend all barriers". For contemporary arguments on territoriality, borders and expansion, see Geoffrey Parker, *The Geopolitics of Domination* (London: Routledge, 1988). Also Giuseppe Sacco, "A Place in the Shade," *European Journal of International Affairs* 12, no. 2 (1991): 5–23.

25. A. I. Asiwaju, ed., *African Boundaries: Barriers, Conduits and Opportunities* (London: C. Hurst, 1996); Sahlins, *Boundaries*.

26. Astrid Suhrke and Lela Garner, *Ethnic Conflict in International Relations* (New York: Praeger, 1977). Also see John C. Welchman, ed., *Rethinking Borders* (Minneapolis: University of Minnesota, 1996); Gloria Anzaldua, *Borderlands/ La Frontera: The New Mestiza* (San Francisco: Aunt Lute, 1987).

27. There are a number of creative studies on questions of identities and borders, and especially on the US–Mexico border. See Daniel D. Arreola and James R. Curtis, *The Mexican Border Cities: Landscape, Anatomy and Place Personality* (Tuscon: University of Arizona Press, 1993); Jorge A. Bustamante, "Demystifying the United States–Mexico Border," *Journal of American History* (September 1992): 485–490; William Langewiesche, "The Border," *Atlantic Monthly* (May 1992): 53–92.

28. W. F. S. Miles and D. A. Rochefort, "Nationalism versus Ethnic Identity in Sub-Saharan Africa," *American Political Science Review* 85 (1991): 393–403.

29. A. I. Asiwaju, *Partitioned Africa* (London: C. Hurst, 1985).

30. Dorothy Woodman, *Himalayan Frontiers: A Political Review of British, Chinese, Indian and Russian Rivalries* (London: Cresset Press, 1969), ix.

31. Sir Thomas Holdich, *Political Frontiers and Boundary Making* (London: Macmillan, 1956), 2. The odd coincidence is that the year Turner published his thesis was also the year in which Durand negotiated the line named after him with the Emir of Afghanistan, which had serious implications for States in South and West Asia, then and later on.

32. George Nathaniel Curzon, *The Romanes Lecture* (London: Clarendon Press, 1907), 7. Alastair Lamb, *The McMahon Line: A Study in Relations between India, China and Tibet 1904 to 1914* (Toronto: University of Toronto Press, 1966).

33. Sir Robert Reid, *History of Frontier Areas Bordering Assam from 1883–1941* (Shillong: The Society for Northeast Hill Regions, 1942), 295.

34. Sir Cyril Radcliffe, *Bengal Boundary Commission Report,* 1947, D50/7/47R, National Library, Calcutta.

35. R. C. Majumdar, *British Paramountcy and Indian Renaissance,* part 1 (Bombay: Bharatiya Vidya Bhavan, 1963).

36. As a contemporary effort a group of historians came together for a colloquium on the Himalayan frontiers, but their efforts were less than satisfactory. N. R. Roy, ed., *Himalayan Frontier in Historical Perspective* (Calcutta: Institute of Historical Studies, 1986).

37. K. G. Vasanthamadhana, "The British Historians on the Himalayan Frontier," in *Himalayan Frontier in Historical Perspective,* ed. N. R. Roy (Calcutta: Institute of Historical Studies, 1986).

38. Paula Banerjee, "Borders as Unsettled Markers in South Asia: A Case Study of the Sino-Indian Border," *International Studies* 35, no. 2 (1998): 179–194.

39. See the collection of essays in Ranabir Samaddar, ed., *Reflections of Partition in the East* (New Delhi: Vikas, 1997).

40. Romila Thapar, "Seminar on Ideas in the Eighteenth and Nineteenth Centuries: A Report," *Enquiry* 1, no. 3 (1964): 114–130.

41. Jawaharlal Nehru, *The Discovery of India* (Calcutta: Signet, 1946), 538–539.

42. Rajni Kothari, *Politics in India* (New Delhi: Orient Longman, 1970).

43. Sudipto Kaviraj, "A Critique of the Passive Revolution," in *State and Politics in India,* ed. Partha Chatterjee (New Delhi: Oxford University Press, 1997), 45–88.

44. M. S. A. Rao and Francine Frankel, *Dominance and State Power in India: Decline of a Social Order* (New Delhi: Oxford University Press, 1990).

45. Alastair Lamb, *The China–India Border* (London: Oxford University Press, 1964); Alastair Lamb, *The Kashmir Problem: A Historical Survey* (New York: Praeger, 1966).

46. Neville Maxwell, *India's China War* (New York: Jonathan Cape, 1970).

47. B. M. Kaul, Untold Story (Bombay: Allied, 1967); K. N. Menon, *The Chinese Betrayal of India* (New Delhi: Contemporary India, 1962); see also P. C. Chakravarti, *Evolution of India's Northern Borders* (London: Asia Publishing House, 1971) and K. Ghosh, *The Chinese Invasion of India* (Calcutta: Banachhaya Ghosh, 1963);.

48. Woodman, *Himalayan Frontiers,* ix.

49. A. K. Ray, "The Case for a Strategic Frontier," *Indian Defence Review* 12, no. 1 (1997): 9–14.

50. Mahnaz Z. Ispahani, *Roads and Rivals: The Politics of Access in the Borderlands of Asia* (London: I. B. Tauris, 1989).

NOTES to Chapter 3

All translations from the Russian, unless otherwise stated, are by the author.

1. Alexander Burnes, *Travels into Bokhara, Being the Account of a Journey from India to Cabool, Tartary and Persia in 1831–1833*, 3 vols. (1834; reprint, New Delhi: Asian Educational Services, 1992); W. Moorcroft and G. Trebeck, *Travels in the Himalayan Provinces of Hindustan and the Punjab, in Ladakh and Kashmir, in Peshwar, Kabul, Kunduz and Bokhara from 1819 to 1825*, 2 vols. (1841; reprint, New Delhi: Asian Educational Services, 1989); Robert Shaw, *Visits to High Tartary, Yarkand and Kashgar* (1871; reprint, Hong Kong: Oxford University Press, 1984); J. Atkinson, *The Expedition into Afghanistan: Notes and Sketches Descriptive of the Country, Contained in a Personal Narrative during the Campaign of 1839 and 1840* (London, 1842); J. P. Ferrier, *Caravan Journeys and Wanderings in Persia, Afghanisatan, Turkestan and Beloochistan, with Historical Notices of the Countries lying between Russia and India*, 2d ed. Translated by William Jesse and edited by H. D. Seymour (London: John Murray, 1857); C. P. Skrine, *Chinese Central Asia: An Account of the Travels in Northern Kashmir and Chinese Turkestan* (Hong Kong: Oxford University Press, 1986); George Nathaniel Curzon, *Russia in Central Asia in 1889 and the Anglo-Russian Question* (London: Frank Cass, 1967); Francis Younghusband, *The Heart of a Continent* (1896; reprint, Hong Kong: Oxford University Press, 1984); George Nathaniel Curzon, *The Pamirs and the Source of the Oxus* (London: The Royal Geographical Society, 1896); P. T. Etherton, *Across the Roof of the World* (London: Constable, 1911).

2. Mahnaz Z. Ispahani, *Roads and Rivals: The Politics of Access in the Borderlands of Asia* (London: I. B. Tauris, 1989), 8.

3. S. A. M. Adshead, *Central Asia in World History* (London: Macmillan, 1993), 3–14.

4. Alexander J. Motyl, "After Empire: Competing Discourses and Inter-State Conflict in Post–Imperial Eastern Europe," in *Post–Soviet Political Order: Conflict and State Building*, eds. Barnett R. Rubin and Jack Snyder (London: Routledge, 1998), 19.

5. G. A. Akhmedjanov, *Rossiskaya Imperiya v Tsentral'noi Azii (Istoriya I Istoriografiya Kolonial'noi Politiki Tsarizma v Turkestane)* [The Russian Empire in Central Asia (History and historiography in the colonial politics of Czarism in Russia)] (Tashkent: Fan, 1995), 37.

6. N. A. Khalfin, *Rossiya i Khanstva Srednei Azii* (Russia and the Khanates of Central Asia) (Moscow: Nauka, 1974), 303–304, 310–311; P. P. Ivanov, *Ocherki po istorii Srednei Azii, XVI seredina XIX veka* (Sketches of the history of Central Asia, sixteenth–mid-nineteenth centuries) (Moscow: RAN, 1968), 31–37.

7. Bill Ashcroft, Gareth Griffiths and Helen Tiffin, *The Empire Writes Back: Theory and Practice in Post–Colonial Literatures* (London: Routledge, 1989), 8–12.

8. To defend their territories and safeguard their spheres of influence the imperial powers endlessly engaged in a process of territorial adjustments to preserve what they called a 'balance of power'. Malcolm Anderson,

Frontiers: Territory and State Formation in the Modern World (Cambridge: Polity Press, 1997), 25.

9. George Nathaniel Curzon, *Persia and the Persian Question*, vol. 1 (London: Frank Cass, 1966), 1:3–4.

10. *Ibid.*, 46.

11. Ferrier's account of his travels describes in great detail how the Wazir of Herat was pitted against the *Sardar* of Kandahar in what he took to be a typical case of incitement by the British. In actuality, this was an example of the age-old rivalry between the rulers of Persian origin and their neighbouring Turkic chieftains who were loyal to the Manghyt ruler of Bukhara. Ferrier, *Caravan Journeys and Wanderings*, 172–179.

12. Khalfin, *Rossiya i Khanstva*, 247–290; N. A. Khalfin and E. F. Rassadina, *N. V. Khanykov: Vostokoved i Diplomat* (Moscow: Nauka, 1974), 13–14, 19–20.

13. Chokan Valikhanov was the local representative of the Czarist authorities who was sent to eastern Turkestan to get acquainted with the vicinity, its geographical and ethnographic characteristics and trading prospects. He was sent there to propagate the idea of establishing direct trade relations between Russia and Kashgar. His outstanding economic survey of eastern Turkestan is entitled, *About the Situation in Altishahr or the Six Eastern Cities of the Chinese Provinces of Nan Ly (Little Bukhara) in 1858–59* (in Russian).

    M. K. Ilusizov, "Ekonomicheskie Vozreniya Kazakhskovo Uchenovo i Prosvetitelya-Demokratiya Ch. Ch. Valikhanova," in *Iz istorii Ekonomicheskoi Mysli Narodov Srednei SSSR* ("Economic views of the Kazakh scientist and enlightened democrat Ch. Ch. Valikhanov," in The history of economic thought of the people of Central Asia)(Moscow: Sotegiz, 1961), 87.

14. Paul B. Henze, "The Great Game in Kashgaria: British and Russian Missions to Yakub Beg," *Central Asian Survey* 8, no. 2 (1989): 62–67.

15. William Moorcroft was a veterinary surgeon who travelled as far as Leh in search of horses for the Bengal Regiment of the East India Company. He had come to India in 1808 at the Company's behest to superintend its stud farm. He travelled to Central Asia and Tibet in search of horses of great speed and stamina.

16. Robert Shaw (1839–1879) was a British tea planter, popularly remembered as the founder of the Royal Geographical Society (RGS) in London and as the uncle of Sir Francis Younghusband. While settled as a tea planter in Kangra in the Himalayas, he explored the markets of eastern Turkestan, and particularly those of Kashgar, to look for prospects for Indian tea in that region.

    George Hayward (1839–1870) was an accomplished British traveller sponsored by the RGS. His mission was to explore the passes between Ladakh and Kashgar. The Vice-President of the RGS and advisor to the Secretary of State for India, Sir Henry Rawlinson, was becoming suspicious of Russian explorations in Central Asia and sent Hayward in 1868 to the Pamirs and the Amu Darya. The purpose was to study the geography of the region, to keep a military watch on the land, the passes and the people, and to try to discover the source of the Amu Darya. He was murdered by local tribesmen in the Pamirs.

17. Paul Titas, "Honour the Baloch, Buy the Pushtun: Stereotypes, Social Organization and History in Western Pakistan," *Modern Asian Studies* 32, no. 3 (1998): 660.

18. The dates of birth, death and adventures of Ney Elias are not mentioned by his biographer, Gerald Morgan. The approximate dates for his exploratory missions to Kashgar, the eastern Pamirs and the upper Amu Darya and Badakhshan are between 1879 and 1882. As the British–Indian government's representative in Leh, he managed to work out a military cooperation between the British–Indian government and China in the 1880s. In his subsequent missions, Elias aimed to create strong buffer zones in Badakhshan in Afghanistan and in Kashgar in Xinjiang. Gerald Morgan, *Ney Elias: Explorer and Envoy Extraordinary in High Asia* (London: George Allen and Unwin, 1971).

19. Younghusband, *Heart of a Continent*; Curzon, *Russia in Central Asia*.

Sir Francis Younghusband (1863–1942), a nephew of Robert Shaw, undertook his first Great Game mission in 1884, in which he explored and reported on the routes and frontiers close to the Khyber Pass. He subsequently worked for the Intelligence Department of the British–Indian government based in Simla, under whose aegis he explored the frontier regions in Kashmir and Manchuria. In 1903 he was dispatched by the Viceroy, Lord Curzon, to Lhasa in Tibet in order to strengthen British–Indian relations with the Dalai Lama. After his retirement from service he became the president of the RGS, London and the chairman of the Mount Everest Committee. He died in 1942, aged 79.

20. Geoffrey Hosking, *Russia, People and Empire 1552–1917* (London: Fontana, 1998), 14.

21. Alfred J. Reiber, "Persistent Factors in Russian Foreign Policy: An Interpretive Essay," in *Imperial Russian Foreign Policy*, ed. Hugh Ragsdale (New York: Cambridge University Press, 1993), 330.

22. David MacKenzie, "The Conquest and Administration of Turkestan 1860–1885," in *Russian Colonial Expansion to 1917*, ed. Michael Rwykin (London: Mansell, 1988), 208.

23. Alton Donnelly, "The Mobile Steppe Frontier: The Russian Conquest and Colonization of Bashkiria and Kazakhstan to 1850," in *Russian Colonial Expansion to 1917*, ed. Michael Rwykin (London: Mansell, 1988), 189–190.

24. The Elder Horde/Larger Horde or Great Horde (*Ulu Zhuz*), literally meaning 'Great Hundred', was based mainly in the east and southeast of Kazakhstan and in the Ili valley. It was dominated by the Usun tribal confederation and comprised of ten distinct tribes of people from the Syr Darya and Semirech'e regions. Similarly, there were *Orta Zhuz* ('Middle Hundred') and *Kiti Zhuz* ('Small Hundred'). 'Horde' implies a common ancestry, although they were more in the nature of tribal federations. They were an extension of the

military unions formed by both Turkic and Mongol tribes. Such unions were called *zhuzi*.

25. Francis Henry Skrine and Edward Denison Ross, *The Heart of Asia: A History of Russian Turkestan and the Central Asian Khanates from the Earliest Times*, (London: Methuen, 1899), 245.

26. See Gorchakov's circular to the Great Powers on 21 November 1864 and General Kuropatkin's address to English tourists in Ashkabad on 25 November 1897. Cited in Dmetrius Charles Boulger, *England and Russia in Central Asia*, Appendices 1 and 2 (London: W. H. Allen, 1879), 417–428.

27. A. M. Khazanov, *Nomads and the Outside World*, trans. Julia Crookenden (Cambridge: Cambridge University Press, 1984), 19, 45. Khazanov refers to certain areas where pastoral nomadism was manifested in its 'purest' form. They are north Eurasia, high inner Asia, the Eurasian steppe, Arabia and the Sahara. Notwithstanding a few cases of economic adaptation, there is clear evidence of opposition between the elements of nomadism and sedentarism. The most important cause of friction was the practice of agriculture. The 'sedentarisation' of the Kazakhs by the Russians began from the end of the eighteenth century.

28. I. Stebelsky, "The Frontier in Central Asia," *Russian Historical Geography*, no. 1 (1983): 158.

29. A. Feoktistov, *Russkie, Kazakhi i Altayi* (Moscow: Alfa i Omega, 1991), 36–37.

30. Khalfin, *Rossiya i Khanstva*, 346.

31. Boulger, *England and Russia*, 318–319.

32. MacKenzie, *"Conquest and Administration,"* 220.

33. N. Ostroumov, *Konstantin Petrovich fon 'Kaufman, ustroitel' Turkestanskovo Kraia; Lychnia Vospominaniia N. Ostroumova (1877–1881 gody)* (Konstantin Petrovich fon Kaufman, the builder of Turkestan province; Personal memoirs of N. Ostroumov [1877–1881])(Tashkent, 1899), 163; Seymour Becker, *Russia's Protectorates in Central Asia: Bukhara and Khiva 1865–1924* (Cambridge: Harvard University Press, 1968), 197.

34. *Turkestanskie Vedomosti* (Tashkent), 22 January 1874, Tashkent: Ali Shir Navoi State Public Library.

35. Territories that were not situated along the course of the Pyandzh river (upper Amu Darya) remained undefined because they were located in inhospitable regions. Among these territories were little principalities within the Bukharan Emirate that adjoined Russian and Afghan territories in the Pamirs. *Entsiklopicheski Slovar*, s. v. "Bukhara." (Leiden, 1891).

36. Madhavan K. Palat, "Tsarist Russian Imperialism," *Studies in History*, 4 (January–December 1988): 294.

37. The internal politics of Afghanistan were closely linked with the foreign policies of Britain and Russia, who had carved out their spheres of influence in Afghan territory. This has been narrated in brief historical memoirs. N. Ostroumov, "'Begstvo': Abdur Rakhman Khana iz Tashkenta v Afghanistan," *Kaufmanskii Sbornik General Adjutanta K. P. fon Kaufmana*

Pervovo, Izdanii v Pamiyat 25 let istekshikh co gnia smerti pokoriteliya I ustroitelya Turkestanskovo Kraia ("'Begdom': Flight of Abdur Rahman Khan from Tashkent to Afghanistan," Kaufman Collection of General Adjutant K. P. fon Kaufman, published in memory of 25 years since the death of the conqueror and builder of Turkestan province)(Moscow, 1910), 100–60.

38. "Afganskoe Razgranichenie 1885–1887 gody," 14–20; "Pamirskoe Razgranichenie 1895 gody," 20–25; in *Ocherki Istorii Formirovaniya Gosudarstvennikh granits mezhdu Rossiei, SSSR i Afganistanom* (Sketches of the history of the formation of State borders between Russia, USSR and Afghanistan)(Moscow: Rossiski Tsentr Strategicheskikh i Mezhdunarodnikh Issledovanyi, 1994).

39. Younghusband, *Heart of a Continent,* 124–188.

40. Information was passed to the Russians of a growing Turkic influence in Afghanistan: Turkic officers were training the Afghan army, and Turkic emissaries were disseminating pan-Islamic propaganda. Since Afghanistan was considered a British protectorate, the Russians assumed that these activities were conducted with British approval, although in reality the level of Turkic propaganda in Afghanistan made both the Russians and the British wary. Suhash Chakravorty, *Anatomy of the Raj: Russian Consular Reports* (New Delhi: Peoples Publishing House, 1981), 262–264.

41. After the revolution, Soviet ideologues argued that the district-wise division of the Turkestan *krai* (Russian frontier region) did not take into account local conditions, and that the indigenous people were left out of the administrative apparatus. They pointed out that the mere division of a geographical space was useless, as it became increasingly unmanageable over time; according to them, the division should have been on the basis of the ethnic stock of the people of the region. "O raionirovani Turkestanskoi Respubliki," in *Materialy Administrativnoi kommissii raionirovanyu Respubliki pri NKVDTASSAR* ("On the Territorial Delimitation of the Turkestan Republic," in Materials of the Adminsitrative Commision Regarding Territorial Demarcation by the National Commissariat of Internal Affairs, Turkestan Autonomous Soviet Socialist Republic) (Tashkent: Tsentral'nyi Gosudarstvennyi Arkhiv [Central State Archives], 1923), 201–202.

NOTES to Chapter 4

The author would like to thank Barun De, Ranabir Samaddar, Muhammad Tajuddin, Joseph Miller, Sunil Kumar and Sumit Guha for comments on an earlier draft of this paper.

1. Ranabir Samaddar, "The Failed Dialectic of Territoriality and Security and the Imperatives of Dialogue," *International Studies* 35, no. 1 (1998): 107–122.

2. Eric Williams, *Capitalism and Slavery* (New York: Capricorn Books, 1966).

3. Seymour Drescher, *Econocide: British Slavery in the Era of Abolition* (Pittsburgh: University of Pittsburgh Press, 1977); David Eltis and James Walvin, eds., *The Abolition of the Atlantic Slave Trade: Origins and Effects in Europe, Africa and the Americas* (Madison: University of Wisconsin Press, 1981); see also Thomas Bender, ed., *The Anti-Slavery Debate: Capitalism and Abolitionism as a Problem in Historical Interpretation* (Berkeley and Los Angeles: University of California Press, 1992); Robin Blackburn, *The Overthrow of Colonial Slavery 1776–1848* (London: Verso, 1996), 517–550.

4. Among a vast and growing literature, the classic is still R. Roberts and S. Miers, eds., *The End of Slavery in Africa* (Madison: University of Wisconsin Press, 1988); also see Suzanne Miers, "Slavery and the Slave Trade as International Issues 1890–1939," *Slavery and Abolition* 19, no. 2 (1998): 16–37; W. G. Clarence-Smith, ed., *The Economics of the Indian Ocean Slave Trade in the Nineteenth Century* (London: Frank Cass, 1989); Elizabeth Savage, *The Human Commodity: Perspectives on the Trans-Saharan Slave Trade* (London: Frank Cass, 1992); M. A. Klein, ed., *Breaking the Chains: Slavery, Bondage and Emancipation in Modern Africa and Asia* (Madison: University of Wisconsin Press, 1993); Alice Moore-Harell, "Slave Trade in the Sudan in the Nineteenth Century and its Suppression in the Years 1877–1880," *Middle Eastern Studies* 34, no. 2 (1998): 113–128.

5. Suzanne Miers, *Britain and the Ending of the Slave Trade* (Bristol: Longman, 1975), 116–117; Suzanne Miers and Martin Klein, introduction in *Slavery and Abolition* 19, no. 2 (1998): 1–15.

6. G. J. Alder, *British India's Northern Frontier 1865–1895: A Study in Imperial Policy* (London: Longman, 1963), 22–55; Wen-Djang Chu, *The Moslem Rebellion in Northwest China 1862–1878: A Study of Government Minority Policy* (The Hague and Paris: Mouton, 1966), 168–169, especially footnote 16.

7. For an account of a Russian male slave taken by the Kyrgyz and sold to the Bukharan ruling house in the latter part of the eighteenth century, see P. M. Kemp, trans. and ed., "The Travells of Filip Yefremov," in *Russian Travellers to India and Persia (1624–1798)* (reprint, New Delhi: Jiwan Prakashan, 1959), 45–93; for a study on Uighur Muslim concubines in eighteenth-century China see James A. Millward, "A Uyghur Muslim in Qianlong's Court: The Meanings of the Fragrant Concubine," *Journal of Asian Studies* 53, no. 2 (1994): 427–458; for families of Hazaras sold into slavery in Bukhara and Khulum as punishment, see I. H. Siddiqi, "Ta'rikh-I Manazil-I-Bukhara: A Source for the

History of Central Asia During the First Decades of the Nineteenth Century," *Studies in Islam* (July 1980): 131–138; and Mohan Lal, *Travels in the Panjab, Afghanistan and Turkistan to Balkh, Bokhara and Herat and a Visit to Great Britain and Germany* (1846; rev. ed., New Delhi: Indian Council for Historical Research, 1977): 54, 58–59; for female and child slaves in Turkestan and Balkh, see Lal, *Travels in the Panjab*, 62–63, 73; for slaves of Russian and Persian origin sold in Bukhara in the mid-nineteenth century, see Alexander Burnes, *Travels into Bokhara, Being the Account of a Journey from India to Cabool, Tartary and Persia in 1831–1833*, 3 vols. (1834; reprint, New Delhi: Asian Educational Services, 1992), 1:256, 275, 281–283, 293–296, 342–244; 2:11–15, 63, 67; Arminius Vambery, *Travels in Central Asia, Being an Account of a Journey from Teheran across the Turkoman Desert on the Eastern Shore of the Caspian to Khiva, Bokhara and Samarcand Performed in the Year 1863* (London: John Murray, 1864), 58–60, 74–75, 77–80, 191–193; Arminius Vambery, *Sketches of Central Asia* (London: W. H. Allen, 1868), 205–230.

8. Helene Carrere D'Encausse, *Islam and the Russian Empire: Reform and Revolution in Central Asia* (reprint, London: I. B. Tauris, 1988), 23–24.

9. Peter Hopkirk, *The Great Game: On Secret Service in High Asia* (Oxford: Oxford University Press, 1990), 85.

10. For first-hand reports on the Russian liberation of slaves in the khanate, see Foreign Political A, September 1873, no. 266, NAI; for the subsequent terms of the treaty between Russia and Khiva regarding the permanent abolition of slavery and trade in men, see, Foreign Secret F, April 1874, nos. 233, 236, 239 and 245, NAI.

11. Charles Marvin, *Reconnoitring Central Asia: Pioneering Adventures in the Region Lying Between Russia and India* (1885; reprint, New Delhi: Asian Educational Services, 1996), 64; Charles Marvin, *Merv, the Queen of the World and the Scourge of the Man-Stealing Turcomans* (London: W. H. Allen, 1881), footnote, 148.

12. G. W. Leitner, *Dardistan in 1866, 1886 and 1893, Being an Account of the History, Religions, Customs, Legends, Fables and Songs of Gilgit, Chilas, Kandia, Dasin, Chitral, Hunsa, Nagyr and Other Parts of the Hindukush* (1890; reprint, New Delhi: Asian Educational Services, 1996), appendix 1, 6–7.

13. *Ibid.*, 10.

14. See an account of the wars in Leitner, *Dardistan*, 85–96.

15. Francis Younghusband, *The Heart of a Continent* (1896; reprint, Hong Kong: Oxford University Press, 1984), 285.

16. *Ibid.*, 236.

17. For the transformation from *ress* (tax paid in labour services) to *begar* (obligatory porterage) within the portering economy of this region after the mid-nineteenth century, see Kenneth Iaian Macdonald, "Push and Shove: Spatial History and the Construction of a Portering Economy in Northern Pakistan," *Comparative Studies in Society and History* 40, no. 2 (1998): 287–317.

According to the author, the toll taken by the obligatory porterage was harsh, as many porters died working on the Gilgit road being constructed under colonial intervention, for which see also Foreign Secret E, December 1890, nos. 152–158, NAI; and E. F. Knight, *Where Three Empires Meet: A Narrative of Recent Travel in Kashmir, Western Tibet, Gilgit and the Adjoining Countries* (1905: reprint, New Delhi: Asian Educational Services, 1993), 163, 245.

18. Knight, *Three Empires*, 215, 227.

19. *Ibid.*, 281.

20. For detailed accounts of slave dealing in this region in the 1830s, see Lal, *Travels in the Panjab*, 58 and *passim*.

21. Robert Shaw, *Visits to High Tartary, Yarkand and Kashgar* (1871; reprint, Hong Kong: Oxford University Press, 1984), 341.

22. *Ibid.*, 343–344.

23. Leitner, *Dardistan*, 93–94.

24. Shaw, *Visits to High Tartary*, 421.

25. For slaves in nomadic communities as sources of stratification, see A. M. Khazanov, *Nomads and the Outside World*, trans. Julia Crookenden (Cambridge: Cambridge University Press, 1984), 153, 159–160.

26. T. K. Beisembiev, "Farghana's Contacts with India in the Eighteenth and Nineteenth Centuries (According to the Khokand Chronicles)," *Journal of Asian History* 28, no. 2 (1994): 126.

27. Vambery, *Travels in Central Asia*, 229.

28. Ram Rahul, *Central Asia: A Historical Survey* (New Delhi: Vikas, 1996), 72.

29. Leitner, *Dardistan*, 56, 96.

30. George Scott Robertson, *The Kafirs of the Hindukush* (1896; reprint, Karachi: Oxford University Press, 1974), 355, 568–569.

31. Knight, *Three Empires*, 348.

32. Shaw, *Visits to High Tartary*, 314.

33. Hopkirk, *Great Game*, 213–229. See also Mary Holdsworth, *Turkestan in the Nineteenth Century: A Brief History of the Khanates of Bukhara, Kokand and Khiva* (Oxford: Central Asian Research Centre and St. Anthony's College, 1959); for Persian slaves in Bukhara see Holdsworth, *Turkestan,* 21–23; for aims of the Russian expedition against Khiva in 1839, which was finally achieved in 1873, see Holdsworth, *Turkestan,* 50–56.

34. Hopkirk, *Great Game*, 219.

35. From the account of the Russian slaves of the eighteenth century, it would appear that female slaves were manumitted even less, partly because of the positions of work and intimacy that they were enmeshed in within the households of their masters, and partly because of the lack of independent access to horses and guns, vital for a getway in that terrain.

36. C. P. Skrine and Pamela Nightingale, *Macartney at Kashgar: New Light on British, Chinese and Russian Activities in Sinkiang 1890–1918* (London: Methuen, 1973), 46–89. See also Peter Hopkirk, *Foreign Devils on the Silk*

Road: The Search for the Lost Cities and Treasures of Chinese Central Asia (Oxford: Oxford University Press, 1980), 73; and Lady Macartney, *An English Lady in Chinese Turkestan* (1931; reprint, Oxford: Oxford University Press, 1985). Her husband, George Macartney, was the son of a Scottish father and a Chinese mother, of whom he never spoke even to his own children, and served for twenty-eight years as Britain's representative in Kashgar.

37. Miers, *Ending of the Slave Trade.*
38. Robert W. Fogel and Stanley L. Engerman, eds., "Philanthropy at Bargain Prices: Notes on the Economics of Gradual Emancipation," in *Without Consent or Contract: The Rise and Fall of American Slavery – Conditions of Slave Life and the Transition to Freedom,* eds. Robert W. Fogel and Stanley L. Engerman (New York and London: W. W. Norton, 1992), 2: 587–605; see also Claudia Goldin, "The Economics of Emancipation," in *Without Consent or Contract: The Rise and Fall of American Slavery – Conditions of Slave Life and the Transition to Freedom,* eds. Robert W. Fogel and Stanley L. Engerman (New York and London: W. W. Norton, 1992), 2: 614–628.
39. Resident in Kashmir to Secretary, GOI, 17 May 1892, Foreign Secret F, February 1893, no. 389, NAI.
40. *Ibid.,* no. 405.
41. *Ibid.,* no. 389.
42. Note by W. J. C[unningham] to Secretary, 13 December 1892, Foreign Secret F, February 1893, no. 389, NAI.
43. Note by W. Hanrahan, n.d., Foreign Secret F, July 1894, 560–610, no. 389, NAI.
44. Demi-official from G. Macartney to H. M. Durand, 12 May 1892, Foreign Secret F, February 1893, no. 396, NAI.
45. *Ibid.*
46. Macartney to British Agent at Gilgit, 1 September 1892, Foreign Secret F, February 1893, no. 404, NAI.
47. O. Patterson, *Slavery and Social Death* (Cambridge, Mas.: Harvard University Press, 1982) 134–146.
48. For the early history of the settlement of Xinjiang, see Joanna Waley-Cohen, *Exile in Mid-Qing China: Banishment to Xinjiang 1758–1820* (New Haven: Yale University Press, 1991).
49. Tor H. Aase, "The Theological Construction of Conflict: Gilgit, Northern Pakistan," in *Muslim Diversity: Local Islam in Global Contexts,* ed. Leif Manger (Richmond: Curzon Press, 1999), 58–79.
50. See Indrani Chatterjee, *Gender, Slavery and the Law in Colonial India* (New Delhi: Oxford University Press, 1999).
51. Amar Singh Chohan, *The Gilgit Agency 1877–1935* (New Delhi: Atlantic, n.d.), 17–21.
52. For further details, see Alder, *British India's Northern Frontier.*
53. See Aase, "Theological Construction," 64–67.
54. Chohan, *Gilgit Agency,* 57–67.

55. See Macartney's report of a "question which Tseng ta lao Yieh asked me why I had taken no steps on behalf of the Chitrali slaves, Chitral, being, as he stated, under Kashmir as well as Nagar, Baltistan, etc.," in a letter to the Resident in Kashmir, 1 February 1894, Foreign Secret F, July 1894, no. 602, NAI.

56. Peshawar Confidential Diary no. 21, 22 December 1888, paragraph 13, Foreign Secret F, January 1889, no. 102, NAI; for the comment that Chitral was a slave State and the mehtar unsympathetic to the abolitionist agenda, see British Agent at Gilgit to Resident in Kashmir, 13 January 1895, Foreign Secret F, August 1895, no. 146, NAI; for details of a Chitrali who was sold as a slave in Kabul, see Gilgit Agency Diary for the fortnight ending 15 December 1894, Foreign Secret F, March 1895, no. 473, NAI.

57. Surgeon-Major Sir George S. Robertson's note on Mr. G. Macartney's letter, 15 October 1892, Foreign Secret F, February 1893, no. 405, NAI.

58. Surgeon-Major Sir George S. Robertson, "Confidential Notes on Certain Points in Connection with Our Future Arrangements in Chitral," 13 August 1895, Foreign Secret F, September 1895, no. 339, NAI.

59. Secretary, GOI to Surgeon-Major Sir George S. Robertson, 17 August 1895, Foreign Secret F, September 1895, no. 347, NAI.

60. H. S. Barnes, Resident in Kashmir, to Secretary, GOI, 25 February 1895, Foreign Secret F, August 1895, no. 145, NAI.

61. Female Chinese slaves who had borne children to their Muslim masters had also been allowed to remain in their masters' houses during the course of the Manchu drive for pacification in the early 1870s, for which see Chu, *Moslem Rebellion*, 154.

62. Translation of Report of the District Magistrate of Yarkand, Foreign Secret F, July 1894, no. 589, NAI.

63. Translated Reply of the Lt. Governor of Xinjiang, n.d., Foreign Secret F, July 1894, no. 577, NAI. This was a response to the regulations drawn up by the District Magistrate of Yarkand after his interviews with Macartney on 1 June 1893, for details of which see, Translation of Report of the District Magistrate of Yarkand, Foreign Secret F, July 1894, nos. 569–575, NAI.

64. Excerpt from Translation of Regulations submitted to the Taotai for Orders, Foreign Secret F, July 1894, no. 590, NAI. The insistence upon assimilation of freedmen into Chinese society may have been particularly pointed in the case of Xinjiang, over which imperial Chinese control had been reestablished only ten years before this date, in 1884. See S. A. M. Adshead, *Central Asia in World History* (London: Macmillan, 1993), 194–196. This may be considered as part of the "administrative Sinicization" urged by Ping-Ti Ho in "In Defense of Sinicization: A Rebuttal of Evelyn Rawski's 'Reenvisioning the Qing,'" *Journal of Asian Studies* 57, no. 1 (1998): 123–155.

65. Macartney to Resident in Kashmir, Foreign Secret F, no. 580, NAI.

66. Regulations submitted to the Taotai, Foreign Secret F, July 1894, no. 590, NAI.

67. Translation of a Report from the District Magistrate of Yarkand to the Taotai of Kashgar, Foreign Secret F, July 1894, no. 603, NAI.

68. Extract from the Diary of Special Assistant for Chinese Affairs (Macartney) to Resident in Kashmir, Foreign Secret F, 30 April 1894, under date 23 April, no. 608, NAI.

69. Macartney to British Agent at Gilgit, 20 November 1894, Foreign Secret F, August 1895, no. 147, NAI.

70. Translation of a Circular Letter from Wang, the Sub-Prefect of Karghallik to the District Magistrate of Yarkand, Taotai of Kashgar, Provincial Treasurer and Provincial Governor of the New Dominions, n.d., Foreign Secret F, August 1895, no. 148, NAI.

71. Extract from Diary of Special Assistant for Chinese Affairs (Macartney) to Resident in Kashmir ending 15 March 1895, Foreign Secret F, July 1895, no. 1155, NAI.

72. Statement of expenses in letter from Special Assistant for Chinese Affairs (Macartney) to Resident in Kashmir, 8 August 1895, Foreign Secret F, December 1895, nos. 229–231, NAI.

73. Shaw, *Visits to High Tartary*, 347.

74. *Ibid.*, 345–346.

75. A Chinese Muslim primer, *Back to the True Faith Earnestly*, listed as one of the disgraceful acts of a Muslim that of the "taking of children of another Muslim into bondage". Cited in Raphael Israeli, *Muslims in China: A Study in Cultural Confrontation* (London and Malmo: Curzon Press; Atlantic Highlands: Humanities Press, 1980) 149–150. For a summary of the revitalisation of Islam in these regions, see Dru C. Gladney, "The Salafiyya Movement in Northwest China: Islamic Fundamentalism among the Muslim Chinese?" in *Muslim Diversity: Local Islam in Global Contexts*, ed. Leif Manger (Richmond, Surrey: Curzon Press, 1999), 102–149; and Dru C. Gladney, ed., *The Legacy of Islam in China* (Cambridge: Harvard University Press, 1989).

76. Hopkirk, *Great Game*, 82, 84–88.

77. Consul at Resht to Secretary of State for Foreign Affairs, 7 November 1873, enclosed in Foreign Secret F, April 1874, no. 245, NAI.

78. Shaw, *Visits to High Tartary*, 273, 297–300.

79. *Ibid.*, 273.

80. Statement of A. Dalgliesh, 7 July 1887, Foreign Secret F, August 1887, no. 326, NAI. While Dalgliesh reported that the men had been left in the charge of the Mir of Hunza who was then murdered by his son, the petition of the slave Turghan says that the men were left in the care of the son, Nafis Khan, who sold them to the *Beg* of Sirikol. Foreign Secret F, August 1887, no. 327, NAI.

81. H. M. Durand advised the Viceroy, Lord Dufferin, to procure the emancipation of the two men with money from the Secret Service Fund, but added that "we cannot touch the Chief of Hunza". See note by H. M. Durand to His Excellency, 7 July 1877, Foreign Secret F, August 1887, no. 326, NAI.

82. Younghusband, *Heart of a Continent*, 177, 179, 199, 209. Younghusband appears to have changed his attitude towards one of them from the beginning

of the march ("a grumbler", etc.), to the end ("the hardest working man I have ever known").

83. Diary of Special Assistant for Chinese Affairs (Macartney) for fortnight ending 15 June 1895, Foreign Secret F, November 1895, no. 86, NAI. For accounts of kinsmen ransoming the Persian slaves in Bukhara in the mid-nineteenth century, see Vambery, *Travels in Central Aisa*, 235–236.

84. See the case of three 'native' slaves in Yangi Hissar, under date 11 April 1897, and that of a Gilgiti slave runaway at Paṣ Robat, under 16 June 1897, Diary of Special Assistant for Chinese Affairs (Macartney) for fortnight ending 15 April 1897 and for fortnight ending 30 June 1897, Foreign Secret F, September 1897, nos. 106 and 217, NAI.

85. Diary of the Special Assistant for Chinese Affairs (Macartney) for fortnight ending 30 April 1897 , under date 20 April 1897, Foreign Secret F, September 1897, no. 209, NAI. This caused the proclamation against re-enslaving in Karghallik by a new District Magistrate.

86. Statement of Expenses to be Borne Entirely by the Kashmir Darbar, Foreign Secret, F December 1895, no. 230, NAI.

87. List of Slaves of British-Kashmiri Origin Released, Foreign Secret F, August 1895, nos. 155 and 168, NAI.

88. Diary of Special Assistant for Chinese Affairs (Macartney) ending 15 January 1895, Foreign Secret F, July 195, no. 1149, NAI. From the list of slaves manumitted in Karghallik in 1894, discussed above, it appears that there were two female salves named Gulbegi. One was a twenty-year-old woman who was the mother of three daughters who were also manumitted along with her. Since the older Gulbegi is also described as the daughter of a released slave, it is likely that it was the younger Gulbegi whose brother was asking to take her back.

89. Studies conducted in the 1980s and 1890s do not show that people represented themselves as having descended from 'Afghan' or 'Kashmiri' ancestors, for which see Colin Mackerras, "Han-Muslim and Intra-Muslim Social Relations in Northwestern China," in *Nationalism and Ethnoregional Identities in China*, ed. William Safran (London and Portland: Frank Cass, 1998); and Matthew Hoddie, "Ethnic Identity Change in the People's Republic of China: An Explanation Using Data from the 1982 and 1990 Census Enumerations," in *Nationalism and Ethnoregional Identities in China*, ed. William Safran (London and Portland: Frank Cass, 1998), Table 1, 28–46, 119–141. However, Gladney's work seems to suggest that assimilation into Hui or other Muslim groups would have led to an 'enclave' existence among the dominant Han society till the 1950s. See Gladney, "The Salafiyya Movement," 112.

90. See details of case in Foreign Political A-I, July 1883, nos. 14–25, NAI.

91. Translated *kharita* (formal missive) from the Agent to the Governor-General for Central India to address of Nawab Shahjahan Begum, 23 June 1883, Foreign Political A-I, January 1884, no. 148, NAI.

NOTES to Chapter 5

All translations from the Russian, unless otherwise stated, are by the author.

1. Malcolm Anderson, *Frontiers: Territory and State Formation in the Modern World* (Cambridge: Polity Press, 1997).

2. Principle decision on the Nationalities Question adopted by the Seventh All Russian Conference of the Russian Social Democratic Labour Party, 1917.

3. Demetrio Boersner, *The Bolsheviks and the National and Colonial Questions* (Geneva: Librarie E. Droz, 1957).

4. Some of V. I. Lenin's writings on the National Question are, "On the Right of Nations to Self-Determination," in vol. 1; "Speech on the National Question at the All Russia Conference of the RSDRP, 12 May 1917," in vol. 2; "Preliminary Draft on the National and Colonial Question for the Second Congress of the Comintern," in vol. 3 of V. I. Lenin, *Selected Works* (Moscow: Progress, 1970); and in "Cultural National Autonomy," in vol. 9; "The Question of Nationalities and Autonomisation," in vol. 9; "Critical Remarks on the National Question," in vol. 20; "National Liberation and the Right of Nations to Self-Determination," in vol. 20 of V. I. Lenin, *Collected Works* (Moscow: Progress, 1964).

5. I. V. Stalin, *Marxism and the National and Colonial Question* (New York: Macmillan, 1936).

6. Lenin's ideas on self-determination and its definition are given in "Right of Nations".

7. "Ko Vsym Trudyashemia Musulmanam Rossi i Vostok," in V. I. Lenin, *O Srednei Azii i Uzbekistane* (About Central Asia and Uzbekistan) (Tashkent: Gosudartsvenoi Isdatelstsvo Uzbekistanskoi SSR, 1957).

8. R. A. Tuzmuhamedov, *How the National Problem was Solved in Soviet Central Asia,* trans. David Fidlon (Moscow: Progress, 1973).

9. *Ibid.,* 71.

10. For an examination of the Russian administrative system see, V. A. Shishkin, ed., *Istoria Uzbekskoi SSR,* vol. 2 (Tashkent: Institut Istorii i Arkheologii, 1967); O. A. Sukhareava, *Kvartalnaya Obshena Poznefeudalnogo Goroda Bukhari* (Blocks of the post–feudal city of Bukhara)(Moscow: Akademia Nayuk SSR, 1967); Richard Pierce, *Russian Central Asia 1867–1917* (Berkeley and Los Angeles: University of California Press, 1960); Demitrius Charles Boulger, *England and Russia in Central Asia* (London: W. H. Allen, 1879); Edward Allworth, ed., *Central Asia: A Century of Russian Rule* (New York and London: Columbia University Press, 1967); Walter Kolarz, *Russia and her Colonies* (New York: Preager, 1952); Seymour Becker, *Russia's Protectorates in Central Asia: Bukhara and Khiva 1865–1924* (Cambridge: Harvard University Press, 1968); Mary Holdsworth, *Turkestan in the Nineteenth Century: A Brief History of the Khanates of Bukhara, Kokand and Khiva* (Oxford: Central Asian Research Centre in association with St. Anthony's College, 1959).

11. K. K. Palen, *Turkestanskogo Kraia,* St. Petersburg, 1909–1911. (INION Collection; New Delhi: IGNCA), microfiche nos. 9501–9518.

12. "Thesis on the National and Colonial Question" adopted by the Second Commintern Congress, 28 July 1920, point 2. Cited in Jane Degras, ed., *The Communist International Documents 1919–1943,* vol. 1 (New York: Oxford University Press, 1956).

13. Tuzmuhamedov, *National Problem,* 95.

14. For a detailed account of the history of delimitation see Shishkin, *Istoria Uzbekskoi,* vol. 3; A. A. Gordiyenko, *Sozdaniye Sovetskoi Natsionalnoi Gosudarts-vennosti v Srednei Azii* (Establishment of Soviet National Statehood in Central Asia)(Moscow: Progress, 1959); M. M. Mumenova, *Istoria Bukhari s Drevneishikh Vpyemini do Nashei Dnei* (History of Bukhara from ancient times to the present) (Tashkent: Gosudartsvenoi Isdatelstgo Uzbekistanskoi SSR, 1976); R. Vaidyanath, *The Formation of the Soviet Central Asian Republics: A Study in Soviet Nationality Policy 1917–1936* (New Delhi: Peoples Publishing House, 1967); Alexander Park, *Bolshevism in Turkestan 1917–1927* (New York: Columbia University Press, 1957).

15. For a detailed discussion on the Commission see, "The Turkestan Commission 1919–1920," *Central Asian Review* 12, no. 1 (1964); Mustafa Chokaev, "Turkestan and the Soviet Regime," *Journal of the Royal Central Asian Society,* no. 18 (1931).

16. From an ECCI appeal on the forthcoming Congress of the Eastern Peoples at Baku, July 1920, cited in Degras, *Communist Documents.*

17. Vaidyanath, *Soviet Central Asian Republics,* 272.

18. Gordiyenko, *Sozdaniye Sovetskoi.*

19. Chokaev, "Turkestan."

20. From the proceedings of the All Russian Muslim Congress, as cited in Serge A. Zenkovsky, *Pan Turkism and Islam in Russia* (Cambridge: Harvard University Press, 1960), 149.

21. Geoffrey Wheeler, *Modern History of Soviet Central Asia* (London: Weidenfeld and Nicholson, 1964).

22. Bukhara was the life and soul of Turkestan, inhabited by large numbers of Uzbeks, Tajiks, Arabs, Mervi, Persians, Hindus and Jews – a sure sign of a metropolis. Arminius Vambery comments on the fact that though his friend Hadji Salih was from Kokand, which was then at war with Bukhara, he was delighted when, in answer to his question as to how he liked Bukhara, Vambery answered rather untruthfully, "[i]t pleases me much". Arminius Vambery, *Travels in Central Asia, Being an Account of a Journey from Tehran Across the Turkoman Desert on the Eastern Shore of the Caspian to Khiva, Bokhara and Samarcand Performed in the Year 1863* (London: John Murray, 1864).

23. Nora Chadwick and Victor Zhirmensky, *Oral Epics of Central Asia* (Cambridge: Cambridge University Press, 1969), 90–91.

24. *Ibid.,* 292–296.

25. *Ibid.,* 93.

26. *Ibid.,* 91.

27. Olaf Caroe, *Soviet Empire, The Turks of Central Asia and Stalinism* (New York: Macmillan, 1967), 32–33.

28. Cited in John A. Armstrong, *Nations before Nationalism* (Chapel Hill: University of North Carolina Press, 1982), 38.

29. A. M. Khazanov, "The Early State among the Eurasian Nomads," in *The Study of the State,* eds. Henri J. M. Classen and Peter Skalnik (The Hague: Mouton, 1981).

30. Lawrence Krader, "The Origin of the State among the Nomads of Asia," in *Soviet and Western Anthropology,* ed. Ernest Gellner (London: Gerald Duckworth, 1980).

31. Armstrong, *Nations,* 45.

32. Arminius Vambery, *History of Bokhara from the Earliest Period down to the Present* (London: John Murray, 1873), 183. Vambery was a Hungarian linguist whose interest in the relations between Hungarian and Turko-Tartaric dialects led him to visit the Central Asian region between 1863 and 1868.

33. Kemal Karpat, "The Old and the New Central Asia," *Central Asian Survey* 12, no. 4 (1993).

34. Holdsworth, *Turkestan,* 2.

35. Milan Hauner, *What is Asia to Us: Russia's Heartland Yesterday and Today* (Boston: Unwin Hyman, 1990).

36. Boulgar, *England and Russia,* 1:2.

37. Alexander Burnes, *Travels into Bokhara, Being the Account of a Journey from India to Cabool, Tartary and Persia in 1831–1833,* 3 vols. (1834; reprint, New Delhi: Asian Educational Services, 1992); Vambery, *Travels in Central Asia,* 144–196, 362–379, 430–438. See also additional chapters on his travels in *Sketches of Central Asia* (London: W. H. Allen, 1868).

38. This is clearly evident in Vambery's account of Bukhara, which is particularly unflattering – though the all-pervasive hypocrisy that Vambery records is also noted by Burnes. One reason for this was possibly the fact that when Vambery arrived in Bukhara in 1863, dressed as a pious dervish, he found a striking contrast between the population there and the people of Khiva he had only just left behind. They had "pelted him with articles of attire and other presents", but "not a farthing" did he get from the people in the "holy city of Bokhara"; in fact, a Bukharan *ishan* (holy man) once tried to pass on to him some useless coins that he had just received from a Turkman. Vambery also arrived at a time when the unfortunate fates of two English officers, Connolly and Stoddart, was a much talked-of affair. It is not surprising, therefore, that he begins his account of Bukhara with the warning words of Mesnevi, a mystical poet, to a Sufi travelling to Bukhara:

> To Bokhara thou goest
> Art thou mad?
> Nought but chains and bondage
> There to be had.

Vambery, *Sketches of Central Asia.*

39. He notes, "Should Russia proceed actively to carry out her designs on Central Asia, the three khanates. . .would by their dissensions furnish the common enemy with the very best arms against themselves". Vambery, *Travels in Central Asia,* 431.

40. Vambery, *History of Bokhara,* 242–243.

41. Burnes, *Travels into Bokhara,* introduction to vol. 1. However, if one looks at the introduction in the book by Mohan Lal, the aim of the journey as being of interest to the British Government is much more explicitly stated. Lal had travelled to Bukhara as Burnes' Persian *munshi* (clerk). Mohan Lal, *Travels in the Punjab, Afghanistan and Turkistan and to Balkh, Bokhara and Herat, and a Visit to Great Britain and Germany* (1846; reprint, Calcutta: K. P. Bagchi, 1977).

42. Burnes travelled as a British captain returning to Europe and Vambery as a dervish, Hadji Mollah Abdur Reshid Efendi.

43. Vambery, *Travels in Central Asia,* 366.

44. Burnes, *Travels into Bokhara,* 2:153–154.

45. *Ibid.,* 2:154.

46. N. Y. Khanikov, *Bokhara, Its Amir and His People,* trans. Baron Clement A. De Bode, (London: James Madden, 1843), 2.

47. Burnes, *Travels into Bokhara,* 2:155. Burnes lists Karakool, Bokhara and seven *tomuns* (districts) around it, Kermina, Meenakal or Katta Koorghan, Samarcand which has five tomuns, Juzzak, Kurshee, Balkh and provinces south of the river. He also notes, "Hissar might be overcome" (1:316). Vambery lists Karakol, Bokhara, Karshe, Samarcand, Kerki, Miyankal, or Kermineh, Kette Kurgan, Chardjuy, Dizzak, Oratepe and Shehr-i-Sabz, which, he pointed out, though equal in size to Samarcand could not be considered wholly subject to the emirate because of its continual struggles with the emir. Vambery, *Travels in Central Asia,* 316.

48. Burnes, *Travels into Bokhara,* 1:376.

49. Vambery, *Travels in Central Asia,* 386.

50. Vambery, *Travels in Central Asia,* 433.

51. Burnes, *Travels into Bokhara,* 2:384.

52. Vambery, *Travels in Central Asia,* 168.

53. *Ibid.;* Burnes, *Travels into Bokhara,* 2:250.

54. Holdsworth, *Turkestan.*

55. For details of this see Dov B. Yavoshevski, "The Central Government and the Peripheral Opposition in Khiva 1910–1924," in *The USSR and the Muslim World: Issues in Domestic and Foreign Policy,* ed. Yaacov Roi (London: George Allen and Unwin, 1984).

56. Holdsworth, *Turkestan,* 3.

57. *Mushtum* 11 (3 October 1924), cited in Edward Allworth, *The Modern Uzbeks From the Fourteenth Century to the Present: A Cultural History* (Stanford: Hoover Institute Press, 1990), 189.

58. See for instance, Donald S. Charlisie, "Soviet Uzbekistan: State and Nation in Historical Perspective," in *Central Asia In Historical Perspective,* ed. Beatrice

Manz (Boulder: Westview Press, 1994). Charlisie looks at the history of the period in terms of the play of politics and the ability of the Uzbek leaders to manipulate Moscow for their own ends.

59. Allworth, *Modern Uzbeks*, 196.
60. *Ibid.*, 190.
61. Vaidyanath, *Soviet Central Asian Republics*, 205, 218.
62. *Ibid.*, 268.
63. *Materialy Dlia Statistichiski Turkestanskogo Krai 1872–1879* (INION Collection; New Delhi: IGNCA), microfiche nos. 11958–11962.
64. I. I. Zarubin, *Naseleniya Samarkandskoi Oblast'* 1926 (INION Collection; New Delhi: IGNCA), microfiche no. 11965, p. 15.
65. Zarubin, *Naseleniya*.
66. *Entsiklopedicheski Slovar,* s. v. "Turkestan." St. Petersburg, 1902.
67. Zarubin, *Naseleniya*, 11.
68. *Ibid.*, 11.
69. Sukhareava, *Kvartalnaya Obshena*.
70. Zarubin, *Naseleniya*, 12.
71. *Ibid.*, 12.
72. V. V. Barthold, *Four Studies on the History of Central Asia* (Leiden: E. J. Brill, 1956).
73. Zarubin, *Naseleniya*, 18.
74. I. I. Gier, *Turkestan* 1909 (INION Collection; New Delhi: IGNCA), microfiche no. 11963, p. 10–37.
75. *Materialy Dlia Statistichiski,* 63.
76. Zarubin, *Naseleniya*.
77. "Turkestan."
78. *Entsiklopedicheski Slovar,* s. v. "Bukhara." St. Petersburg, 1902.
79. *Materialy Dlia Statistichiski,* 80.
80. Allworth, *Modern Uzbeks*.
81. Rakhim Masov, *History of the Axe Type Division,* trans. Anonymous (Dushanbe: Irfon, 1991).
82. Martha Brill Olcott, "The Myth of Tsentral'naya Azia," *Orbis* (Fall 1994).

NOTES to Chapter 6

1. Achin Vanaik, "Mediation is the Message," *The Telegraph,* 26 July 1999.
2. For a survey of the Kargil conflict in the press, see Sabyasachi Basu Ray Chaudhury and Shahid Fiaz, eds., "The Ten Week War in Kargil: From the News Files," SAFHR Paper Series no. 7, South Asia Forum for Human Rights, Kathmandu, Nepal, November 1999.
3. A. G. Noorani, "Kargil Diplomacy," *Frontline,* 13 August 1999.
4. Kanti P. Bajpai, P. R. Chari, Pervaiz Iqbal Cheema, Stephen P. Cohen and Sumit Ganguly, *Brasstacks and Beyond: Perception and Management of Crisis in South Asia* (Urbana: University of Illinois Press, 1995), 13.
5. Ranabir Samaddar, "Those Accords: A Bunch of Documents," SAFHR paper series no. 4, South Asia Forum for Human Rights, Kathmandu, Nepal, September 1999.
6. Sugata Bose and Ayesha Jalal, *Modern South Asia* (New Delhi: Oxford University Press, 1997), 200.
7. Sisir Gupta, *India's Relations with Pakistan 1954–1957* (New Delhi: Indian Council of World Affairs, 1958).
8. Ayesha Jalal, *The State of Martial Rule: The Origins of Pakistan's Political Economy of Defence* (Cambridge: Cambridge University Press, 1990), 50–60.
9. See Sreedhar and J. Kaniyalil, *India–Pakistan Relations: A Documentary Study* (New Delhi: ABC, 1993).
10. Ministry of External Affairs, "India–Pakistan Relations: Correspondence between the Prime Ministers of India and Pakistan, 15 July – 9 August 1951," *White Paper* (New Delhi, 1951).
11. Cited in S. Gupta, *India's Relations.*
12. Hari Ram Gupta, *The Rann of Kutch Affair* (New Delhi: U. C. Kapur, 1969), 45–46.
13. Ayub Khan, *Friends Not Masters* (Karachi: Oxford University Press, 1967). See also B. R. Nanda, *India's Foreign Policy: The Nehru Years* (New Delhi: Radiant, 1976).
14. Zulfiqar A. Bhutto, *Foreign Policy of Pakistan* (Karachi: Oxford University Press, 1964), 3.
15. *Dawn* (Karachi), 13 January 1966; see also *Reuter* (Karachi), 1 September 1968.
16. Kuldip Nayar, *Distant Neighbours* (New Delhi: Vikas, 1972), 122–123.
17. Mahtab A. Rashidi, "Indo-Pakistan Relations," Pakistan Study Circle occasional paper, University of Sind, Sind, 1988, 17–20. See also R. P. Anand, "The Kutch Award," vol. 2 in *International Relations and Foreign Policy of India,* ed. V. Grover (New Delhi: Deep and Deep, 1992); and H. R. Gupta, *Rann of Kutch Affair.*
18. *The Times of India* (New Delhi), 22 February 1968; *The Hindustan Times* (New Delhi), 22 February 1968.
19. Cited in Anand, "The Kutch Award." See also H. R. Gupta, *Rann of Kutch Affair.*

20. G. T. Keith Pitman, "The Role of the World Bank in Enhancing Cooperation and Resolution of Conflict: The Case of the Indus Basin," in *International Watercourses: Enhancing Cooperation and Managing Conflict. Proceedings of a World Bank Seminar*, eds. Salman M. A. and Laurence Boisson de Chazournes. World Bank technical paper no. 414, n.d., 155–165.

21. Dipak Gyawali, "Water Accords in South Asia" (paper presented at the Audit for Peace, Dhulikhel, Nepal, September 1999).

22. Bhabani Sen Gupta and Amit Gupta, "Changing Patterns of Regional Conflict in South Asia," in *Regional Cooperation and Development in South Asia*, ed. Bhabani Sen Gupta (New Delhi: Centre for Policy Research, 1988), 250.

23. J. N. Dixit, *Anatomy of a Flawed Inheritance: India–Pakistan Relations 1954–1970* (New Delhi: Konarak, 1995), 26.

24. Rafi Raza, *Z. A. Bhutto and Pakistan 1967–1977* (Karachi: Oxford University Press, 1992), 200. Rafi Raza was the industry minister in Bhutto's Cabinet. See also Ali Mehrunissa, "The Simla Agreement," *Pakistan Horizon* 25, no. 3 (1972): 53–74. Senior foreign ministry official D. P. Dhar, who was part of Indira Gandhi's negotiating team in Simla when the agreement was drawn up, has, in a series of recent articles, claimed that there was a secret understanding between Bhutto and Gandhi that Pakistan would eventually recognise the LoC as the international border.

25. Raza, *Bhutto and Pakistan*, 222–223.

26. Raza, *Bhutto and Pakistan*. See also Mani S. Aiyar, *Pakistan Papers* (New Delhi: UBS, 1996), 16–21.

27. Samina Ahmed, "Public Opinion, Democratic Governance and the Makings of Pakistan's Nuclear Policy," in *Nuclear Weapons and Arms Control in South Asia after the Test Ban*, ed. Eric Arnet (Oxford: Oxford University Press, 1998), 15–73.

28. Zia-ul-Haq, interview by author in Rajendra Sareen, *Pakistan, The India Factor* (New Delhi: Allied, 1984), 155–156 .

29. Sreedhar and Kaniyalil, *India–Pakistan Relations.*

30. K. M. Arif, *Working with Zia* (Karachi: Oxford University Press, 1995), 220–224.

31. Bajpai *et al., Brasstacks and Beyond*, 13.

32. Prime Minister Nawaz Sharif, through Pakistan's spokesperson, had indicated that Pakistan was willing to demilitarise the Siachin Glacier simultaneously with India. But he was forced to backtrack following the army chief General Karamat's public opposition to the withdrawal of troops. See "No Troop Withdrawal: CoAS," *The News* (Islamabad), 26 March 1997.

33. Dixit, *Anatomy of a Flawed Inheritance*, 79.

34. Kanti P. Bajpai, "CBMs, Contexts, Achievements and Futures" ·(paper presented at a Regional Centre for Strategic Studies conference, Colombo, June 1999).

35. See Dixit, *Anatomy of a Flawed Inheritance*, 1. Dixit quotes Sattar, then High Commissioner, who called on him in mid-July 1992: "I do not think India and Pakistan can be friends or have normal relations in our lifetimes."

36. In 1993, the Kashmiri militants who had laid siege to the Hazaratbal mosque in Srinagar were ousted through political negotiations involving safe passage to Pakistan.

37. Dixit, *Anatomy of a Flawed Inheritance.*

38. Rita Manchanda, "The Political Dilemma – To Trade or Not to Trade," *The Economic Times on Sunday* (New Delhi), 16 March 1997.

39. Amit Baruah, "Pakistan Hardliners Blocking Trade with India," *The Hindu* (New Delhi), 8 March 1998; also Rita Manchanda, "India–Pakistan Trade Hit by Political Rhetoric," *The Economic Times* (New Delhi), 1 September 1997.

40. Amir Mir, "The RAW Factor," *Newsline,* April (1998): 41–43.

41. Rajan Alexander, "Victory No, Compromise Yes," *The Deccan Herald* (Bangalore), 25 July 1999.

42. Ayesha Jalal, in her comparative study on civil–military relations, discusses the peculiar circumstance of scholars on both sides of the border accepting the territorial bifurcation as a divide in their historical and political analysis of the political processes in the sub-continent as well. Jalal, *State of Martial Rule.*

43. Pakistan–India Forum for Peace and Democracy, Proceedings, Recommendations and Declaration of the Third Joint Convention (Calcutta, 28–31 December 1996).

44. Rita Manchanda, "Pakistan's Most Favoured Nation," *The Pioneer* (New Delhi), 24 July 1997; Dixit, *Anatomy of a Flawed Inheritance*, 229–230.

45. Dixit, *Anatomy of a Flawed Inheritance*, 234–235.

46. Manchanda, "The Political Dilemma."

47. Nadeem Malik, "Normalisation Must Precede Pak-India Trade, says Sartaj," *The News* (Islamabad), 31 July 1997, international edition.

48. Sondeep Waslekar, "Track Two Diplomacy in South Asia," ACDIS Occasional Paper, University of Illinois, Urbana, March 1994.

49. Findings of the non-official round of talks reported in Navneeta C. Behra, Gowhar Rizvi and Paul Evans, *Beyond Boundaries: A Report on the State of Non-Official Dialogues on Peace, Security and Cooperation in South Asia* (Ontario: University of Toronto–York University, 1997).

50. For an example of regional consultations on refugees, see T. K. Bose and Rita Manchanda, eds., *States, Citizens and Outsiders: The Uprooted Peoples of South Asia* (Kathmandu: South Asia Forum for Human Rights, 1997).

51. Behra *et al., Beyond Boundaries*, 27, 31.

52. Amir Abbasi, "Options on Kashmir," *The Frontier Post* (Peshawar), 26 February 1997; and Amir Abbasi, "Beyond Stereotypes," *The Pioneer* (New Delhi), March 1997.

53. Pakistan–India Peoples Forum for Peace and Democracy, Proceedings and Recommendations (New Delhi, 24–25 February 1995).

   A similar people-to-people dialogue was set up in Cyprus recently between Greek and Turkish Cypriots. Youth from both sides, ignoring the political divide, stated their desire to get to know each other. See *The Hindu,* (Hyderabad), 3 September 2001.

54. Pakistan–India Forum for Peace and Democracy, Proceedings, Recommendations and Declaration of the Third Joint Convention (Calcutta, 28–31 December 1996).

55. Cited in Pakistan–India Forum for Peace and Democracy, Proceedings, Recommendations and Declaration of the Third Joint Convention (Calcutta, 28–31 December 1996).

56. Rita Manchanda, "A Peshawar Journey," The Hindu Sunday Magazine (New Delhi), 13 December 1998.

NOTES to Chapter 7

1. The Indian prime minister, Mr. Atal Behari Vajpayee, travelled by bus from New Delhi to Lahore in February 1999 as a gesture of reconciliation with Pakistan.

2. Jacques Derrida, *The Politics of Friendship* (London: Verso, 1997).

3. There is a plethora of such strategic studies that argue that arms control is a matter of strategy and has little to do with disarmament (even nuclear disarmament) and peace; such studies make my point clear. See for example, William H. Lewis and Stuart E. Johnson, eds., *Weapons of Mass Destruction: New Perspectives on Counterproliferation* (Washington, D.C.: National Defense University Press, 1995).

4. John Lewis Gaddis, "The Long Peace: Elements of Stability in the Post-War International System," in *The Long Peace: Inquiries into the History of the Cold War*, ed. John Lewis Gaddis (New York: Oxford University Press, 1987).

5. A representative example of this view is the collection of articles in Jorn Gjelstad and Olav Njolstad, eds., *Nuclear Rivalry and International Order* (Oslo: International Peace Research Institute, 1996), especially the articles by John Lewis Gaddis, "Nuclear Weapons and Cold War History," 40–54; and John Mueller, "Nine Propositions about the Historical Impact of Nuclear Weapons," which show how the discourse of control of nuclear weaponry was subsumed under the discourse of deterrence and what Gaddis called "nuclear logic".

6. Tom Nairn, "A Civic-Nationalist Divorce: Czechs and Slovaks," in *Faces of Nationalism: Janus Revisited*, ed. Tom Nairn, (London: Verso, 1997), 150–156.

7. In April 1922, in the small Italian town of Rapallo, Germany and the USSR entered into a bilateral agreement to cancel their debts and economic claims and to provide mutual support to each other. The agreement was modest in scope, yet it came to symbolise Germany's desire for, and capacity to, strike a relationship with the power in the east independent of its relationship with the West. The Treaty of Locarno in 1925–26 settled the issue of Germany's western borders with regard to Alsace-Lorraine and the demilitarisation of the Rhineland. Germany's relationship with France never completely negated the Treaty of Rapallo. In fact, to be true to recent history, Locarno has lived under the shadow of the 'Eastern Locarno'; while Germany's relationship with Poland has been set right, France has yet to free itself from the 'German Question'. In a sense, the 'spirit of Rapallo' has lived on.

   Thus Germany's search for its place in Europe could not be subsumed under the disarmament negotiations between the USA and the USSR that involved, above all else, the issue of Europe. Questions regarding Germany's alliances with Russia and the West have reappeared with German reunification, which again shows that dialogues for stability cannot be monolithic and monothematic in nature. See Ranabir Samaddar, "Germany unto France," *Liberal Times* (Special issue on Fifty Years of Germany) 7, no. 2 (1999): 40–47.

8. Paul Kennedy, *The Rise and Fall of Great Powers* (New York: Vintage, 1987). He writes of the "imperial overreach" that caused the decline of the major powers. The point is whether the powers can ever free themselves from overreaching.

9. Brahma Chellaney, "The Spread of Weapons of Mass Destruction and the Regional Arms Balance in South Asia;" Dhruba Kumar, "Proliferation, Deterrence and Security Delusions in South Asia;" Nazir Kamal, "Regional Arms Balance and Weapons of Mass Destruction in South Asia;" and Zia Mian, "The Search for Military Security as Self-Destruction in South Asia," in *Sustainable Development: Environmental Security, Disarmament and Development Interface in South Asia,* ed. D. D. Khanna (New Delhi: Macmillan, 1997), 299–406.

10. My main objection to the standard writings on this issue is that the writers take as their base for analysis a static situation, whereas I view it as dynamic. See for example, T. T. Poulose, "India's Nuclear Option and National Security;" and P. R. Chari, "India's Nuclear Options: Future Directions," in *Nuclear Non-Proliferation in India and Pakistan: South Asian Perspectives,* eds. P. R. Chari, Pervaiz Iqbal Cheema and Iftekharuzzman (Colombo: Regional Centre for Strategic Studies; New Delhi: Manohar, 1996), 42–86.

11. Kanti P. Bajpai, P. R. Chari, Pervaiz Iqbal Cheema, Stephen P. Cohen and Sumit Ganguly, "A Chronology of Cooperation 1947–1995," appendix 1 to *Brasstacks and Beyond: Perception and Management of Crisis in South Asia* (1995; reprint New Delhi: Manohar, 1997), 115–139.

12. Imtiaz Bokhari and Thomas Perry Thornton, *The 1972 Simla Agreement: An Asymmetrical Negotiation* (Washington, D.C.: School of Advanced International Studies, Johns Hopkins University Press, 1988).

13. Raymond Cohen, *Negotiating Across Cultures: Communication Obstacles in International Diplomacy* (Washington, D.C.: United States Institute of Peace, 1991).

14. The Indus Waters Treaty was signed by India and Pakistan in 1960 to govern the sharing of the Indus river waters by the two countries. In 1984, India began construction of a barrier on the Jhelum river downstream of the Wular Lake to make the river navigable during the lean period between late October and mid-February. Construction stopped in 1987 when Pakistan, referring to the construction as a barrage meant for water storage, accused India of violating the Indus Waters Treaty. The two sides almost reached an agreement in October 1991, when Pakistan added a final condition, which India refused to accept.

15. I have written earlier on the language of dialogue, taking the Farakka Barrage dispute as an example. Ranabir Samaddar, "Flowing Waters and the Nationalist Metaphor," *Studies in Conflict and Terrorism* 20, no. 2, (1997): 195–206.

16. Maya Chadda, *Ethnicity, Security and Separatism in India* (New York: Columbia University Press, 1997), 12.

17. A. G. Noorani, "Indo-Pak Impasse," *The Statesman* (Calcutta) 2 and 3 December 1998), part 1.
18. Nehru to the cabinet secretary on 6 April 1953, cited in Noorani, "Indo-Pak Impasse".
19. Shelton Kodikara, ed., *External Compulsions of South Asian Politics* (New Delhi: Sage, 1993); Iftekharuzzaman, ed., *South Asia's Security: Primacy of Internal Dimension* (Dhaka: Academic, 1994). My main objection to their views is that these considerations of externality and internality are not integral to conflicts; both authors take a legalistic view, and ignore the inherent regional and global aspects of the issues.
20. John F. Kennedy as a presidential candidate in 1960 had said, "It is an unfortunate fact that we can only secure peace by preparing for war". This security discourse has been, in a sense, a century old. Indeed, European history of the nineteenth century tells us that what Charles Kegley, Jr. and Eugene Wittkopf call the "military path to peace" led to a peace maintained by wars, and thus became the marker of "failed security". Not unnaturally, perceptive observers like the British military officer Sir John Frederick Maurice admitted in 1881 that, "I went into the British Army believing that if you want peace, you must prepare for war. I now believe that if you prepare thoroughly for war, you will get it." Both the citations are from Charles W. Kegley, Jr. and Eugene R. Wittkopf, *World Politics: Trends and Transformations* (New York: St. Martin's Press, 1995), 468.
21. I. William Zartman, ed., *Elusive Peace: Negotiating an End to Civil Wars* (Washington, D.C.: Brookings Institution Press, 1995).
22. I have in mind as an example the two significant proposals, in the form of draft treaties, prepared and circulated in 1999 by the Citizens' Peace Committee, Islamabad, a member of the Pakistan Coalition for Peace. These draft treaties propose measures for preventing a sudden missile attack by either of the two countries, mutually available early warning systems, mutually available risk-reduction measures and inspection facilities. Draft paper, Pakistan Coalition for Peace and Pakistan Institute of Labour Education and Research (PILER), Karachi, 1999.
23. I borrow these terms and also some of the underlying ideas from Emmanuel Levinas, "Bible and the Greeks," in *In the Time of the Nations* (London: Athlone Press, 1994), 135.
24. Bajpai, *et al. Brasstacks and Beyond,* 115–139.

NOTES to Chapter 8

1. John Lewis Gaddis, "The Long Peace: Elements of Stability in the Post–War International System," in *The Long Peace: Inquiries into the History of the Cold War*, ed. John Lewis Gaddis (New York: Oxford University Press, 1987), 216.

2. *Ibid.*, 245.

3. Subir Bhaumik, *India's North-East: Insurgency Crossfire* (New Delhi: Lancer, 1996).

4. Although the two major post–1945 wars saw the deployment of multinational armies, rapid use of new weaponry, colossal loss of life and desperate and painstaking efforts by third parties for peace, they were, in the end, localised wars without a worldwide significance.

   Pre-nineteenth-century wars were open, transparent and declared. Secret diplomacy flourished with the formation of modern States, the establishment of the Westphalian system and the use of the concept of 'the balance of power' as a major deterrent to hostility in the European state-systems, which led to secret diplomacies characterised by pacts, ententes and alliances. But with the abolition of secret diplomacy characteristic of nineteenth-century world politics, and with the invention and manufacture of modern weaponry of mass murder and total destruction, wars are once again being perceived as 'barbaric'. Because new means of espionage make all styles of diplomacy virtually transparent and rule out the possibility of secret influences and covert attempts at peace, nations now engage in wars that, in terms of brutality, resemble those of earlier ages. 'Modern' wars are now akin to 'olden' wars – and modernisation in this respect has spelt regression.

5. While historians of world politics remain preoccupied with global peace (long peace), local wars (short wars) are almost constantly being waged. If peace is the condition of war, as Clausewitz argued, then one can say that civic peace in the world (of the sort Gaddis and other historians of arms control admired) is made up of 'uncivil' (or barbaric) wars.

6. Geoffrey Blainey, "The Causes of War," in *The Long Peace: Inquiries into the History of the Cold War*, ed. John Lewis Gaddis (New York: Oxford University Press, 1987), 217.

7. On the origins of area conciousness see Ranabir Samaddar, *Whose Asia is it Anyway? Nation and the Region in South Asia* (Calcutta: Maulana Abul Kalam Azad Institute of Asian Studies and Pearl, 1996).

8. Joyce Kolko and Gabriel Kolko, *The Limits of Power: The World and The United States Foreign Policy 1945–1954* (New York: Pantheon, 1972); Thomas G. Paterson, *Soviet–American Confrontation: Post–War Reconstruction and the Origins of the Cold War* (Baltimore: Johns Hopkins University Press, 1973).

9. Cited in Gaddis, "Long Peace," 219. In South Asia, for example, conflicts like those in Kashmir, Sind, the Chittagong Hill Tract, Sri Lanka and Afghanistan have shown, both internal and external linkages with remarkable consistency.

One insurgency analyst has chosen to describe the situation in terms of "crossfire". See Bhaumik, *India's North-East*.

10. The formation of new States developed from two phenomena – decolonisation, and the Great Powers' strategy of partition to include large chunks of territory in their respective spheres of influence. These two phenomena were linked to each other but were not the same. The cold war/long peace discourse mentions the second phenomenon only to explain the state of world politics post the Second World War, and completely ignores the first; it mentions only the one history instead of the many.

11. The same comment applies to the other imperial powers when, at the end of the First World War, a new world order was sought to be made. For a comparative discussion involving the aftermath of the two World Wars and the attempts to create new world systems following the decline of old imperial powers, see Robert K. Schaeffer, *Severed States: Dilemmas of Democracy in a Divided World* (New York: Rowman and Littlefield, 1999), 9–39.

12. Radha Kumar, *Divide and Fall? Bosnia in the Annals of Partition* (London: Verso, 1997); see also the review essay by Arvind N. Das, "The End of Geography," *Biblio* (March–April 1998): 8–9; Clive J. Christie, "Partition, Separatism and National Identity: A Reassessment," *Political Quarterly* 63, no. 1 (1992): 68–72.

13. Old political regions and their attendant problems, such as the question of central Europe and the Balkan problem, have reappeared with the re-creation of 'one' Europe. The impact of political regions in the making of Europe has been discussed by, among others, Charles Tilly, *The Formation of Nation-States in Western Europe* (Princeton: Princeton Univeristy Press, 1975). For the geopolitical element in the earlier phases of State formation (for example of the 'Eastern Question') see D. Turnock, *The Making of Eastern Europe* (London: Routledge, 1988); D. Thompson, *Europe Since Napoleon* (London: Longmans, 1960; J. A. R. Marriott, *The Eastern Question* (Oxford: Oxford University Press, 1969); I. Banac, *The National Question in Yugoslavia: Origin, History and Politics* (Ithaca: Cornell University Press, 1984).

14. On the impact of Wilsonism see M. P. Leffler, *The Elusive Quest: America's Pursuit of European Stability and French Security 1919–1933* (Chapel Hill: University of North Carolina Press, 1979); for an analysis of Wilsonian 'liberal' policies against Bolshevism see David S. Fogelsong, *America's Secret War against Bolshevism: U.S. Intervention in the Russian Civil War* (Chapel Hill: University of North Carolina Press, 1995).

15. Some of the debates in European political circles reflected in the pages of the *European Journal of International Affairs* give an idea of what Europe thinks of the 'Americanisation' of the continent today: see, for example, the views of an ex-prime minister of Belgium in "An Interview with Mark Eyskens," *European Journal of International Affairs* 7, no. 4 (1990); and also of the co-editor of *Frankfurter Allgemeine Zeitung* in "A Conversation with Joachim Fest," *ibid.;* Guiseppe Sacco, the well-known columnist in "Europe and the

World," *European Journal of International Affairs* 10, no. 4 (1990); the whole section on "De Gaulle and his Century," *European Journal of International Affairs* 9, no. 3 (1990); "Britain in Today's World: An Interview with Michael Heseltine," *European Journal of International Affairs* 6, no. 3 (1989); William Safran, "Is France becoming America?" *European Journal of International Affairs* 6, no. 3 (1989); Marie-France Toinet, "Convergence in Disguise," *ibid.*

16. Mary Kaldor, *The Baroque Arsenal* (New York: Hill and Wang, 1981).

17. Johan Galtung, "Regional Security Commissions: A Proposal," in *Cooperation in Europe*, eds. Johan Galtung and Sverre Lodgaard (Oslo: Universitetsforlaget; Assen: International Peace Research Institute, 1970), 73–83.

18. The mystery seems to be most acute to the celebrated campaigners of peace. Of the nine Nobel Peace Prize recipients between 1971 and 1980 only two were concerned with human rights violations and popular protests: Amnesty International (1977) and Adolfo Perez Esquivel (1980). The rest represented the worries of a world in which only the presence or absence of nuclear weapons counted, and were proponents of the typical conflict-resolution mumbo-jumbo of the cold war age – Willy Brandt (1971), Henry Kissinger (1973), Eisaku Sato (1974), Andrei Sakharov (1975), Menachem Begin and Mohamed Anwar Al-Sadat (1978), Lech Walesa (1983), International Physicians For The Prevention of Nuclear War (1985), the XIVth Dalai Lama (1989), and the person most singularly incapable of addressing the question of war and peace in the Third World, Mikhail Sergeyevich Gorbachov (1990). The Nobel Peace Lectures are instructive in that they show how the peace movement in the 1970s and '80s had only the Atlantic world in mind when they spoke of "global" dangers. See Tore Frangsmyr, ed., *Nobel Lectures*, 2 vols. (Singapore: Scientific Press, 1997). This myopia is addressed partly in Mary Durfee and James N. Rosneau, "Playing Catch-Up: International Relations Theory and Poverty," *Millennium: Journal of International Studies* 25, no. 3 (1996): 521–545.

19. There is a growing literature on the issue of peacekeeping, peace enforcing and helping the State to stand on its feet, which begins with the evaluation of the Military Staff Committee of the UN. See, for example, Jonathan Soffer, "All for One or All for All: The UN Military Staff Committee and the Contradictions within American Internationalism," *Diplomatic History* 21, no. 1 (1997): 45–69; Eva Bertram, "Reinventing Governments: The Promise and Perils of United Nations Peace Building," *Journal of Conflict Resolution* 39, no. 3 (1995): 387–418; D. Holiday and W. Stanley, "Building the Peace: Preliminary Lessons from El Salvador," *Journal of International Affairs* 46, no. 2 (1993): 415–438.

20. The triumphalist literature varies across a wide spectrum. However, the reader can get an idea of this disparity from Francis Fukuyama, *The End of History and the Last Man* (London: Penguin, 1992); John Lewis Gaddis, "International Relations Theory and the End of the Cold War," *International*

Security 17, no. 3 (1992–93); Paul Kennedy, *Preparing for the Twenty-First Century* (New York: Random House, 1993); W. C. Wohlforth, "Realism and the End of the Cold War," *International Security* 19, no. 3 (1994–95); A. Varsori, ed., *Europe 1945–1990: The End of an Era?* (London: Macmillan, 1995); Thomas J. McCormick, "Troubled Triumphalism: Cold War Veterans Confront a Post–Cold War World," *Diplomatic History* 21, no. 3 (1997); S. P. Huntington, "The Clash of Civilizations?" *Foreign Affairs* 72, no. 3 (1993): 22–49; S. P. Huntington, "If not Civilizations, What? Paradigms of the Post–Cold War World," *Foreign Affairs* 72, no. 5 (1993): 186–194.

Several historians, like Gaddis, recall the last century while discussing peace. Theodore Draper, "Prophets of the 'Cold War,'" in *Present History: On Nuclear War, Détente, and Other Controversies,* ed. Theodore Draper (New York: Random House, 1983), 371–399, recounts the theme as it had featured in the nineteenth century, and discusses in that context the famous remark made by Alexis de Tocqueville more than a hundred years ago about Russo-American control of the globe.

21. Eric Hobsbawm, *The Age of Revolution: Europe 1789–1848* (London: Weidenfeld and Nicholson, 1975).

22. In 1648, after seven years of protracted negotiations, the Peace of Westphalia was signed in this German province. It was a landmark in international relations not only because it brought anarchy under control but also because it created a new system for dealing with war. Among the several important innovations of the Peace was the gathering of all the participants in the Thirty Years' War at one place, and the all-embracing terms of the treaties; but the Peace also heralded a more fundamental transformation – wars became 'national' for the next three hundred years, and supranational causes for war such as religion lost the power to determine a State's foreign policy. This situation changed only after 1948.

23. There is some literature on the question of forming the State anew. One author, on the basis of the experiences of a restructured State in sub-Saharan Africa, speaks of "degrees of Statehood". See Christopher Clapham, "Degrees of Statehood," *Review of International Studies,* no. 24 (1998): 143–157; see also Richard Devetak, "Incomplete States: Theories and Practices of Statecraft," in *Boundaries in Question: New Directions in International Relations,* eds. John Macmillan and Andrew Linklater (London: Pinter, 1995), 19–40.

24. A recent and thorough guide to international relations literature is Malcolm Anderson, *Frontiers: Territory and State Formation in the Modern World* (Cambridge: Polity Press, 1997).

25. On the role of the Church in stabilising post–War Europe, the entire collection of essays in the *European Journal of International Affairs* 12, no. 2 (1992), is rewarding.

26. Etienne Balibar, "Racism and Nationalism," in *Race, Nation, Class: Ambiguous Identities,* eds. Etienne Balibar and Immanuel Wallerstein (London: Verso, 1991), 38–45.

27. Christie, "Partition, Separatism and National Identity". Christie's argument about the need to separate two kinds of partition, ideological and identity-generated, can be accepted only in a broad format of decolonisation where the simultaneous processes of partition, decolonisation and new State formation were ushered in by war and the decline of an old imperial tradition.

28. See Ranabir Samaddar, *The Marginal Nation: Transborder Migration from Bangladesh to West Bengal* (New Delhi: Sage, 1999); See also the collection of essays in *Reflections on Partition in the East*, ed. Ranabir Samaddar (Delhi: Vikas; Calcutta: Calcutta Research Group, 1997).

29. On the entire Chakma question including its impact on the Northeast, see Subir Bhaumik, Meghna Guhathakurta and Sabyasachi Basu Ray Chaudhury, eds., *Living on the Edge: Essays on the Chittagong Hill Tracts* (Kathmandu: South Asia Forum for Human Rights; Calcutta: Calcutta Research Group, 1997); For a wide ranging survey of the conditions of uprooted peoples in South Asia, see T. K. Bose and Rita Manchanda, eds., *States, Citizens and Outsiders: The Uprooted Peoples of South Asia* (Kathmandu: South Asia Forum for Human Rights, 1997); For more on Myanmar see Bertil Lintner, *Burma in Revolt: Opium and Insurgency since 1948* (Bangkok: White Lotus, 1994).

30. T. K. Oomen, "Conceptualising the Linkage between Citizenship and National Identity," in *Citizenship and National Identity: From Colonialism to Globalism*, ed. T. K. Oomen (New Delhi: Sage, 1997) 13–51. He notes the conflation, but considers it a mistake. My argument has been, however, the opposite, as I consider that the reality of massive immigration and its links to statehood makes such a conflation an understandable occurrence.

31. On this topic, the reader may find helpful the papers contributed to the Strasbourg Conference on Human Rights hosted by the Council of Europe in 1995. See Jurgen Axer, ed., *The Human Rights Community and Conflict Resolution in South Asia: The Applicability of European Examples* (Brussels: Friedrich Naumann Stiftung, 1996).

32. A. Minc, cited in Alfonso Alfonsi, "Citizenship and National Identity: The Emerging Stirrings in Western Europe," in *Citizenship and National Identity: From Colonialism to Globalism*, ed. T. K. Oomen (New Delhi: Sage, 1997), 64; D. Thranhardt, ed., *Europe: A New Immigration Continent*, (Munich: Lit, 1992); David Carment and Patrick James, "Internal Constraints and Interstate Ethnic Conflict: Towards a Crisis-Based Assessment of Irredentism," *Journal of Conflict Resolution* 39, no. 1 (1995): 82–109.

33. Myron Weiner, "Security, Stability and International Migration," in *Global Dangers – Changing Dimensions: International Security*, eds. Sean M. Lynn-Jones and Steven E. Miller (Cambridge: MIT Press, 1995), 183–218. It is significant to note that to this close observer of the migration scene the issue of trans-border population movements does not appear as a problematic in international relations theory; it is at best a problem for the State to manage, particularly in terms of security.

34. For a broad survey, see the introduction in Virginia Yans-MacLaughlin, ed., *Immigration Reconsidered: History, Sociology and Politics* (New York: Oxford University Press, 1990).

35. Gil Loescher and John Scanlan, *Calculated Kindness: Refugees and America's Half-Open Door 1945 – Present* (New York: Free Press, 1986).

36. See in this connection Sita Bali, "Migration and Refugees," in *Issues in World Politics*, eds. Brian White, Richard Little and Michael Smith (London: Macmillan, 1997), 200–221. It is inconceivable that any such study today would leave out the 'new issue' of immigration, in stark contrast to the power studies and system studies of yesteryear; but these new studies still carry the traces of an uncertain comprehension of the state of the world today.

37. Two narrative accounts that suggest this continuity have influenced my view: Neal Ascherson, *Black Sea* (London: Jonathan Cape, 1995), and the set of essays on riots in modern history in Paul R. Brass, ed., *Riots and Pogroms* (London: Macmillan, 1996).

38. I. William Zartman, ed., *Elusive Peace: Negotiating an End to Civil Wars* (Washington, D.C.: Brookings Institution Press, 1995), 7–12. Zartman admits that these asymmetries make any politics of negotiation to end civil wars uncertain. The case studies presented by him, including ones that centre on non-State persons, show that these conflicts with inbuilt asymmetries make the State once again an issue of international relations.

39. Michael J. Hogan, ed., *America in the World – The Historiography of American Foreign Relations since 1941* (New York: Cambridge University Press, 1995); also by Michael J. Hogan, *The End of the Cold War: Its Meaning and Implications* (Cambridge and New York: Cambridge University Press, 1992). Indeed the historiography of the cold war brings out the still inconclusive debate as to the relative importance of geopolitical considerations and cultural factors in the making of the cold war. There were uncertainties even in the early phase of the cold war – was it, for example, being waged for territorial gains or for political-cultural considerations? The uncertainty in the debate on the origins of the cold war reflects the ambiguity that lay in its beginnings. Massive immigration today has brought back these uncertainties, which had been successfully covered up by the certainties of the cold war decades.

40. I have gained immensely from the succinct historical overview of the two interlinked processes of globalisation and fragmentation in Ian Clark, *Globalization and Fragmentation: International Relations in the Twentieth Century* (New York: Oxford University Press, 1997).

Bibliography

Primary Sources

National Archives of India, New Delhi

Foreign Political A, September 1873, no. 266

Foreign Political A–I, July 1883, nos. 14–25.

Foreign Secret E, December 1890, nos. 152–158

Foreign Secret F, April 1874, nos. 233, 236, 239, and 245.

Barnes, H. S., Resident in Kashmir, to Secretary, GOI, 25 February 1895, Foreign Secret F, August 1895, no. 145.

British Agent at Gilgit to Resident in Kashmir, 13 January 1895, Foreign Secret F, August 1895, no. 146.

"Confidential Notes on Certain Points in Connection with Our Future Arrangements in Chitral" by Sir George S. Robertson, 13 August 1895, Foreign Secret F, September 1895, no. 339.

Consul at Resht to Secretary of State for Foreign Affairs, 7 November 1873, enclosed in Foreign Secret F, April 1874, no. 245.

Diary of Special Assistant for Chinese Affairs (Macartney) to Resident in Kashmir, Foreign Secret F, 30 April 1894, under date 23 April, no. 608.

Diary of Special Assistant for Chinese Affairs (Macartney) to Resident in Kashmir, ending 15 March 1895, Foreign Secret F, July 1895, no. 1155.

Diary of Special Assistant for Chinese Affairs (Macartney) for fortnight ending 15 January 1895, Foreign Secret F, July 1895, no. 1149.

Diary of Special Assistant for Chinese Affairs (Macartney) for fortnight ending 15 June 1895, Foreign Secret F, November 1895, no. 86.

Diary of Special Assistant for Chinese Affairs (Macartney) for fortnight ending 15 April 1897, under date 11 April 1897, and for fortnight ending 30 June 1897, under date 16 June 1897, Foreign Secret F, September 1897, nos. 106 and 217.

Diary of the Special Assistant for Chinese Affairs (Macartney) for fortnight ending 30 April 1897, under date 20 April 1897, Foreign Secret F, September 1897, no. 209.

Demi-official from G. Macartney to H. M. Durand, 12 May 1892, Foreign Secret F, February 1893, no. 396.

Gilgit Agency Diary for the fortnight ending 15 December 1894, Foreign Secret F, March 1895, no. 473.

Kharita from the Agent to the Governor-General for Central India to Address of Nawab Shahjahan Begum, 23 June 1883, Foreign Political A–I, January 1884, no. 148.

List of Slaves of British-Kashmiri Origin Released, Foreign Secret F, August 1895, nos. 155 and 168.

Macartney to British Agent at Gilgit, 1 September 1892, Foreign Secret F, February 1893, no. 404.

Macartney to Resident in Kashmir, Foreign Secret, F, no. 580.

Macartney's letter to Resident in Kashmir, 1 February 1894, Foreign Secret, F, July 1894, no. 602.

Macartney to British Agent at Gilgit, 20 November 1894, Foreign Secret F, August 1895, no. 147.

Note by C[unningham], W. J., to Secretary, 13 December 1892, Foreign Secret F, February 1893, no. 389.

Note by Durand, H. M., to His Excellency, 7 July 1877, Foreign Secret, F, August 1887, no. 326.

Note by Hanrahan, W., n.d., Foreign Secret F, July 1894, 560–610, no. 389.

Peshawar Confidential Diary no. 21, 22 December 1888, paragraph 13, Foreign Secret F, January 1889, no. 102.

Regulations Submitted to the Taotai, Foreign Secret F, July 1894, no. 590.

Resident in Kashmir to Secretary, GOI, 17 May 1892, Foreign Secret F, February 1893, nos. 389, 405.

Secretary, GOI to Surgeon-Major Sir George S. Robertson, 17 August 1895, Foreign Secret F, September 1895, no. 347.

Statement of Dalgliesh, A., 7 July 1887, Foreign Secret F, August 1887, nos. 326, 327.

Statement of expenses in letter from Special Assistant for Chinese Affairs (Macartney) to Resident in Kashmir, 8 August 1895, Foreign Secret F, December 1895, Nos. 229–231.

Statement of Expenses to be Borne Entirely by the Kashmir Darbar, Foreign Secret F, December 1895, no. 230.

Surgeon-Major Sir George S. Robertson's Note on Mr. George Macartney's letter, 15 October 1892, Foreign Secret F, February 1893, no. 405.

Translation of Circular Letter from Tseng, Sub-Prefect of Karghallik, to the District Magistrate of Yarkand, Taotai of Kashgar, Provincial Treasurer and Provincial Governor of the New Dominions, n.d., Foreign Secret F, August 1895, no. 148.

Translation of Regulations Submitted to the Taotai for Orders, Foreign Secret F, July 1894, no. 590.

Translation of Report of the District Magistrate of Yarkand, Foreign Secret, F, July 1894, nos. 569–575.

Translation of a Report from the District Magistrate of Yarkand to the Taotai of Kashgar, Foreign Secret F, July 1894, no. 603.

Translation of Report of the District Magistrate of Yarkand, Foreign Secret F, July 1894, no. 589.

Translated Reply of the Lt. Governor of Xinjiang, n.d., Foreign Secret F, July 1894, no. 577.

Articles in Newspapers and Magazines

Abbasi, Amir. "Options on Kashmir." *The Frontier Post* (Peshawar), 26 February 1997.

———. "Beyond Stereotypes." *The Pioneer* (New Delhi), March 1997.

Alexander, Rajan. "Victory No, Compromise Yes." *The Deccan Herald* (Bangalore), 25 July 1999.

Baruah, Amit. "Pakistan Hardliners Blocking Trade with India." *The Hindu* (New Delhi), 8 March 1989.

Dawn (Karachi), 13 January 1966.

Economic Times on Sunday, The, (New Delhi), 31 July 1997.

Hindu, The, (Hyderabad), 3 September 2001.

Hindustan Times, The (New Delhi), 22 February 1968.

Malik, Nadeem. "Normalisation Must Precede Pak–India Trade, says Sartaj." *The News* (Islamabad), 31 July 1997, international edition.

Manchanda, Rita. "India–Pakistan Trade hit by Political Rhetoric." *The Economic Times* (New Delhi), 1 September 1997.

————. "Pakistan's Most Favoured Nation." *The Pioneer* (New Delhi), 24 July 1997.

————. "A Peshawar Journey." *The Hindu Sunday Magazine* (New Delhi), 13 December 1998.

————. "The Political Dilemma – To Trade or Not to Trade." *The Economic Times on Sunday* (New Delhi), 16 March 1997.

Mir, Amir. "The RAW Factor." *Newsline*, April 1998.

"No Troop Withdrawal: COAS." *The News* (Islamabad), 26 March 1997.

Noorani, A. G. "Indo–Pak Impasse." *The Statesman* (Calcutta), 2 and 3 December 1998.

————. "Kargil Diplomacy." *Frontline*, 13 August 1999.

Reuter (Karachi), 1 September 1968.

Times of India, The (New Delhi), 22 February 1968.

Vanaik, Achin. "Mediation is the Message." *The Telegraph*, 26 July 1999.

Government of India Publications

White Paper, 1951, on "India–Pakistan Relations: Correspondence between the Prime Ministers of India and Pakistan. 15 July 1951–9 August 1951. Ministry of External Affairs, New Delhi.

Library of the Indira Gandhi National Centre for the Arts, New Delhi

Gier, I. I. *Turkestan*. 1909. INION Collection. Microfiche no. 11963.

Materialy Dlia Statistichiski Turkestanskogo Krai 1872–1879. INION Collection. Microfiche nos. 11958–11962.

Palen, K. K. *Turkestanskogo Kraia*. St Petersburg, 1909–1911. INION Collection. Microfiche nos. 9501–9518.

Zarubin, I. I. *Naseleiniya Samarkandskoi Oblast'*. 1926. INION Collection. Microfiche no. 11965.

Interviews

"Britain in Today's World: An Interview with Michael Heseltine." *European Journal of International Affairs* 6, no. 3 (1989).

"Conversation with Joachim Fest, A." *European Journal of International Affairs* 7, no. 4 (1990).

"Interview with Mark Eyskens, An." *European Journal of International Affairs* 7, no. 4 (1990).

National Library, Calcutta

Radcliffe, Sir Cyril. Bengal Boundary Commission Report. 1947/ D/50/7/47R.

Publications in Russian

"Afganskoe Razgranichenie 1885–1887 gody;" "Pamirskoe Razgranichenie 1895 gody," 20–25; in *Ocherki Istorii Formirovaniya Gosudarstvennikh granits mezhdu Rossiei, SSSR i Afganistanom* (Sketches of the history of the formation of State borders between Russia, USSR and Afghanistan). Moscow: Rossiski Tsentr Strategicheskikh i Mezhdunarodnikh Issledovanyi, 1994.

"O raionirovani Turkestanskoi Respubliki." in *Materialy Administrativnoi kommissii raionirovanyu Respubliki pri NKVDTASSAR* ("On the territorial delimitation of the Turkestan Republic," in Materials of the Adminsitrative Commission regarding territorial demarcation by the National Commissariat of Internal Affairs, Turkestan Autonomous Soviet Socialist Republic). Tashkent: Tsentral'nyi Gosudarstvennyi Arkhiv [Central State Archives], 1923.

Akhmedjanov, G. A. *Rossiskaya Imperiya v Tsenralnoi Azii* (The Russian Empire in Central Asia [History and historiography in colonial politics of Czarism in Russia]). Tashkent: Fan, 1995.

Entsiklopedicheski Slovar. S. v. "Bukhara." Leiden, 1891.

Entsiklopedicheski Slovar. S. v. "Bukhara." St. Petersburg, 1902.

Entsiklopedicheski Slovar. S. v. "Turkestan." St. Petersburg, 1902.

Feoktistov, A. *Russkie, Kazakhi i Altayi.* Moscow: Alfa i Omega 1991

Ilusizov, M. K. "Ekonomicheskie Vozreniya Kazakhskovo Uchenovo i Prosvetitelya-Demokratiya Ch. Ch. Valikhanova." In *Iz Istorii Ekonomicheskoi Mysli Narodov Srednei SSSR* ("Economic views of the Kazakh scientist and enlightened democrat Ch. Ch. Valikhanov." In The history of economic thought of the people of Central Asia). Moscow: Sotegiz, 1961.

Ivanov, P. P. *Ocherki po istorii Srednei Azii, XVI seredina XIX veka* (Sketches of the history of Central Asia, sixteenth–mid-nineteenth centuries). Moscow: RAN, 1968.

Khalfin, N. A. *Rossiya i Khanstva Srednei Azii* (Russia and the Khanates of Central Asia). Moscow: Nauka, 1974.

Khalfin, N. A. and E. F. Rassadina. *N. V. Khanykov: Vostokoved i Diplomat.* Moscow: Nauka, 1974.

Lenin, V. I. "Ko Vsym Trudyashemia Musulmanam Rossi i Vostok." In *O Srednei Azii i Uzbekistane* (About Central Asia and Uzbekistan). Tashkent: Gosudartsvenoi Isdatelstgo Uzbekistanskoi SSR, 1957.

Mumenova, M. M. *Istoria Bukhari s Drevneishikh Vpyemini do Nashei Dnei* (History of Bukhara from ancient times to the present). Tashkent: Gosudartsvenoi Isdatelstgo Uzbekistanskoi SSR, 1976.

Ostroumov, N. *"'Begstvo': Abdur Rakhman Khana iz Tashkenta v Afghanistan," Kaufmanskii Sbornik General Adjutanta K. P. fon Kaufmana Pervovo, Izdanii v Pamiyat 25 let istekshikh co gnia smerti pokoriteliya I ustroitelya Turkestanskovo Kraia* ("'Begdom': Flight of Abdur Rahman Khan from Tashkent to Afghanistan," Kaufman Collection of General Adjutant K. P. fon Kaufman, published in memory of 25 years since the death of the conqueror and builder of Turkestan province). Moscow, 1910.

Ostroumov, N. Konstantin Petrovich fon Kaufman, ustroitel' Turkestanskovo Kraia, Lychnia Vospominaniia N. Ostroumova (1877–1881 godi) (Konstantin Petrovich fon Kaufman, the builder of Turkestan province. Personal memoirs of N. Ostroumov [1877–1881]). Tashkent, 1899.

Shishkin, V. A., ed. *Istoria Uzbekskoi SSR*. Vols. 2 and 3. Tashkent: Institut Istorii i Arkheologii, 1967.

Sukhareava, O. A. *Kvartalnaya Obshena Poznefeudalnogo Goroda Bukhari* (Blocks of the post–feudal city of Bukhara). Moscow: Akademia Nayuk SSR, 1967.

Turkestanskie Vedomosti (Tashkent), 22 January 1874. Ali Shir Navoi State Public Library.

Papers

Bajpai, Kanti P. "CBMs, Contexts, Achievements and Futures." Paper presented at the Regional Centre for Strategic Studies Conference, Colombo, June 1999.

Chaudhury, Sabyasachi Basu Ray, and Shahid Fiaz. "The Ten Week War in Kargil: From the News Files." SAFHR Paper Series no. 7, South Asia Forum for Human Rights, Kathmandu, Nepal, November 1999.

Draft Treaties, Citizens' Peace Committee, Islamabad, 1999. Pakistan Coalition for Peace and Pakistan Institute of Labour Education and Research (PILER), Karachi.

Falk, R. A. "Regionalism and World Order after the Cold War." Draft Paper presented for WIDER/IPSA Workshop and Panel, Berlin, Germany, 20–23 August 1994.

Kristof, Ladis K. D. "Geopolitics as a Field of Study." In The Ford Foundation Lectures in International Relations Studies, Maharaja Sayajirao University, Baroda, 1992.

Pakistan–India Peoples Forum for Peace and Democracy. Convention on Peace and Democracy. New Delhi, 24–25 February 1995.

————. Proceedings, Recommendations and Declaration of the Third Joint Convention, Calcutta, 28–31 December 1996.

Pitman, G. T. Keith. "The Role of the World Bank in Enhancing Cooperation and Resolution of Conflict: The Case of the Indus Basin." In *International Watercourses: Enhancing Cooperation and Managing Conflict. Proceedings of a World Bank Seminar,* eds. Salman M. A. and Laurence Boisson ed Chazournes. World Bank technical paper no. 414, n. d.

Samaddar, Ranabir. "Those Accords: A Bunch of Documents." Paper Series no. 4, South Asia Forum for Human Rights, Kathmandu, Nepal, September 1999.

Waslekar, Sondeep. *Track Two Diplomacy in South Asia.* Arms Control, Disarmament and International Studies Occasional Paper, University of Illinois, Urbana, March 1994.

Secondary Sources

Aase, Tor H. "The Theological Construction of Conflict: Gilgit, Northern Pakistan." In *Muslim Diversity: Local Islam in Global Contexts,* ed. Leif Manger. Richmond: Curzon Press, 1999.

Adams, W. M. "Sustainable Development." In *Geographies of Global Change: Remapping the World in the Late Twentieth Century,* ed. R. J. Johnston, P. J. Taylor and M. J. Watts. Oxford: Blackwell, 1995.

Adshead, S. A. M. *Central Asia in World History.* London: Macmillan, 1993.

Agnew, J. *Geopolitics: Re-Visioning World Politics.* London: Routledge, 1998.

Agnew, J., and S. Corbridge. *Mastering Space: Hegemony, Territory and International Political Economy.* London: Routledge, 1995.

Ahmar, M. "The Emergence of Three Asias." *World Affairs: The Journal of International Issues* 2, no. 2 (1998).

Ahmed, Samina. "Public Opinion, Democratic Governance and the Makings of Pakistan's Nuclear Policy." In *Nuclear Weapons and Arms Control in South Asia after the Test Ban,* ed. Eric Arnet. Oxford: Oxford University Press, 1998.

Aiyar, Mani S. *Pakistan Papers.* New Delhi: UBS, 1996.

Akerman, James R. "Cartography and the Emergence of Territorial States in Western Europe." In *Proceedings of the Tenth Annual Meeting of the Western Society for French History,* ed. J. F. Sweets. Lawrence: University of Kansas Press, 1984.

Akiner, S. "Environmental Degradation in Central Asia." *Central Asia and the Caucasus Review* 3, no. 7 (1994).

Alder, G. J. *British India's Northern Frontier 1865–1895: A Study in Imperial Policy.* London: Longmans, 1963.

Alfonsi, Alfonso. "Citizenship and National Identity: The Emerging Stirrings in Western Europe." In *Citizenship and National Identity: From Colonialism to Globalism,* ed. T. K. Oomen. New Delhi: Sage, 1997.

Allworth, Edward. *The Modern Uzbeks From the Fourteenth Century to the Present: A Cultural History.* Stanford: Hoover Institute Press, 1990.

———. ed. *Central Asia: A Century of Russian Rule.* New York and London: Columbia University Press, 1967.

Anand, R. P. "The Kutch Award." In *International Relations and Foreign Policy of India*, ed. V. Grover. Vol. 2. New Delhi: Deep and Deep, 1992.

Ancel, J. *Geopolitics*. Paris: Les Frontieres, 1938.

Anderson, Malcom. *Frontiers: Territory and State Formation in the Modern World*. Cambridge: Polity Press, 1997.

――――. *Frontiers: Territory and State Formation in the Modern World*. New York: Blackwell, 1997.

Anzaldua, Gloria. *Borderlands/La Frontera: The New Mestiza*. San Francisco: Aunt Lute, 1987.

Arif, K. M. *Working with Zia*. Karachi: Oxford University Press, 1995.

Armstrong, John A. *Nations before Nationalism*. Chapel Hill: University of North Carolina Press, 1982.

Arreola, Daniel D. and James R. Curtis. *The Mexican Border Cities: Landscape, Anatomy and Place Personality*. Tuscon: University of Arizona Press, 1993.

Ascherson, Neal. *Black Sea*. London: Jonathan Cape, 1995.

Ashcroft, Bill, Gareth Griffiths and Helen Tiffin. *The Empire Writes Back: Theory and Practice in Post–Colonial Literatures*. London: Routledge, 1989.

Asiwaju, A. I. *Partitioned Africa*. London: C. Hurst, 1985.

――――. ed. *African Boundaries: Barriers, Conduits and Opportunities*. London: C. Hurst, 1996.

Atkinson, J. *The Expedition into Afghanistan: Notes and Sketches Descriptive of the Country, Contained in a Personal Narrative during the Campaign of 1839 and 1840*. London: 1842.

Axer, Jurgen, ed. *The Human Rights Community and Conflict Resolution in South Asia: The Applicability of European Examples*. Brussels: Friedrich Naumann Stiftung, 1996.

Bajpai, Kanti P., P. R. Chari, Pervaiz Iqbal Cheema, Stephen P. Cohen and Sumit Ganguly, eds. *Brasstacks and Beyond: Perception and Management of Crisis in South Asia*. Urbana: University of Illinois Press, 1995. Reprint, New Delhi: Manohar, 1997.

Bali, Sita. "Migration and Refugees." In *Issues in World Politics*, ed. Brian White, Richard Little and Michael Smith. London: Macmillan, 1997.

Balibar, Etienne. "Racism and Nationalism." In *Race, Nation, Class: Ambiguous Identities*, ed. Etienne Balibar and Immanuel Wallerstein. London: Verso 1991.

Bameazizi, A., and M. Weiner, eds. *The New Geopolitics of Central Asia and its Borderlands*. London: I. B. Tauris, 1994.

Banac, I. *The National Question in Yugoslavia: Origin, History and Politics*. Ithaca: Cornell University Press, 1984.

Banerjee, Paula. "Borders as Unsettled Markers in South Asia: A Case Study of Sino-Indian Border." *International Studies* 35, no. 2 (1998).

Barthold, V. V. *Four Studies on the History of Central Asia*. Leiden: E. J. Brill, 1956.

Bassin, M. "Friedrich Ratzel." *Geographers: Bibliographical Studies*, no. 11 (1987).

――――. "Russia between Europe and Asia: The Ideological Construction of Geographical Space." *Slavic Review*, no. 50 (1991).

Baud, Michiel and Willem Van Schendel. "Toward a Comparative History of Borderlands." *Journal of World History* 8, no. 2 (1997).

Becker, Seymour. *Russia's Protectorates in Central Asia: Bukhara and Khiva, 1865–1924.* Cambridge: Harvard University Press, 1968.

Behra, Navneeta C., Paul M. Evans and Gowher Rizvi. *Beyond Boundaries: A Report on the State of the Non-Official Dialogue on Peace, Security and Cooperation in South Asia.* Ontario: University of Toronto–York University, 1997.

Beisembiev, T. K. "Farghana's Contacts with India in the Eighteenth and Nineteenth Centuries (According to the Khokand Chronicles)." *Journal of Asian History* 28, no. 2 (1994).

Bender, Thomas, ed. *The Anti-Slavery Debate: Capitalism and Abolitionism as a Problem in Historical Interpretation.* Berkeley and Los Angeles: University of California Press, 1992.

Bertram, Eva. "Reinventing Governments: The Promise and Perils of United Nations Peace-Building." *Journal of Conflict Resolution* 39, no. 3 (1995).

Berube, Michael. *Marginal Forces/Cultural Centres: Tolson, Pinchon and the Politics of Canon.* Ithaca: Cornell University Press, 1992.

Bhaumik, Subir. *India's North-East: Insurgency Crossfire.* New Delhi: Lancer, 1996.

Bhaumik, Subir, Meghna Guhathakurta and Sabyasachi Basu Ray Chaudhury, eds. *Living on the Edge: Essays on the Chittagong Hill Tracts.* Kathmandu: South Asia Forum for Human Rights; Calcutta; Calcutta Research Group, 1997.

Bhutto, Zulfiqar A. *Foreign Policy of Pakistan.* Karachi: Oxford University Press, 1964.

Blackburn, Robin. *The Overthrow of Colonial Slavery 1776–1848.* 1988. Reprint, London: Verso, 1996.

Blainey, Geoffrey. "The Causes of War." In *The Long Peace: Inquiries into the History of the Cold War,* ed. John Lewis Gaddis. New York: Oxford University Press, 1987.

Boersner, Demetrio. *The Bolsheviks and the National and Colonial Questions.* Geneva: Librarie E. Droz, 1957.

Boggs, S. Whittemore. *International Boundaries: A Study of Boundary Functions and Problems.* New York: Special Libraries Association, 1940.

Bokhari, Imtiaz, and Thomas Perry Thornton. *The 1972 Simla Agreement: An Asymmetrical Negotiation.* Washington, D.C.: Johns Hopkins University Press, 1988.

Bose, Sugata, and Ayesha Jalal. *Modern South Asia.* New Delhi: Oxford University Press, 1997.

Bose, T. K., and Rita Manchanda, eds. *States, Citizens and Outsiders: The Uprooted Peoples of South Asia.* Kathmandu: South Asia Forum for Human Rights, 1997.

Boulger, Dmetrius Charles. *England and Russia in Central Asia.* London: W. H. Allen, 1879.

Brass, Paul R., ed. *Riots and Pogroms.* London: Macmillan, 1996.

Burnes, Alexander. *Travels into Bokhara, Being the Account of a Journey from India to Cabool, Tartary and Persia in 1831–1833.* 3 vols. 1834. Reprint, New Delhi: Asian Educational Services, 1992.

Bustamante, Jorge A. "Demystifying the United States–Mexico Border." *Journal of American History* (September 1992).

Carment, David, and Patrick James. "Internal Constraints and Interstate Ethnic Conflict: Towards a Crisis-Based Assessment of Irredentism." *Journal of Conflict Resolution* 39, no. 1 (1995).

Caroe, Olaf. *Soviet Empire, the Turks of Central Asia and Stalinism.* New York: Macmillan, 1967.

Chadda, Maya. *Ethnicity, Security and Separatism in India.* New York: Columbia University Press, 1997.

Chadwick, Nora and Victor Zhirmensky. *Oral Epics of Central Asia.* Cambridge: Cambridge University Press, 1969.

Chakravarti, P. C. *Evolution of India's Northern Borders.* London: Asia Publishing House, 1971.

Chakravorty, Suhash. *Anatomy of the Raj: Russian Consular Reports.* New Delhi: Peoples Publishing House, 1976.

Chappell, David A. "Ethnogenesis and Frontiers." *Journal of World History* 4, no. 2 (1993).

Chari, P. R. "India's Nuclear Options: Future Directions." In *Nuclear Non-Proliferation in India and Pakistan: South Asian Perspectives,* eds. P. R. Chari, Pervaiz Iqbal Cheema and Iftekharuzzaman. Colombo: Regional Centre for Strategic Studies; New Delhi: Manohar, 1996.

Charlisie, Donald S. "Soviet Uzbekistan: State and Nation in Historical Perspective." In *Central Asia in Historical Perspective,* ed. Beatrice Manz. Boulder: Westview Press, 1994.

Chellaney, Brahma. "The Spread of Weapons of Mass Destruction and the Regional Arms Balance in South Asia." In *Sustainable Development: Environmental Security, Disarmament and Development Interface in South Asia,* ed. D. D. Khanna. New Delhi: Macmillan, 1997.

Chohan, Amar Singh. *The Gilgit Agency 1877–1935.* New Delhi: Atlantic, n.d.

Chokaev, Mustafa. "Turkestan and the Soviet Regime." *Journal of the Royal Central Asian Society,* no. 18 (1931).

Christie, Clive J. "Partition, Separatism and National Identity: A Reassessment." *Political Quarterly* 63, no. 1 (1992).

Chu, Wen-Djang. *The Moslem Rebellion in Northwest China 1862–1878: A Study of Government Minority Policy.* The Hague and Paris: Mouton, 1966.

Clark, Ian. *Globalization and Fragmentation: International Relations in the Twentieth Century.* New York: Oxford University Press, 1997.

Clapham, Christopher. "Degrees of Statehood." *Review of International Studies,* no. 24 (1998).

Clarence-Smith, W. G., ed. *The Economics of the Indian Ocean Slave Trade in the Nineteenth Century.* London: Frank Cass, 1989.

Cohen, Raymond. *Negotiating Across Cultures: Communication Obstacles in International Diplomacy.* Washington, D. C.: United States Institute of Peace, 1991.

Cohen, S. B. "Geopolitics in the New World Era: A New Perspective on an Old Discipline." In *Reordering the World: Geopolitical Perspectives on the Twenty-First Century*, ed. G. J. Demko and W. B. Wood. Boulder: Westview Press, 1994.

Cohn, B. S. "Representing Authority in Victorian India." In *The Invention of Tradition*, ed. E. Hobsbawm and R. Ranger. Cambridge: Cambridge University Press, 1996.

Curzon, George Nathaniel. *The Pamirs and the Source of the Oxus*. London: The Royal Geographical Society, 1896.

————. *Persia and the Persian Question*. Vol. 1. London: Frank Cass, 1966.

————. *The Romanes Lecture*. London: Clarendon Press, 1907.

————. *Russia in Central Asia in 1889 and the Anglo-Russian Question*. London: Frank Cass, 1967.

D'Encausse, Helene Carrere. *Islam and the Russian Empire: Reform and Revolution in Central Asia*. Reprint, London: I. B. Tauris, 1988.

Dalby, S. *Creating the Second Cold War: The Discourse of Politics*. London: Pinter, 1990.

————. "Ecopolitical Discourse: 'Environmental Security' and 'Political Geography'. *Progress in Human Geography* 16, no. 4 (1992).

————. "Geopolitical Discourse: The Soviet Union as Other." *Alternatives*, no. 13 (1988).

————. Introduction to *The Geopolitics Reader*, edited by G. Ó Tuathail, S. Dalby and P. Routledge. London: Routledge, 1998.

Dalby S., and G. Ó Tuathail. "The Critical Geopolitics Constellation: Problematizing Fusions of Geographical Knowledge and Power." *Political Geography* 15, no. 6/7 (1996).

Damodaran, A. K. "Before Non-Alignment." In *Interpreting World Politics: Essays for A. P. Rana*, ed. Kanti P. Bajpai and H. C. Shukul. New Delhi: Sage, 1995.

Darwin, C. *Journal of Researches into the Geology and Natural History of the Various Countries Visited by the H. M. S. Beagle*. London: Henry Colburn, 1839.

Das, Arvind N. "The End of Geography." *Biblio* (March–April 1998).

Dawisha, K., and B. Parrot. *Conflict, Cleavage and Change in Central Asia and the Caucasus*. Cambridge: Cambridge University Press, 1997.

De, B. "Moving Beyond Boundaries: Contradictions Between People and Territory." In *States, Citizens and Outsiders: The Uprooted Peoples of South Asia*, ed. T. K. Bose and Rita Manchanda. Kathmandu: South Asia Forum for Human Rights, 1997.

"De Gaulle and his Century." (Issue on Charles De Gaulle) *European Journal of International Affairs* 9, no. 3 (1990).

Degras, Jane, ed. *The Communist International Documents 1919–1943*. Vol. 1. New York: Oxford University Press, 1956.

Derrida, Jacques. *The Politics of Friendship*. London: Verso, 1997.

Devetak, Richard. "Incomplete States: Theories and Practices of Statecraft." In *Boundaries in Question: New Directions in International Relations*, ed. John Macmillan and Andrew Linklater. London: Pinter, 1995.

Dixit, J. N. *Anatomy of a Flawed Inheritance: India–Pakistan Relations 1954–1970.* New Delhi: Konarak, 1995.

Dodds, K. J., and J. D. Sidaway. "Locating Critical Geopolitics." *Environment and Planning; D: Society and Space,* no. 12 (1994).

Donnelly, Alton. "The Mobile Steppe Frontier: The Russian Conquest and Colonization of Bashkiria and Kazakhstan to 1850." In *Russian Colonial Expansion to 1917,* ed. Michael Rwykin. London: Mansell, 1988.

Draper, Theodore. "Prophets of the 'Cold War'." In *Present History: On Nuclear War, Détante and Other Controversies.* New York: Random House, 1983.

Drescher, Seymour. *Econocide: British Slavery in the Era of Abolition.* Pittsburgh: University of Pittsburgh Press, 1977.

Durfee, Mary, and James N. Rosneau. "Playing Catch-Up: International Relations Theory and Poverty." *Millenium: Journal of International Studies* 25, no. 3 (1996).

Elliott, J. *The Frontier 1837–1947: The Story of the Northwest Frontier of India.* London: Cassell, 1968.

Eltis, David, and James Walvin, eds. *The Abolition of the Atlantic Slave Trade: Origins and Effects in Europe, Africa and the Americas.* Madison: University of Wisconcin Press, 1981.

Etherton, P. T. *Across the Roof of the World.* London: Constable, 1911.

European Journal of International Affairs 12, no 2 (1992).

Falk, R. A. *On Human Governance: Towards a New Global Politics.* Cambridge: Polity Press, 1995.

Ferrier, J. P. *Caravan Journeys and Wanderings in Persia, Afghanistan, Turkestan and Beloochistan, with Historical Notices of the Countries lying between Russia and India.* 2d ed. Trans. William Jesse and ed. H. D. Seymour. London: John Murray, 1857.

Fisher, M. H. *The Politics of British Annexation of India 1757–1857.* New Delhi: Oxford University Press, 1993.

Fogel, Robert W., and Stanley L. Engerman. "Philanthropy at Bargain Prices: Notes on the Economics of Gradual Emancipation." In *Without Consent or Contract: The Rise and Fall of American Slavery – Conditions of Slave Life and the Transition to Freedom,* ed. Robert W. Fogel and Stanley L. Engerman. Vol. 2. New York and London: W. W. Norton, 1992.

"Formation of Ethnic Identities in Frontier Societies, The." *Journal of World History* 4, no. 2 (1993).

Fogelsong, David S. *America's Secret War against Bolshevism: U. S. Intervention in the Russian Civil War.* Chapel Hill: University of North Carolina Press, 1995.

Frangysmyr, Tore, ed. *Nobel Lectures.* 2 vols. Singapore: Scientific Press, 1997.

Fukushama, Y. "Political Geographers of the Past; X: Japanese Geopolitics and its Background: What is the Real Legacy of the Past?" *Political Geography* 16, no. 5 (1997).

Fukuyama, Francis. *The End of History and the Last Man.* London: Penguin, 1992.

Fürer-Haimendrof, C. von. *Tribes of India: The Struggle for Survival.* New Delhi: Oxford University Press, 1982.

Gaddis, John Lewis. "The Long Peace: Elements of Stability in the Post–War International System." In *The Long Peace: Inquiries into the History of the Cold War,* ed. John Lewis Gaddis. New York: Oxford University Press, 1987.

———. "International Relations Theory and the End of the Cold War." *International Security* 17, no. 3 (1992–1993).

Galtung, Johan. "Regional Security Commissions: A Proposal." In *Cooperation in Europe,* ed. Johan Galtung and Sverre Lodgaard. Oslo: Universitetsforlaget; Assen: International Peace Research Institute, 1970.

Ghosh, K. *The Chinese Invasion of India.* Calcutta: Banachhaya Ghosh, 1963.

Gjelstad, Jorn, and Olav Njolstad, eds. *Nuclear Rivalry and International Order.* Oslo: International Peace Research Institute, 1996.

Gladney, Dru C., ed. *The Legacy of Islam in China.* Cambridge: Harvard University Press, 1989.

———. "The Salafiyya Movement in Northwest China: Islamic Fundamentalism among the Muslim Chinese?" In *Muslim Diversity: Local Islam in Global Contexts,* ed. Leif Manger. Richmond: Curzon Press, 1999.

Glassner, M. I. *Political Geography.* New York: John Wiley, 1995.

Goldin, Claudia. "The Economics of Emancipation." In *Without Consent or Contract: The Rise and Fall of American Slavery: Conditions of Slave Life and the Transition to Freedom,* ed. Robert W. Fogel and Stanley L. Engerman. New York and London: W. W. Norton, 1992.

Gray, C. S. *The Geopolitics of the Nuclear Area: Heartlands, Rimlands and the Technological Revolution.* New York: Crane, Russak, 1977.

———. *The Geopolitics of Superpower.* Lexington: University of Kentucky Press, 1988.

Gupta, Hari Ram. *The Rann of Kutch Affair.* New Delhi: U. C. Kapur, 1969.

Gupta, Karunakar. *Spotlight on the Sino-Indian Frontier.* Calcutta: New Book, 1982.

Gupta, Sisir. *India's Relations with Pakistan 1954–1957.* New Delhi: Indian Council of World Affairs, 1958.

Hale, D. "Is Asia's High Growth Era Over?" *National Interest* 47 (Spring 1997).

Hauner, Milan. *What is Asia to Us? Russia's Heartland Yesterday and Today.* Boston: Unwin Hyman, 1990.

Hennessy, Alistair. *The Frontier in Latin American History.* London: Edward Arnold, 1978.

Henze, Paul B. "The Great Game in Kashgaria: British and Russian Missions to Yakub Beg." *Central Asian Survey* 8, no. 2 (1989).

Hepple, L. W. "Metaphor, Geopolitical Discourse and the Military in South America." In *Writing Worlds: Discourse, Text and Metaphor in the Representation of Landscape,* ed. T. Barnes and J. Duncan. London: Routledge, 1992.

Hitchcock, D. I. "Internal Problems in East Asia." *Washington Quarterly* 21, no. 2 (1998).

Ho, Ping-Ti. "In Defense of Sinicization: A Rebuttal of Evelyn Rawski's 'Reenvisioning the Qing'." *Journal of Asian Studies* 57, no. 1 (1998).

Hobsbawm, Eric. *The Age of Revolution: Europe 1789–1848.* London: Weidenfeld and Nicholson, 1975.

Hoddie, Matthew. "Ethnic Identity Change in the People's Republic of China: An Explanation Using Data from the 1982 and 1990 Census Enumerations." In *Nationalism and Ethnoregional Identities in China,* ed. William Safran. London and Portland: Frank Cass, 1998.

Hofstadter, Richard and Seymour Martin Lipset, eds. *Turner and the Sociology of Frontiers.* New York: Basic Books, 1968.

Hogan, Michael J. *The End of the Cold War: Its Meanings and Implications.* Cambridge and New York: Cambridge University Press, 1992.

————, ed. *America in the World: The Historiography of American Foreign Relations since 1941.* New York: Cambridge University Press, 1995.

Holdar, S. "The Political Geographers of the Past; IX: The Ideal State and the Power of Geography: The Life-Work of Rudolf Kjellen." *Political Geography* 11, no. 3 (1992).

Holdich, Sir Thomas. *Political Frontiers and Boundary Making.* London: Macmillan, 1956.

Holdsworth, Mary. *Turkestan in the Nineteenth Century: A Brief History of the Khanates of Bukhara, Kokand and Khiva.* Oxford: Central Asian Research Centre and St. Anthony's College, 1959.

Holiday, D., and W. Stanley. "Building the Peace: Preliminary Lessons from El Salvador." *Journal of International Affairs* 46, no. 2 (1993).

Hopkirk, Peter. *Foreign Devils on the Silk Road: The Search for the Lost Cities and Treasures of Chinese Central Asia.* Oxford: Oxford University Press, 1980.

————. *The Great Game: On Secret Service in High Asia.* Oxford: Oxford University Press, 1990.

Hosking, Geoffrey. *Russia, People and Empire 1552–1917.* London: Fontana, 1998.

Houbert, J. "Russia in the Geopolitics of Settler Colonization and Decolonization." *Round Table,* no. 344 (1997).

Huntington, S. P. "The Clash of Civilizations?" *Foreign Affairs* 72, no. 3 (1993).

————. "If Not Civilizations, What? Paradigms of the Post–Cold War World." *Foreign Affairs* 72, no. 5 (1993).

Iftkahruzzaman, ed. *South Asia's Security: Primacy of Internal Dimension.* Dhaka: Academic, 1994.

Ispahani, Mahnaz Z. *Roads and Rivals: The Politics of Access in the Borderlands of Asia.* London: I. B. Tauris, 1989.

Israeli, Raphael, *Muslims in China: A Study in Cultural Confrontation.* London and Malmo: Curzon Press; Atlantic Highlands: Humanities Press, 1980.

Jalal, Ayesha. *The State of Martial Rule: The Origins of Pakistan's Political Economy of Defence.* Cambridge: Cambridge University Press, 1990.

Jones, Stephen B. *Boundary Making: A Handbook for Statesmen, Treaty Editors and Boundary Commissioners.* Washington, D.C.: Carnegie Endowment for International Peace, 1945.

Kaldor, M. *The Baroque Arsenal.* New York: Hill and Wang 1981.

————. "The World Economy and Militarization." In *Towards Just World Peace: Perspectives from Social Movements,* ed. S. Mendelovittz and R. B. J. Walker. London: Butterworths, 1987.

Kamal, Nazir. "Regional Arms Balance and Weapons of Mass Destruction in South Asia." In *Sustainable Development: Environmental Security, Disarmament and Development Interface in South Asia,* ed. D. D. Khanna. New Delhi: Macmillan, 1997.

Karpat, Kemal. "The Old and the New Central Asia." *Central Asian Survey,* 12, no. 4 (1993).

Kaul, B. M. *Untold Story.* Bombay: Allied, 1967.

Kaviraj, Sudipto. "A Critique of the Passive Revolution." In *State and Politics in India,* ed. Partha Chatterjee. New Delhi: Oxford University Press, 1997.

Kegley, Charles W., Jr., and Eugene R. Wittkopf. *World Politics: Trends and Transformations.* New York: St. Martin's Press, 1995.

Kemp, P. M., trans. and ed. "The Travells of Filip Yefremov." In *Russian Travellers to India and Persia (1624–1798).* Reprint, New Delhi: Jiwan Prakashan, 1959.

Kennedy, Paul. *Preparing for the Twenty-First Century.* New York: Random House, 1993.

———. *The Rise and Fall of Great Powers.* New York: Vintage, 1987.

Khan, Ayub. *Friends Not Masters.* Karachi: Oxford University Press, 1967.

Khanikov, N. Y. *Bokhara, its Amir and his People.* Trans. Baron Clement A. De Bode. London: James Madden, 1843.

Khazanov, A. M. "The Early State Among the Eurasian Nomads." In *The Study of the State,* ed. Henri J. M. Classen and Peter Skalnik. The Hague: Mouton, 1981.

———. *Nomads and the Outside World.* Trans. Julia Crookenden. Cambridge: Cambridge University Press, 1984.

Klein, J. "Reflections on Geopolitics: From Pangermanism to the Doctrines of Living Space and Moving Frontiers." In *On Geopolitics: Classical and Nuclear,* ed. C. Zoppo and C. Zorgbibe. Dordrecht: Martinus Nijhoff, 1985.

Klein, M. A., ed. *Breaking the Chains: Slavery, Bondage and Emancipation in Modern Africa and Asia.* Madison: University of Wisconsin Press, 1993.

Knight, E. F. *Where Three Empires Meet: A Narrative of Recent Travel in Kashmir, Western Tibet, Gilgit and the Adjoining Countries.* 1905. Reprint, New Delhi: Asian Educational Services, 1993.

Knox, P., and J. Agnew. *The Geography of the World Economy: An Introduction to Economic Geography.* London: Edward Arnold, 1994.

Kodikara, Shelton. *External Compulsions of South Asian Politics.* New Delhi: Sage, 1993.

Kolarz, Walter. *Russia and her Colonies.* New York: Preager, 1952.

Kolko, Joyce, and Gabriel Kolko. *The Limits of Power: The World and The United States Foreign Policy 1945–1954.* New York: Pantheon, 1972.

Kost, K. "The Conception of Politics in Political Geography and Geopolitics in Germany until 1945." *Political Geography* 8, no. 4 (1989).

Kothari, Rajni. *Politics in India.* New Delhi: Orient Longman, 1970.

Krader, Lawrence. "The Origin of the State among the Nomads of Asia." In *Soviet and Western Anthropology,* ed. Ernest Gellner. London: Gerald Duckworth, 1980.

Krishna, G. "India and the International Order: Retreat from Idealism." In *The Expansion of International Society,* ed. H. Bull and A. Watson. Oxford: Clarendon Press, 1984.

Krishna, Sankaran, *Post–Colonial Insecurities.* New Delhi: Oxford University Press, 1999.

Kumar, Dhruba. "Proliferation, Deterrence and Security Delusions in South Asia." In *Sustainable Development: Environmental Security, Disarmament and Development Interface in South Asia,* ed. D. D. Khanna. New Delhi: Macmillan, 1997.

Kumar, Radha. *Divide and Fall? Bosnia in the Annals of Partition.* London: Verso, 1997.

Lal, D. "Eco-Fundamentalism." *International Affairs* 71, no. 3 (1995).

Lal, Mohan. *Travels in the Panjab, Afghanistan and Turkistan to Balkh, Bokhara and Herat and a Visit to Great Britain and Germany.* 1846. Revised edition, New Delhi: Indian Council for Historical Research, 1977. Reprint, Calcutta: K. P. Bagchi, 1977.

Lamb, Alastair. *The China–India Border.* London: Oxford University Press, 1964.

———. *The Kashmir Problem: A Historical Survey.* New York: Praeger, 1966.

———. *The McMahon Line: A Study in Relations Between India, China and Tibet 1904–1914.* Toronto: University of Toronto Press, 1966.

Lapradelle, P. de. *La Frontiere: Etude de Droit Internationale.* Paris: Les Editions Internationales, 1928.

Lauderdale, P. "Frank Justice Rather Than Frankenstein Injustice: Homogenous Development as Deviance in the Diverse World." In *The Underdevelopment of Development: Essays in Honour of Andre Gunder Frank.* S. C. Chew and R. A. Danemark. Thousand Oaks: Sage, 1996.

Leitner, G. W. *Dardistan in 1866, 1886 and 1893, Being an Account of the History, Religions, Customs, Legends, Fables and Songs of Gilgit, Chilas, Kandia, Dasin, Chitral, Hunsa, Nagyr and Other Parts of the Hindukush.* 1890. Reprint, New Delhi: Asian Educational Services, 1996.

Leffler, M. P. *The Elusive Quest: America's Pursuit of European Stability and French Security 1919–1933.* Chapel Hill: University of North Carolina Press, 1979.

Lenin, V. I. "Critical Remarks on the National Question." In *Collected Works.* Vol. 20. Moscow: Progress, 1964.

———. "Cultural National Autonomy." In *Collected Works.* Vol. 9. Moscow: Progress, 1964.

———. "National Liberation and the Right of Nations to Self-Determination." In *Collected Works.* Vol. 20. Moscow: Progress, 1964.

———. "On the Right of Nations to Self-Determination." In *Selected Works.* Vol. 2. Moscow: Progress, 1970.

———. "Preliminary Draft on the National and Colonial Question for the Second Congress of the Comintern." In *Selected Works.* Vol. 3. Moscow: Progress, 1970.

———. "Speech on the National Question at the All Russia Conference of the RSDRP." In *Selected Works.* Vol. 2. Moscow: Progress, 1970.

————. "The Question of Nationalities and Autonomisation." In *Collected Works*. Vol. 9. Moscow: Progress Publishers, 1964.

Levinas, Emmanuel. "Bible and the Greeks." In *In the Time of the Nations*, ed. Emmanuel Levinas. London: Athlone Press, 1994.

Lewis, William H., and Stuart E. Johnson, eds. *Weapons of Mass Destruction: New Perspectives on Counterproliferation*. Washington, D.C.: National Defense University Press, 1995.

Lintner, Bertil. *Burma in Revolt: Opium and Insurgency since 1948*. Bangkok: White Lotus, 1994.

Loescher, Gil, and John Scanlan. *Calculated Kindness: Refugees and America's Half-Open Door, 1945 – Present*. New York: Free Press, 1986.

Louis, Wm. R. "The Era of the Mandate System and the Non-European World." In *The Expansion of International Society*, ed. H. Bull and A. Watson. Oxford: Clarendon Press, 1984.

Luard, D. E. T. *The International Regulation of Frontier Disputes*. London: Thames and Hudson, 1970.

Macartney, Lady. *An English Lady in Chinese Turkestan*. 1931. Reprint, Oxford: Oxford University Press, 1985.

Macdonald, Kenneth Iaian. "Push and Shove: Spatial History and the Construction of a Portering Economy in Northern Pakistan." *Comparative Studies in Society and History* 40, no. 2 (1998).

MacKenzie, David. "The Conquest and Administration of Turkestan 1860–1868." In *Russian Colonial Expansion to 1917*, ed. Michael Rwykin. London: Mansell, 1988.

Mackerras, Colin. "Han-Muslim and Intra-Muslim Social Relations in Northwestern China." In *Nationalism and Ethnoregional Identities in China*, ed. William Safran. London and Portland: Frank Cass, 1998.

Majumdar, R. C. *British Paramountcy and Indian Renaissance*. Part 1. Bombay: Bharatiya Vidya Bhavan, 1963.

Marriott, J. A. R. *The Eastern Question*. Oxford: Oxford University Press, 1969.

Marvin, Charles. *Merv, the Queen of the World and the Scourge of the Man-Stealing Turcomans*. London: W. H. Allen, 1881.

————. *Reconnoitring Central Asia: Pioneering Adventures in the Region Lying Between Russia and India*. 1885. Reprint, New Delhi: Asian Educational Services 1996.

Masov, Rakhim. *The History of the Axe Type Division*. Anonymously translated. Dushanbe: Irfon, 1991.

Maxwell, Neville. *India's China War*. New York: Jonathan Cape, 1970.

McCormick, Thomas J. "Troubled Triumphalism: Cold War Veterans Confront a Post–Cold War World." *Diplomatic History* 21, no. 3 (1997).

Mehrunissa, Ali. "The Simla Agreement." *Pakistan Horizon* 25, no. 3 (1972).

Melville, A. "Post–Communist Russia: Problems of Transition." *World Affairs: The Journal of International Issues* 2, no. 2 (1998).

Menon, K. N. *The Chinese Betrayal of India*. New Delhi: Contemporary India, 1962.

Metcalf, T. *Ideologies of the Raj*. Cambridge: Cambridge University Press, 1996.

Mian, Zia, "The Search for Military Security as Self-Destruction in South Asia." In *Sustainable Development: Environmental Security, Disarmament and Development Interface in South Asia*, ed. D. D. Khanna. New Delhi: Macmillan, 1997.

Miers, Susanne. *Britain and the Ending of the Slave Trade*. Bristol: Longman, 1975.

———. "Slavery and the Slave Trade as International Issues 1890–1939." *Slavery and Abolition* 19, no. 2 (1998).

Miers, Susanne, and Martin Klein, eds. Introduction in *Slavery and Abolition* 19, no. 2 (1998), 1–15.

Miles, W. F. S. and D. A. Rochefort. "Nationalism versus Ethnic Identity in Sub-Saharan Africa." *American Political Science Review*, 85 (1991).

Millward, James A. "A Uyghur Muslim in Qianlong's Court: The Meanings of the Fragrant Concubine." *Journal of Asian Studies* 53, no. 2 (1994).

Moodie, A. E. *Geography Behind Politics*. London: Hutchinson, 1947.

Moorcroft, W. and G. Trebeck. *Travels in the Himalayan Provinces of Hindustan and the Punjab, in Ladakh and Kashmir, in Peshwar, Kabul, Kunduz and Bokhara from 1819 to 1825*. 2 vols. 1841. Reprint, New Delhi: Asian Educational Services, 1989.

Moore-Harell, Alice. "Slave Trade in the Sudan in the Nineteenth Century and its Suppression in the Years 1877–1880." *Middle Eastern Studies* 34, no. 2 (1998).

Morgan, Gerald. *Ney Elias: Explorer and Envoy Extraordinary in High Asia*. London: George Allen and Unwin, 1971.

Motyl, Alexander J. "After Empire: Competing Discourses and Inter-State Conflict in Post–Imperial Eastern Europe." In *Post–Soviet Political Order: Conflict and State Building*, ed. Barnett R. Rubin, and Jack Snyder. London: Routledge, 1998.

Mulgan, R. "Should Indigenous Peoples Have Special Rights?" In *One World, Many Voices: Global Perspectives on Political Issues*, ed. G. Hastedt. Eaglewood Cliffs: Prentice Hall, 1995.

Nairn, Tom. "A Civic–Nationalist Divorce: Czechs and Slovaks." In *Faces of Nationalism: Janus Revisited*, ed. Tom Nairn. London: Verso, 1997.

Nanda, B. R. *India's Foreign Policy: The Nehru Years*. New Delhi: Radiant, 1976.

Nayar, Kuldip. *Between the Lines*. Bombay: Allied, 1969.

———. *Distant Neighbours*. New Delhi: Vikas, 1972.

Nehru, Jawaharlal. *Discovery of India*. Calcutta: Signet Press, 1946.

Neumann, I. B. "The Geopolitics of Delineating 'Russia' and 'Europe': The Creation of the 'Other' in European and Russian Tradition." In *Geopolitics in Post–Wall Europe: Security, Territory and Identity*, ed. O. Tunander, P. Baev and I. Einagel. London: Sage, 1997.

Nijman, J. *Geopolitics of Conflict and Power: Superpowers in the International System*. London: Belhaven Press, 1993.

———. "The Limits of Superpower: The United States and the Soviet Union Since World War II." *Annals of the Association of American Geographers* 82, no. 4 (1992).

Olcott, Martha Brill. "The Myth of Tsentral'naya Azia." *Orbis* (Fall 1994).

Ó Loughlin, J., and H. Heske. "From 'Geopolitik' to 'Geopolitique': Converting a Discipline for War to a Discipline for Peace." In *The Political Geography of*

Conflict and Peace, ed. N. Kliot and S. Waterman. London: Belhaven Press, 1991.

Oomen, T. K. "Conceptualising the Linkage between Citizenship and National Identity." In *Citizenship and National Identity: From Colonialism to Globalism,* ed. T. K. Oomen. New Delhi: Sage, 1997.

Ó Tuathail, G. *Critical Geopolitics: The Politics of Writing Global Space.* London: Routledge, 1996.

————. Introduction to *The Geopolitics Reader,* ed. G. Ó Tuathail, S. Dalby and P. Routledge. London: Routledge, 1998.

————. "Second Cold War." In *Dictionary of Geopolitics,* ed. J. O'Loughlin. Westport: Greenwood Press, 1994.

————. "(Dis)placing Geopolitics: Writing on the Maps of Global Politics." *Environment and Planning; D: Society and Space,* no. 12 (1994).

————. "Critical Geopolitics and the Development Theory: Intensifying the Dialogue." *Transactions of the Institute of British Geographers,* no. 19 (1994).

Ó Tuathail, G., and J. Agnew. "Geopolitics and Discourse: Practical Geopolitical Reasoning in American Foreign Policy." *Political Geography* 11, no. 2 (1992).

Ó Tuathail, G., and S. Dalby. "Critical Geopolitics: Unfolding Spaces for Thought in Geography and Global Politics." *Environment and Planning; D: Society and Space* 12, no. 5 (1994).

Ó Tuathail, G., A. Herod and S. M. Roberts. "Negotiating Unruly Problematics." In *Unruly World: Globalization, Governance and Geography,* ed. G. Ó Tuathail, A. Herod and S. M. Roberts. London: Routledge, 1998.

Oye, Anthony. *The Settlement of Boundary Disputes in International Law.* Dobbs Ferry: Manchester University Press, 1967.

Palat, Madhavan K. "Tsarist Russian Imperialism." *Studies in History* 4 (January–December 1988).

Pannikkar, K. M. *Asia and Western Dominance: A Survey of the Vasco Da Gama Epoch of Asian History 1498–1945.* London: George Allen and Unwin, 1959.

Park, Alexander. *Bolshevism in Turkestan 1917–1927.* New York: Columbia University Press, 1957.

Parker, G. *Geopolitics: Past, Present and Future.* London: Pinter, 1998.

————. *The Geopolitics of Domination.* London: Routledge, 1988.

————. *Western Geopolitical Thought in the Twentieth Century.* London: Croom Helm, 1988.

Paterson, Thomas G. *Soviet–American Confrontation: Post–War Reconstruction and the Origins of the Cold War.* Baltimore: Johns Hopkins University Press, 1973.

Patterson, O. *Slavery and Social Death.* Cambridge: Harvard University Press, 1982.

Pierce, Richard. *Russian Central Asia 1867–1917.* Berkley and Los Angeles: University of California Press, 1960.

Portus, G. V. "Americans and Australians." *Australian Quarterly* (June 1942).

Poulose, T. T. "India's Nuclear Option and National Security." In *Nuclear Non-Proliferation in India and Pakistan: South Asian Perspectives,* ed. P. R. Chari,

Pervaiz Iqbal Cheema and Iftekharuzzaman. Colombo: Regional Centre for Strategic Studies; New Delhi: Manohar, 1996.

Pounds, Norman J. G. *Political Geography.* New York: McGraw Hill, 1972.

Prescott, J. R. V. *Political Frontiers and Boundaries.* London: Routledge, Chapman and Hall, 1987.

Puri, M. M. "Central Asian Geopolitics: The Indian View." *Central Asian Survey* 16, no. 2 (1997).

Rahul, Ram. *Central Asia: A Historical Survey.* New Delhi: Vikas, 1996.

Rajan, M. S. *Nonalignment and Nonaligned Movement: Retrospect and Prospect.* New Delhi: Vikas, 1990.

Rana, A. P. "Back to Basics: Non-Alignment after the Cold War." *World Affairs: The Journal of International Issues* 1, no. 2 (1997).

———. "The Non-Hegemonical Imperative: The Non-Aligned Regulation of India's National Security Problematic and the Universalisation of International Society." *Indian Journal of Social Science* 4, no. 1 (1991).

Rao, M. S. A. and Francine Frankel. *Dominance and State Power in India: Decline of a Social Order.* New Delhi: Oxford University Press, 1990.

Ratzel, Friedrich. *Politische Geographie.* Munich: Oldenburg, 1897.

Ray, A. K. "The Case for a Strategic Frontier." *Indian Defence Review* 12, no. 1, (1997).

Raza, Rafi. Z. A. *Bhutto and Pakistan 1967–1977.* Karachi: Oxford University Press, 1992.

Reiber, Alfred J. "Persistent Factors in Russian Foreign Policy: An Interpretive Essay." In *Imperial Russian Foreign Policy,* ed. Hugh Ragsdale. New York: Cambridge University Press, 1993.

Reid, Sir Robert. *History of Frontier Areas Bordering Assam from 1883–1941.* Shillong: The Society for Northeast Hill Regions, 1942.

Roberts, R., and S. Miers, eds. *The End of Slavery in Africa.* Madison: University of Wisconsin Press, 1988.

Robertson, George S. *The Kafirs of the Hindukush.* 1896. Reprint, Karachi: Oxford University Press, 1974.

Routledge, P. "Critical Geopolitics and Terrains of Resistance." *Political Geography* 15, no. 6–7 (1996).

———. Introduction to *The Geopolitics Reader,* ed. G. Ó Tuathail, S. Dalby and P. Routledge. London: Routledge, 1998.

Roy, N. R., ed., *Himalayan Frontier in Historical Perspective.* Calcutta: Institute of Historical Studies, 1986.

Roy-Choudhury, R. "The Indian Ocean Rim-Association for Regional Co-operation: An Overview." *World Affairs: The Journal of International Issues* 1, no. 3 (1997).

Rubinstein, A. Z. "Russia in Search of a New Role: Changing Geopolitical Compulsions in Central Asia." *World Affairs: The Journal of International Issues* 1, no. 2 (1997).

Sack, D. R. *Conceptions of Space in Social Thought.* Minneapolis: University of Minnesota Press, 1980.

————. *Human Territoriality: Its Theory and History.* Cambridge: Cambridge University Press, 1980.

Sacco, Giuseppe. "A Place in the Shade." *European Journal of International Affairs* 12, no. 2 (1991).

Safran, William. "Is France becoming America?" *European Journal of International Affairs* 6, no. 3 (1989).

Sahlins, Peter. *Boundaries: The Making of France and Spain in the Pyrenees.* Berkeley and Los Angeles: University of California Press, 1989.

Samaddar, Ranabir. *Memory, Identity, Power: Politics in the Jungle Mahals 1890–1950* Madras: Orient Longman, 1997.

————. ed., *Reflections on Partition in the East.* New Delhi: Vikas; Calcutta: Calcutta Research Group, 1997.

————. *The Marginal Nation: Transborder Migration from Bangladesh to West Bengal.* New Delhi: Sage, 1999.

————. *Whose Asia is it Anyway? Nation and the Region in South Asia,* Calcutta: Pearl, 1996.

————. "Flowing Waters and the Nationalist Metaphor." *Studies in Conflict and Terrorism* 20, no. 2, (1997).

————. "Germany unto France." *Liberal Times* 7 no. 2 (1999).

————. "The Failed Dialectic of Territoriality and Security and the Imperatives of Dialogue." *International Studies* 35, no. 1 (1998).

Sareen, Rajendra. *Pakistan, The India Factor.* New Delhi: Allied, 1984.

Savage, Elizabeth. *The Human Commodity: Perspectives on the Trans-Saharan Slave Trade.* London: Frank Cass, 1992.

Schaeffer, Robert K. *Severed States: Dilemmas of Democracy in a Divided World.* New York: Rowman and Littlefield, 1999.

Sen Gupta, Bhabani, and Amit Gupta. "Changing Patterns of Regional Conflict in South Asia." In *Regional Cooperation and Development in South Asia.* ed. Bhabani Sen Gupta. New Delhi: Centre for Policy Research, 1988.

Sharp, P. F. "Three Frontiers: Some Comparative Studies of Canadian, American and Australian Settlements." *Pacific Historical Review* (1955).

Shaw, Robert. *Visits to High Tartary, Yarkand and Kashgar.* 1871. Reprint, Hong Kong: Oxford University Press, 1984.

Shiva, V. *Ecology and the Politics of Survival: Conflicts Over Natural Resources in India.* New Delhi: Sage, 1995.

————. "The Greening of the Global Reach." In *Global Visions: Beyond the New World Order,* ed. J. Brecher, J. B. Childs and J. Cutler. Boston: New End Press, 1993.

Siddiqi, I. H. "Ta'rikh-i-Manazil-i-Bukhara: A Source for the History of Central Asia during the First Decades of the Nineteenth Century." *Studies in Islam* (July 1980).

Skrine, C. P. *Chinese Central Asia: An Account of the Travels in Northern Kashmir and Chinese Turkestan.* Hong Kong: Oxford University Press, 1986.

Skrine, C. P. and Pamela Nightingale. *Macartney at Kashgar: New Light on British, Chinese and Russian Activities in Sinkiang 1890–1918.* London: Methuen, 1973.

Skrine, Francis Henry and Edward Denison Ross. *The Heart of Asia: A History of Russian Turkestan and the Central Asian Khanates from the Earliest Times.* London: Methuen, 1899.

Sloan, G. *Geopolitics in the United States Strategic Policy 1890–1987.* Brighton: Wheatsheaf Books, 1988.

Smith, D. L. "Central Asia: A New Great Game?" *Asian Affairs* 23, no. 3 (1996).

Smith, G. "Ends, Geopolitics and Transitions." In *The Challenge for Geography: A Changing World, A Changing Discipline,* ed. R. J. Johnston. Oxford: Blackwell, 1993.

Soffer, Jonathan. "All for One or All for All: The UN Military Staff Committee and the Contradictions within American Internationalism." *Diplomatic History* 21, no. 1 (1997).

Sreedhar, and J. Kaniyalil. *India–Pakistan Relations: A Documentary Study.* New Delhi: ABC, 1993.

Stalin, I. V. *Marxism and the National and Colonial Question.* New York: Macmillan, 1936.

Stebelsky, I. "The Frontier in Central Asia." *Russian Historical Geography,* no. 1 (1983).

Suhrke, Astrid and Lela Garner. *Ethnic Conflict in International Relations.* New York: Praeger, 1977.

Taylor, P. J. *Political Geography: World Economy, Nation-State and Locality.* 3d ed. Essex: Longman Scientific and Technical, 1993.

———. "Geopolitical World Orders." In *Political Geography of the Twentieth Century: A Global Analysis,* ed. P. J. Taylor. London: Belhaven Press, 1993.

———. "From Heartland to Hegemony: Changing the World in Political Geography." *Geoforum* 25, no. 4 (1994).

Thapar, Romila. "Seminar on Ideas in the Eighteenth and Ninteenth Centuries: A Report." *Enquiry* 1, no. 3 (1964).

Thien, T. T. "New Alignments, New Realities: East Asia in the Post–Cold War Setting." *World Affairs: The Journal of International Issues* 1, no. 1 (1997).

Thompson, D. *Europe Since Napoleon.* London: Longmans, 1960.

Thranhardt, D., ed. *Europe: A New Immigration Continent.* Munich: Lit, 1992.

Tilly, Charles. *The Formation of Nation-States in Western Europe.* Princeton: Princeton University Press, 1975.

Titas, Paul. "Honour the Baloch, Buy the Pushtun: Stereotypes, Social Organization and History in Western Pakistan." *Modern Asian Studies* 32, no. 3 (1989).

Toinet, Marie-France. "Convergence in Disguise." *European Journal of International Affairs* 6, no. 3 (1989).

Treadgold, Donald W. *The Great Siberian Migration: Government and Peasants in Resettlement from Emancipation to the First World War.* Princeton: Princeton University Press, 1957.

———. "Russian Expansion in the Light of Turner's Study of the American Frontier." *Agricultural History* (October 1962).

"Turkmenistan Commission 1919–1920, The." *Central Asian Review* 12, no. 1 (1964).

Turner, Frederick Jackson. "The Significance of the Frontier in American History." In *Selected Essays of Frederick Jackson Turner,* ed. R. A. Billington. New Jersey: Holt, Rinehart and Winston, 1961.

Turnock, D. *The Making of Eastern Europe.* London: Routledge, 1988.

Tuzmuhamedov, R. A. *How the National Problem was Solved in Soviet Central Asia.* Trans. David Fidlon. Moscow: Progress, 1973.

Vaidyanath, R. *The Formation of the Soviet Central Asian Republics: A Study in Soviet Nationality Policy 1917–1936.* New Delhi: Peoples Publishing House, 1967.

Vambery, Arminius. *History of Bokhara from the Earliest Period down to the Present.* London: John Murray, 1873.

———. *Sketches of Central Asia.* London: W. H. Allen, 1868.

———. *Travels in Central Asia, Being an Account of a Journey from Tehran Across the Turkoman Desert on the Eastern Shore of the Caspian to Khiva, Bokhara and Samrcand, Perfomed in the year 1863.* London: John Murray, 1864.

Varsori, A., ed. *Europe 1945–1990: The End of an Era?* London: Macmillan, 1995.

Vasanthamadhana, K. G. "The British Historians on the Himalayan Frontier." In *Himalayan Frontier in Historical Perspective,* ed. N. R. Roy. Calcutta: Institute of Historical Studies, 1986.

Visvanathan, S. "Mrs. Brundtland's Disenchanted Cosmos." In *The Geopolitics Reader,* ed. G. Ó Tuathail, S. Dalby and P. Routledge. London: Routledge, 1998.

Vlasto, A. P. "The Entry of the Slavs into Christendom." In *Introduction to the Medieval History of the Slavs.* Cambridge: Cambridge University Press, 1970.

Waley-Cohen, Joanna. *Exile in Mid-Qing China: Banishment to Xinjiang 1758–1820.* New Haven: Yale University Press, 1991.

Walker, M. *The Cold War and the Making of the Modern World.* London: Fourth Estate, 1993.

Weinbaum, M. G. "The Three Asias: Security, Economic and Cultural Linkages Across Central, West and South Asia." *Swords and Ploughshares,* no. 10 (1996–97).

Weiner, Myron. "Security, Stability and International Migration." In *Global Dangers – Changing Dimensions: International Security,* ed. Sean M. Lynn-Jones and Steven E. Miller. Cambridge: MIT Press, 1995.

Welchman, John C., ed. *Rethinking Borders.* Minneapolis: University of Minnesota Press, 1996.

Wheeler, Geoffrey. *Modern History of Soviet Central Asia.* London: Weidenfeld and Nicholson, 1964.

Williams, Eric. *Capitalism and Slavery.* New York: Capricorn, 1966.

Wilmer, F. *The Indigenous Voice in World Politics: Since Time Immemorial.* Newbury Park: Sage, 1993.

Wohlforth, W. C. "Realism and the End of the Cold War." *International Security* 19, no. 3 (1994–1995).

Woodman, Dorothy. *Himalayan Frontiers: A Political Review of British, Chinese, Indian and Russian Rivalries.* London: Cresset Press, 1969.

Wyman, W. V. and C. B. Kroeber. *The Frontier in Perspective*. Madison: University of Wisconsin Press, 1957.

Yans-McLaughlin, Virginia. *Immigration Reconsidered: History, Sociology and Politics*. New York: Oxford University Press, 1990.

Yavoshevski, Do. B. "The Central Government and the Peripheral Opposition in Khiva 1910–1924." In *The USSR and the Muslim World: Issues in Domestic Policies,* ed. Yaacov Roi. London: George Allen and Unwin, 1984.

Younghusband, Francis. *The Heart of a Continent*. 1896. Reprint, Hong Kong: Oxford University Press, 1984.

Zartman, William, I., ed. *Elusive Peace: Negotiating an End to Civil Wars*. Washington, D. C.: Brookings Institution Press, 1995.

Zenkovsky, Serge A. *Pan Turkism and Islam in Russia*. Cambridge: Harvard University Press, 1960.

Glossary

adamzad	ruling clan (of Chitral)
aksaqal	representative, village elder
amban	governor (in Chinese Turkestan)
ataliq Ghazi	Guardian Warrior
aul	peasant village
autarchie	economic self-sufficiency
bandeirantes	expeditionary groups who captured indigenous slaves during the colonial period
beg	chief
begar	obligatory porterage
begum	lady
caravanbashi	leader of the caravan
darbar	government (of Kashmir)
dari	Persian language
distansii	sub-divisions
emir	chief
ezhegodnik	statistical yearbook
haji	a person who has been on the Haj pilgrimage
ishan	holy man
jamadar dadkhwah	chief of the artillery
jus sanguinis	right of blood
jus soli	right of soil
kampf	struggle
khan	chief
kharita	formal missive
kilaochi	fort commander
kiti Zhuz	'Small Hundred'
kolonizatsiya	colonisation
koori	unit of currency
krai	Russian frontier region
kvartal	block
lebensraum	living space
limites naturelles	natural boundaries
mehtar	ruler (of Chitral)
mir	chief (of Hunza)
mission civilastrice	modernisation
mitteleuropa	Central Europe
mujahideen	Islamic guerilla fighters
mullah	Muslim cleric

narodno'st	nationality
oblast'	province
odtel	division
okrug	territorial administrative unit in a province
orgbyuro	Organisational Bureau of the Central Committee of the Turkestan Commission
orta Zhuz	'Middle Hundred'
ostpolitik	politics towards the East
panchayat	village council
pansadbashi	commander of five hundred
raionirovanie	delimitation of territories
razgranichenie	border demarcation
ress	tax paid in labour services
sarbaz	infantrymen
sardar	ruler
seer	a measure
shah	ruler
sredazbyuro	Central Asian Bureau
stanitsy	settlements
sultan pravitel	local ruler (of the Kazakhs)
svetlost	Illustrious
tamozhennoe uchrezhdenie	Department of Customs
tanga	unit of currency
tillah	unit of currency
toman	district
topchibashi	commandant of artillery
totaler krieg	total war
tsungli yamen	Foreign Office
turkbyuro	Turkestan Bureau
turkkommissia	Turkestan Commission
uezd	district
ulu zhuz	'Great Hundred' or Elder/Larger/Great Horde
vilayet	province
volost	sub-division of a district
Vysochestvo	Highness
vysokoprevoskodichelstvo	His Highness
vysokostepenstvo	Highest Honour
wazir	ruler
zvoevaniya	conquest
ziaketchik	customs collector

Index

RELATED TITLES FROM ORIENT LONGMAN

Competing Nationalisms in South Asia: Essays in Honour of Asghar Ali Engineer
Ed. Paul Brass and Achin Vanaik

India in a Changing World
Achin Vanaik

Nation and National Identity
S. L. Sharma and T. K. Oomen

Trade and Politics in the Himalaya-Karakoram Borderlands
D. P. Choudhury

NEW AND FORTHCOMING TITLES

The Human Landscape
Ed. Geeti Sen and Ashis Banerjee

Jharkhand: Politics of Development and Identity
Amit Prakash

Reclaiming Identity: Realist Theory and the Predicament of Postmodernism
Paula M. L. Moya and Michael R. Hames-Gracia

After Pokhran: A Tract on India's Nuclear Power
Kanti P. Bajpai

Prisoners of the Nuclear Dream
Ed. M. V. Ramana and Rammonohar Reddy